LIFE IN THE FAR WEST

THE AMERICAN EXPLORATION
AND TRAVEL SERIES

Trappers (Alfred Jacob Miller)

*"A prominent feature in the character of the hunters of the far west
is their quick determination and resolve in cases
of extreme difficulty and peril"*

LIFE
IN THE
FAR WEST

BY

GEORGE FREDERICK RUXTON

EDITED BY LEROY R. HAFEN

WITH A FOREWORD BY

MAE REED PORTER

UNIVERSITY OF OKLAHOMA PRESS

NORMAN

ISBN: 0-8061-1534-3

Life in the Far West is Volume 14 in The American Exploration and Travel Series.

10 11 12 13 14 15 16 17 18

FOREWORD

IN THE LITERATURE of the early Far West, no work excels in color, charm, or authenticity George Frederick Ruxton's *Life in the Far West,* which has long been recognized by students of the fur trade as a classic of its kind. Despite this recognition, and despite the wide influence *Life in the Far West* has had on the innumerable histories and novels about this colorful era, the book itself has not often been available to the interested modern reader. For this reason I welcome the opportunity to say a few words in this new edition of *Life in the Far West,* which has been admirably edited and annotated by LeRoy R. Hafen, and to record a few of the many pleasures that Ruxton's works have given both myself and my husband, Clyde Porter.

The final opening of the hitherto unpaved gaps in the Pan-American Highway between El Paso and Mexico City brought realization of a long-held desire of ours to set eyes on the localities that in 1846 were visited by young George Ruxton, and in June, 1950, with his two books as guides, we traversed the more than two thousand miles between Veracruz and the bone-dry deserts of present-day New Mexico and Arizona that Ruxton had traveled on horseback, over a century ago, to arrive in the Far West of the trappers and traders about which he was to write.

The new highway obligingly follows quite closely Ruxton's own route, so we were able without inconvenience to add to our knowledge of formerly accessible places, acquired in two earlier jaunts to the southern extremities of his travels, impressions of the towns below Chihuahua—Mapimi, Frésnillo, Zacatecas, Aguascalientes, Lagos, and others which cannot have changed greatly since Ruxton wrote of them, cut off as they were by all but impassable roads for anything but the most primitive means of travel.

The deeper we penetrated into these regions the greater our wonderment mounted, until it seemed a veritable miracle that a person on horseback could have traversed such barren and rugged country and lived to write of it. These natural obstacles overcome, it must have taken genuine bravery to pass alone, save for a cowardly servant or two, through the dread Apache and Comanche country of northern Mexico.

To today's gregarious society, the solitary life led by Ruxton in his wanderings seems beyond endurance. One marvels that a man reared in refinement and luxury could sacrifice all the comforts of home and turn so frequently from the civilized world as did Ruxton in his brief twenty-seven years. One wonders, too, that he found time and opportunity for literary efforts; it is indeed remarkable that, with his schooling coming to a close as it did in his thirteenth year, he was able to write with such style and apparent ease a book now recognized as perhaps unique in quality.

In one hundred years civilization's tide has all but obliterated the footprints on the moccasin trails of the West, but Ruxton through the printed page has breathed the breath of life into some of the strangest yet most fascinating of God's mortals, the Mountain Men. It took a young man out of England, a born adventurer and explorer, to write a "Who's Who," a "What's What," and a vocabulary for that breed.

MAE REED PORTER

Kansas City

CONTENTS

ILLUSTRATIONS

INTRODUCTION

SELDOM do we find in one individual the passion for rugged adventure, the hardihood to survive it, and the literary ability to portray it vividly. But such were the talents of George Frederick Ruxton.

Ruxton was first among writers to use the Mountain Man as literary material. In doing so he cast aside the romantic approach of J. Fenimore Cooper and portrayed his heroes in a realistic pattern. Having roasted buffalo humps and rolled in a blanket before a trapper campfire, Ruxton knew the heart that beat beneath fringed buckskin. He could describe the fascinating life of fur men and express their thoughts in their own distinctive jargon. With such an approach and presentation, he has given us, in *Life in the Far West*, one of the classics of American literature.

For the story of Ruxton's own remarkable career we refer the reader to our companion volume, *Ruxton of the Rockies*. Its availability makes unnecessary the giving here of anything more than a brief biographical sketch.

Although born in a quiet English countryside and receiving there the sound rudiments of education, his spirit was never caged in the boundaries of Oxfordshire or Kent. "I was a vagabond in all my propensities," he writes of his youth. "Everything quiet or commonplace I detested and my spirit chafed within me to see the world and participate in scenes of novelty and danger."[1]

[1] See Chapter I of *Ruxton of the Rockies* (edited by LeRoy R. Hafen [Norman, 1950]).

So it is not surprising that when sent to military college he was soon in rebellion. Consequent expulsion came as a relief.

With father dead and his mother and brothers unable to restrain him, he was off to Spain to test his mettle in the civil war. His courage and ability, soon apparent, won for him the Cross of the Order of San Fernando.

Returning to England—a military veteran at seventeen—he enlisted in Her Majesty's Eighty-ninth Regiment. After an uneventful period of service in England and Ireland, he was sent to Canada. Here, though he found novelty in this wild, wooded country alive with game, he fretted at barracks routine. To escape boredom he sold his lieutenant's commission and pushed deep into the forests of Upper Canada, there to revel in the unhampered freedom of the hunter's life.

A short visit back home and he was off to Africa, making two separate trips into the dark continent. With the outbreak of the Mexican War Ruxton sailed for Veracruz. Traveling generally alone, he journeyed to Mexico City, then northward to Durango, El Paso, and on to Santa Fé. With unconcealed relief he left the settlements behind and though it was midwinter headed for the wild frontier.

After solitary hunting trips to South Park and the vicinity of Pike's Peak, he wrote:

"Although liable to an accusation of barbarism, I must confess that the very happiest moments of my life have been spent in the wilderness of the Far West; and I never recall but with pleasure the remembrance of my solitary camp in the Bayou Salado, with no friend near me more faithful than my rifle, and no companions more sociable than my good horses and mules, or the attendant coyote which nightly serenaded us."[2]

At a traders' fort on the site of present Pueblo, Colorado, he found congenial companions. Here with the trappers and hunters he spent most of the winter and spring of 1847 and absorbed the facts and flavor which were to enrich his principal literary work.

[2] *Ruxton of the Rockies,* 262.

Ruxton's unfettered spirit was kin to the carefree trappers he met on the upper Arkansas. As blood brothers they sat in campfire glow to vicariously live each other's adventures.

Ruxton could tell of fratricidal battles in Spain, of glorious hunting trips with Chippewas in the crisp white woods of Upper Canada, or of his recent trip through the length of warring Mexico.

What he heard in return are the adventures related in this book.

The young Englishman was a good listener. From a stored memory and fragmentary notes, aided by his own experiences in the region and a genius for repeating the picturesque language of his trapper companions, he created the dramatic narrative, *Life in the Far West.*

The story told here is of Killbuck, La Bonté, and their carefree companions. We follow them along mountain streams to trap beaver, join them in fighting or eluding hostile Indians, are lured into New Mexico, and make a horse-stealing raid into California.

But the book is more than a story of adventure, it is a portrayal of the fascinating life of a picturesque period—the fur trade days of Western America.

During the first half of the nineteenth century, the fur gatherers, pushing into the Western wilds, were the first to thoroughly explore this newly acquired territory. They were the trailmakers of the frontier, the real pioneers of the Far West. Once lured beyond the settlements, they quickly lost the thin veneer of civilization and were soon wedded to their new life.

These weathered sons of Kentucky and Missouri, with an admixture of Frenchmen, Mexicans, and other nationalities, were a reckless breed of men. With bronzed faces and long hair, it was difficult to distinguish one from another, or all from a band of Indians. The trapper dressed in what is perhaps the only original American costume—the fringed buckskin suit.

With powder horn, bullet mold, muzzle-loading rifle, and knife, he was self-supporting and independent. Primitive barter supplied his simple wants; beaver skins served him for money.

Most fur men were without book learning, but they were educated for the life they led. They could read the tracks of moccasins, the sign of beaver, the trace of travois; they could mold their bullets from bars of lead and strike a fire with flint and steel. An Indian-style tipi furnished their winter shelter; a buffalo robe beneath the stars sufficed for summer nights. A horse to ride, one to carry his trappings, others for his squaw and children if he had been in the country long—and he could journey wherever trails led, or did not lead. Even his language was a conglomerate, understood only by the initiated. He soon became a distinct breed and gloried in the name of Mountain Man.

Such men and conditions are the actors and setting of Ruxton's book. They have never had a more effective portrayal.

Life in the Far West is fictionized history. The story is not a reliable historical chronicle, but it is factual. While it was running serially in *Blackwood's Edinburgh Magazine* during the summer of 1848, Ruxton wrote to the editors:

"With regard to the incidents of Indian attacks, starvation, cannibalism, etc., I have invented not one out of my own head. They are all matters of history in the mountains; but I have, no doubt, jumbled the *dramatis personæ* one with another, and may have committed anachronisms in the order of their occurrence."[3]

Thus he admits that the chronological order of events as given is not to be depended upon, and the persons listed in association on particular occasions may not have actually been together at the time indicated.

"The reader is informed that 'Life in the Far West' is *no fiction*. The scenes and incidents described are strictly true. The characters are real (the names being changed in two or

[3] Extracts from Ruxton's letters reproduced in Appendix A at the end of this volume.

three instances only), and all have been, and are, well known in the Western country."

Killbuck and La Bonté, heroes of the story, are the characters whose names are changed. Their identity will be discussed in Appendix B, at the end of this volume.

Only a few of the narrated incidents were Ruxton's own experiences. The remainder were gathered by observation or through conversation with trappers of the Far West. At Fort Pueblo on the upper Arkansas and around mountain campfires he listened to thrilling adventures of hunters and Indian fighters told in their own mountainesque words and metaphors.

So keen and capable was this young English traveler that in four short months he had mastered the language and lore which enabled him to present the most lively, flavorful, and complete picture of the Mountain Man and his time that has ever been written.

The story was prepared during the winter of 1847–48 and ran serially in *Blackwood's Edinburgh Magazine*, June to November, 1848. It was published in book form the next year and since then has been reissued many times. There were English editions of 1849, 1850, 1851, 1861, and 1867; American editions in 1849, 1855, 1859, and 1915; and a German edition in 1852.

While lecturing on American history at the University of Glasgow, 1947–48, I took an early opportunity to visit Edinburgh and call at the publication office on George Street of *Blackwood's Magazine* (founded in 1817). Dubiously I asked if there might possibly be preserved the back numbers of 1848, carrying Ruxton's serial, "Life in the Far West." Mr. Blackwood, the personable young representative of the famous old publishing house, was most gracious. He sent to the back files and presently brought out the century-old numbers; and, almost equally surprising to an American, gave these prized magazines at the original price, 2s, 6d (50 cents) each.

This serial publication, with only minor typographical

changes, has been followed for the present edition. Chapter divisions are as they appeared in the first book publication. Ruxton's own footnotes are identified by his name, though numbered along with the notes supplied by the editor.

In the proofreading and the preparation of notes I have had the assistance of my ever-helpful wife and collaborator, Ann Hafen.

LeRoy R. Hafen

Henry E. Huntington Library
San Marino, California

LIFE IN THE FAR WEST

The lost greenhorn (Alfred Jacob Miller)

"*Wagh,* he's *some—*he *is!*"

CHAPTER I

AWAY TO THE HEAD WATERS of the Platte, where several small streams run into the south fork of that river, and head in the broken ridges of the "Divide" which separates the valleys of the Platte and Arkansa, were camped a band of trappers on a creek called Bijou.[1] It was the month of October,[2] when the early frosts of the coming winter had crisped and dyed with sober brown the leaves of the cherry and quaking asp, which belted the little brook; and the ridges and peaks of the Rocky Mountains were already covered with a glittering mantle of snow, which sparkled in the still powerful rays of the autumn sun.

The camp had all the appearance of being a permanent one; for not only did one or two unusually comfortable shanties form a very conspicuous object, but the numerous stages on which huge strips of buffalo meat were hanging in process of cure, showed that the party had settled themselves here in order to lay in a store of provisions, or, as it is termed in the language of the mountains, "make meat." Round the camp were feeding some twelve or fifteen mules and horses, having their fore-legs confined by hobbles of raw hide, and, guarding these animals, two men paced backwards and forwards, driving in the strag-

[1] Bijou Creek was named for Joseph Bijeau, guide and interpreter with Major Stephen H. Long's 1820 expedition to the Rocky Mountains. The various branches of this north-flowing stream rise in high, grass-covered Bijou Basin, located some thirty miles northeast of the city of Colorado Springs, Colorado.

[2] The year is 1847, according to the references presently to the murder of Bent at Taos (which occurred in January of 1847), and later to Tharp's death (May 28, 1847). At another time Ruxton infers that the meeting was in 1846, since after spending the winter with the Utes, Killbuck and La Bonté meet Ruxton in South Park in the spring of 1847.

glers; and ever and anon ascending the bluffs which overhung the river, and, leaning on their long rifles, would sweep with their eyes the surrounding prairie. Three or four fires were burning in the encampment, on some of which Indian women were carefully tending sundry steaming pots; whilst round one, which was in the centre of it, four or five stalwart hunters, clad in buckskin, sat cross-legged, pipe in mouth.

They were a trapping party from the north fork of Platte, on their way to wintering-ground in the more southern valley of the Arkansa; some, indeed, meditating a more extended trip, even to the distant settlements of New Mexico, the paradise of mountaineers. The elder of the company was a tall gaunt man, with a face browned by a twenty years' exposure to the extreme climate of the mountains; his long black hair, as yet scarcely tinged with gray, hung almost to his shoulders, but his cheeks and chin were cleanly shaved, after the fashion of the mountain men. His dress was the usual hunting-frock of buckskin, with long fringes down the seams, with pantaloons similarly ornamented, and mocassins of Indian make. As his companions puffed their pipes in silence, he was narrating a few of his former experiences of western life; and whilst the buffalo "hump-ribs" and "tender loin" are singing away in the pot, preparing for the hunters' supper, we will note down the yarn as it spins from his lips, giving it in the language spoken in the "far west":

" 'Twas about 'calf-time,' maybe a little later, and not a hundred year ago, by a long chalk, that the biggest kind of rendezvous was held 'to' Independence, a mighty handsome little location away up on old Missoura. A pretty smart lot of boys was camp'd thar, about a quarter from the town, and the way the whisky flowed that time was 'some' now, I can tell you. Thar was old Sam Owins—him as got 'rubbed out'[3] by the Spaniards at Sacramenty, or Shihuahuy, this hos doesn't know which, but he 'went under'[4] any how. Well, Sam had his train along,

[3] Killed, } both terms adapted from the Indian figurative language. Ruxton's note.
[4] Died,

4

ready to hitch up for the Mexican country—twenty thunderin big Pittsburg waggons; and the way *his* Santa Fé boys took in the liquor beat all—eh, Bill?"[5]

[5] Samuel Owens, prominent merchant of Independence and trader on the Santa Fé Trail, enlisted in the Mexican War and was killed at the Battle of Sacramento, February 28, 1847.

Here are brief accounts of the figures mentioned in the following paragraph:

William Bent, one of the sons of Judge Silas Bent of St. Louis, was the principal owner and operator of famous Bent's Fort, located on the north bank of the Arkansas River about seven miles northeast of the present La Junta, Colorado.

Bill Williams, one of the most picturesque figures among the Mountain Men and fur trappers, has been portrayed by various writers. See A. H. Favour, *Old Bill Williams* (Chapel Hill, 1936), and Chauncey P. Williams, *Lone Elk, the Life Story of Bill Williams, Trapper and Guide of the Far West* (Denver, 1935). A more definitive biography, by Frederic Voelker of St. Louis, is about ready for publication.

William Tharp was killed on the Walnut Creek branch of the Arkansas in May of 1847, while on his way to the States. See *Ruxton of the Rockies*, 270–71, and Lewis Garrard, *Wah-To-Yah and the Taos Trail* (edited by R. P. Bieber [Glendale, California, 1938]), 173.

John Hatcher, prominent on the Santa Fé Trail, is given a lead part in Lewis Garrard's excellent historical narrative, *Wah-To-Yah and the Taos Trail*. R. P. Bieber gives biographical data on Hatcher in his edition of Garrard's book, p. 219.

Bill Garey (William Guerrier) was one of William Bent's traders at Bent's Fort on the Arkansas. Guerrier married a Cheyenne woman. See George B. Grinnell, "Bent's Old Fort and Its Builders," in the Kansas State Historical Society *Collections*, Vol. XV (1919), 37–38; and "The W. M. Boggs Manuscript about Bent's Fort, Kit Carson, the Far West, and Life Among the Indians," in the *Colorado Magazine*, Vol. VII, No. 2 (March, 1930), 49.

Jean Baptiste Charbonneau, son of Sacajawea (Bird Woman) of the Lewis and Clark expedition of 1804–1806, had a colorful career. Adopted and educated by William Clark, he accompanied Prince Paul of Wurttemburg to Europe in 1823 and remained there with the Prince until 1829. Returned to the United States, he joined a trapping expedition to the Rockies and for fifteen years was in the wilds as a Mountain Man. In 1846 he served as hunter and guide to Colonel St. George Cooke on the march of the Mormon Battalion from Santa Fé to San Diego. In his later years Charbonneau returned to his Shoshone relatives on the Wind River Reservation of Wyoming. Here he married into the tribe and remained until his death. See Ann W. Hafen, "Baptiste Charbonneau, Son of Bird Woman," in *The Westerners Brand Book* (Denver, 1950).

William Bent lived until May 19, 1869. It was his brother, Charles Bent, who was killed and scalped at Taos on January 19, 1847, during the uprising against Americans. Charles Bent had been appointed by General S. W. Kearny as the first American governor of New Mexico.

Ceran St. Vrain went to New Mexico in 1824 and was in a trapper band on the Gila River of Arizona as early as 1826. In 1831 he joined Charles Bent

"*Well*, it did."

"Bill Bent—his boys camped the other side the trail, and they was all mountain men, wagh!—and Bill Williams, and Bill Tharpe (the Pawnees took his hair on Pawnee Fork last spring): three Bills, and them three's all 'gone under.' Surely Hatcher went out that time; and wasn't Bill Garey along, too? Didn't him and Chabonard sit in camp for twenty hours at a deck of Euker? Them was Bent's Indian traders up on Arkansa. Poor Bill Bent! them Spaniards made meat of him. He lost his topknot to Taos. A 'clever' man was Bill Bent as *I* ever know'd trade a robe or 'throw' a bufler in his tracks. Old St Vrain could knock the hind-sight off him though, when it come to shootin, and old silver heels spoke true, she did: 'plum-center' she was, eh?"

"*Well*, she was'nt nothin else."

"The Greasers[6] payed for Bent's scalp, they tell me. Old St Vrain went out of Santa Fé with a company of mountain men, and the way they made 'em sing out was 'slick as shootin.' He 'counted a coup' did St Vrain.[7] He throwed a Pueblo as had on poor Bent's shirt. I guess he tickled that niggur's hump-ribs. Fort William[8] aint the lodge it was, an' never will be agin, now he's gone under; but St Vrain's 'pretty much of a gentleman,' too; if he aint, I'll be dog-gone, eh, Bill?"

"He is *so-o*."

"Chavez had his waggons along. He was only a Spaniard any

---

to form Bent, St. Vrain and Co., thereafter prominent in the Santa Fé trade. Ceran's younger brother, Marcelline, a trapper and trader with the Indians, was a famous hunter. See T. M. Marshall, "St. Vrain's Expedition to the Gila in 1826," in *The Pacific Ocean in History* (edited by H. M. Stephens and H. E. Bolton [New York, 1917]), 429–38; and [P. A. St. Vrain], *The de Lassus St. Vrain Family* [1944].

6 The Mexicans are called "Spaniards" or "Greasers" (from their greasy appearance) by the Western people. Ruxton's note.

7 Captain St. Vrain led a company of volunteers in Colonel Sterling Price's campaign to put down the uprising of January, 1847.

8 Bent's Indian trading fort on the Arkansa. Ruxton's note. Fort William, named for William Bent and generally known as Bent's Fort, was established in 1832 and was the most famous trading post of the Southwest. See Grinnell, "Bent's Old Fort and Its Builders."

how, and some of his teamsters put a ball into him his next trip, and made a raise of *his* dollars, wagh! Uncle Sam hung 'em for it, I heard, but can't b'lieve it, no-how.[9] If them Spaniards wasn't born for shootin', why was beaver made? You was with us that spree, Jemmy?"

"No *sirre-e;* I went out when Spiers[10] lost his animals on Cimmaron: a hundred and forty mules and oxen was froze that night, wagh!"

"Surely Black Harris[11] was thar; and the darndest liar was Black Harris—for lies tumbled out of his mouth like boudins out of a bufler's stomach. He was the child as saw the putrefied forest in the Black Hills. Black Harris come in from Laramie; he'd been trapping three year an' more on Platte and the 'other side'; and, when he got into Liberty, he fixed himself right off like a Saint Louiy dandy. Well, he sat to dinner one day in the tavern, and a lady says to him:

"Well, Mister Harris, I hear you're a great travler."

"Travler, marm," says Black Harris, "this niggur's no travler; I ar' a trapper, marm, a mountain-man, wagh!"

"Well, Mister Harris, trappers are great travlers, and you goes over a sight of ground in your perishinations, I'll be bound to say."

"A sight, marm, this coon's gone over, if that's the way your

[9] Don Antonio José Chavez left New Mexico in February of 1843 with two wagons, fifty-five mules, furs, and some $10,000 in gold and silver. He was going to Missouri to purchase trade goods. When nearing his destination he was robbed and murdered by a gang of ruffians led by John McDaniel. The outlaws were later apprehended and tried in St. Louis. John McDaniel and his brother David were hanged, and others of the gang were imprisoned. See R. E. Twitchell, *The Leading Facts of New Mexican History* (5 vols., Cedar Rapids, Iowa, 1911–17), II, 83–84.

[10] Albert Speyer and Dr. Henry Connelly lost some three hundred mules in a storm on the Cimarron in the early winter of 1844. J. L. Collins' report in Twitchell, *ibid.*, 126.

[11] Moses ("Black") Harris divides with Jim Bridger the honor of being the biggest liar among the Mountain Men. Harris, prominent trapper, was later an important emigrant guide.

'stick floats.'[12] I've trapped beaver on Platte and Arkansa, and away up on Missoura and Yaller Stone; I've trapped on Columbia, on Lewis Fork, and Green River; I've trapped, marm, on Grand River and the Heely (Gila). I've fout the 'Blackfoot' (and d——d bad Injuns they are); I've 'raised the hair'[13] of more *than one* Apach, and made a Rapaho 'come' afore now; I've trapped in heav'n, in airth, and h——, and scalp my old head, marm, but I've seen a putrefied forest."

"La, Mister Harris, a what?"

"A putrefied forest, marm, as sure as my rifle's got hindsights, and *she* shoots center. I was out on the Black Hills, Bill Sublette[14] knows the time—the year it rained fire—and every body knows when that was.[15] If thar wasn't cold doin's about that time, this child wouldn't say so. The snow was about fifty foot deep, and the bufler lay dead on the ground like bees after a beein'; not whar we was tho', for *thar* was no bufler, and no meat, and me and my band had been livin' on our mocassins (leastwise the parflesh),[16] for six weeks; and poor doin's that feedin' is, marm, as you'll never know. One day we crossed a 'canon' and over a 'divide,' and got into a periara, whar was green grass, and green trees, and green leaves on the trees, and birds singing in the green leaves, and this in Febrary, wagh! Our animals was like to die when they see the green grass, and we all sung out, 'hurraw for summer doin's.'

" 'Hyar goes for meat,' says I, and I jest ups old Ginger at one of them singing birds, and down come the crittur elegant;

---

[12] Meaning, if that's what you mean! The "stick" is tied to the beaver trap by a string; and, floating on the water, points out its position, should a beaver have carried it away. Ruxton's note.

[13] Scalped. Ruxton's note.

[14] William Sublette was the most prominent of five brothers—Milton, Andrew, Solomon, and Pinckney, being the others. He was one of the business successors of W. H. Ashley in the Rocky Mountain fur trade and was founder, with Robert Campbell, of Fort William (later Fort Laramie) on the Laramie Fork of the North Platte. One of his purposes in going into the mountains was to combat tuberculosis; but he succumbed to the disease in 1845.

[15] The "Year the Stars Fell"—the meteoric shower of November 12, 1833.

[16] Soles made of buffalo hide. Ruxton's note.

its darned head spinning away from the body, but never stops singing, and when I takes up the meat, I finds it stone, wagh!

"Hyar's damp powder and no fire to dry it," I says quite skeared.

" 'Fire be dogged,' says old Rube.[17] 'Hyar's a hos as'll make fire come'; and with that he takes his axe and lets drive at a cottonwood. Schr-u-k—goes the axe agin the tree, and out comes a bit of the blade as big as my hand. We looks at the animals, and thar they stood shaking over the grass, which I'm dog-gone if it wasn't stone, too. Young Sublette comes up, and he'd been clerking down to the fort on Platte, so he know'd something. He looks and looks, and scrapes the tree with his butcher knife, and snaps the grass like pipe stems, and breaks the leaves a-snappin' like Californy shells.

" 'What's all this, boy?' I asks.

" 'Putrefactions,' says he, looking smart, 'putrefactions, or I'm a niggur.' "

"La, Mister Harris," says the lady; "putrefactions, why, did the leaves, and the trees, and the grass smell badly?"

"Smell badly, marm," says Black Harris, "would a skunk stink if he was froze to stone? No, marm, this child didn't know what putrefactions was, and young Sublette's varsion wouldn't 'shine' nohow, so I chips a piece out of a tree and puts it in my trap-sack, and carries it in safe to Laramie. Well, old Captain Stewart[18] (a clever man was that, though he was an Englishman), he comes along next spring, and a Dutch doctor chap was along too. I shows him the piece I chipped out of the tree, and he called it a putrefaction too; and so, marm, if that wasn't a putrefied peraira, what was it? For this hos doesn't know, and *he* knows 'fat cow' from 'poor bull,' anyhow."

"Well, old Black Harris is gone under too, I believe. He went to the 'Parks' trapping with a Vide Pôche Frenchman, who shot

---

[17] Rube Herring, whom Ruxton met at the Mormon settlement near Pueblo, Colorado, early in 1847. See *Ruxton of the Rockies*, 255–56. He is to appear subsequently in this story.

[18] Captain William Drummond Stewart, famed Scottish traveler and hunter, who first came into the West in 1833.

9

him for his bacca and traps.[19] Darn them Frenchmen, they're no account any way you lays your sight. (Any 'bacca in your bag, Bill? this beaver feels like chawing.)

"Well, any how, thar was the camp, and they was goin to put out the next morning; and the last as come out of Independence was that ar Englishman. He'd a nor-west[20] capôte on, and a two-shoot gun rifled. Well, them English are darned fools; they can't fix a rifle any ways; but that one did shoot 'some'; leastwise *he* made it throw plum-center. He made the bufler 'come,' *he* did, and fout well at Pawnee Fork too.[21] What was his name? All the boys called him Cap'en, and he got his fixings from old Choteau;[22] but what he wanted out thar in the mountains, I never jest rightly know'd. He was no trader, nor a trapper, and flung about his dollars right smart. Thar was old grit in him, too, and a hair of the black b'ar at that.[23] They say he took the bark off the Shians when he cleared out of the village with old Beaver Tail's squaw. He'd been on Yaller Stone afore that: Leclerc know'd him in the Blackfoot, and up in the Chippeway country; and he had the best powder as ever I flashed through life, and his gun was handsome, that's a fact. Them thar locks was grand; and old Jake Hawken's nephey (him as trapped on Heely [Gila] that time), told me, the other day, as he saw an English gun on Arkansa last winter as beat all off hand.[24]

[19] This report is false, as Black Harris died of cholera at Independence on May 6, 1849.

[20] The Hudson Bay Company, having amalgamated with the American North West Company, is known by the name "North West" to the southern trappers. Their employes usually wear Canadian *capôtes*. Ruxton's note.

[21] The reference is to William Drummond Stewart. Bernard De Voto calls Killbuck's references to Stewart "embroidery," and thinks the Scotsman never traveled the Santa Fé Trail and fought at Pawnee Fork. However, Stewart's movements in the spring of 1834 may possibly have brought him to Pawnee Fork. See Bernard De Voto, *Beyond the Wide Missouri* (Boston, 1947), 46, 420.

[22] Pierre Choteau and Company were successors to the Western Department of the American Fur Company at St. Louis and did an outfitting business.

[23] A spice of the devil. Ruxton's note.

[24] Jake and Samuel Hawken were famous gunsmiths at St. Louis. Samuel

"Nigh upon two hundred dollars I had in my possibles, when I went to that camp to see the boys afore they put out; and you know, Bill, as I sat to 'Euker' and 'seven up'[25] till every cent was gone.

" 'Take back twenty, old coon,' says Big John.

" 'H——'s full of such takes back,' says I; and I puts back to town and fetches the rifle and the old mule, puts my traps into the sack, gets credit for a couple of pounds of powder at Owin's store, and hyar I ar on Bijou, with half a pack of beaver, and running meat yet, old hos: so put a log on, and let's have a smoke.

"Hurraw, Jake, old coon, bear a hand, and let the squaw put them tails in the pot; for sun's down, and we'll have to put out pretty early to reach 'Black Tail' by this time tomorrow. Who's fust guard, boys: them cussed 'Rapahos' will be after the animals to-night, or I'm no judge of Injun sign. How many did you see, Maurice?"

"Enfant de Gârce, me see bout honderd, when I pass Squirrel Creek, one dam war-party, parce-que, they no hosses, and have de lariats for steal des animaux. May be de Yutes in Bayou Salade."[26]

"We'll be having trouble to-night, I'm thinking, if the devils are about. Whose band was it, Maurice?"

"Slim-Face—I see him ver close—is out; mais I think it White Wolf's."

"White Wolf, maybe, will lose his hair if he and his band knock round here too often. That Injun put me afoot when he

---

went to the new town of Denver in 1859 and set up a gunsmith shop there. Among early trappers the Hawken was the most prized weapon of the West.

Ruxton calls the person "John Hawkens" who entertained him at Pueblo on the Arkansas in January of 1847, and this is doubtless the person referred to here. The English gun mentioned would be Ruxton's own, which he showed the trappers at Pueblo.

[25] "Euker," "poker," and "seven-up," are the fashionable games of cards. Ruxton's note.

[26] Bayou Salade (Salt Valley), now known as South Park (Colorado), was a hunter's paradise. It took its name from the salt spring and marsh at the southern end of this high mountain valley.

was out on 'Sandy' that fall. This niggur owes him one, any how."

"H——'s full of White Wolves: go ahead, and roll out some of your doins across the plains that time."

"You seed sights that spree, eh, boy?"

"*Well*, we did. Some of em got their flints fixed this side of Pawnee Fork, and a heap of mule-meat went wolfing. Just by Little Arkansa we saw the first Injun. Me and young Somes was ahead for meat, and I had hobbled the old mule and was 'approaching' some goats,[27] when I see the critturs turn back their heads and jump right away for me. 'Hurraw, Dick!' I shouts, 'hyars brown-skin acomin,' and off I makes for the mule. The young greenhorn sees the goats runnin up to him, and not being up to Injun ways, blazes at the first and knocks him over. Jest then seven darned red heads top the bluff, and seven Pawnees come a-screechin upon us. I cuts the hobbles and jumps on the mule, and, when I looks back, there was Dick Somes ramming a ball down his gun like mad, and the Injuns flinging their arrows at him pretty smart, I tell you. 'Hurraw, Dick, mind your hair,' and I ups old Greaser and let one Injun 'have it,' as was going plum into the boy with his lance. *He* turned on his back handsome, and Dick gets the ball down at last, blazes away, and drops another. Then we charged on em, and they clears off like runnin cows; and I takes the hair off the heads of the two we made meat of; and I do b'lieve thar's some of them scalps on my old leggings yet.

"Well, Dick was as full of arrows as a porkypine: one was sticking right through his cheek, one in his meat-bag, and two more 'bout his hump ribs. I tuk 'em all out slick, and away we go to camp (for they was jost a-campin' when we went ahead), and carryin' the goat too. Thar was a hurroo when we rode in with the scalps at the end of our guns. 'Injuns! Injuns!' was the cry from the greenhorns; 'we'll be 'tacked to-night, that's certain.'

" "Tacked be ——,' says old Bill; 'ain't we men too, and

[27] Antelope are frequently called "goats" by the mountaineers. Ruxton's note.

white at that. Look to your guns, boys; send out a strong hos'-guard with the animals, and keep your eyes skinned.'

"Well, as soon as the animals were unhitched from the wag-gons, the guvner sends out a strong guard, seven boys, and old hands at that. It was pretty nigh upon sundown, and Bill had just sung out to 'corral.' The boys were drivin' in the animals, and we were all standin' round to get 'em in slick, when, 'howgh-owgh-owgh-owgh,' we hears right behind the bluff, and 'bout a minute and a perfect crowd of Injuns gallops down upon the animals. Wagh! war'nt thor hoopin'! We jump for the guns, but before we get to the fires, the Injuns were among the cavayard. I saw Ned Collyer and his brother, who were in the hos'-guard, let drive at 'em; but twenty Pawnees were round 'em before the smoke cleared from their rifles, and when the crowd broke the two boys were on the ground, and their hair gone. Well, that ar Englishman just saved the cavayard. He had his horse, a reglar buffalo-runner, picketed round the fire quite handy, and as soon as he sees the fix, he jumps upon her and rides right into the thick of the mules, and passes through 'em, firing his two-shoot gun at the Injuns, and by Gor, he made two come. The mules, which was a snortin' with funk and run-ning before the Injuns, as soon as they see the Englishman's mare (mules'ill go to h—— after a horse, you all know), fol-lowed her right into the corral, and thar they was safe. Fifty Pawnees come screechin' after 'em, but we was ready that time, and the way we throw'd 'em was something handsome, I tell you. But three of the hos'-guards got skeared—leastwise their mules did, and carried 'em off into the peraira, and the Injuns having enough of *us*, dashed after 'em right away. Them poor devils looked back miserable now, with about a hundred red varmints tearin' after their hair, and whooping like mad. Young Jem Bulcher was the last; and when he seed it was no use, and his time was nigh, he throw'd himself off the mule, and standing as upright as a hickory wiping stick, he waves his hand to us, and blazes away at the first Injun as come up, and dropped him slick; but the moment after, you may guess, *he* died.

"We could do nothin,' for, before our guns were loaded, all three were dead and their scalps gone. Five of our boys got rubbed out that time, and seven Injuns lay wolf's meat, while a many more went away gut-shot, I'll lay. How'sever, seven of us went under, and the Pawnees made a raise of a dozen mules, wagh!"

Thus far, in his own words, we have accompanied the old hunter in his tale; and probably he would have taken us, by the time that the Squaw Chili-pat had pronounced the beaver tails cooked, safely across the grand prairies—fording Cotton Wood, Turkey Creek, Little Arkansa, Walnut Creek, and Pawnee Fork—passed the fireless route of the Cook Creeks; through a sea of fat buffalo meat, without fuel to cook it; have struck the big river, and, leaving at the "Crossing" the waggons destined for Santa Fé, have trailed us up the Arkansa to Bent's Fort; thence up Boiling Spring, across the divide over to the southern fork of the Platte, away up to the Black Hills, and finally camped us, with hair still preserved, in the beaver-abounding valleys of the Sweet Water, and Câche la Poudre, under the rugged shadow of the Wind River mountains; if it had not so befell, that at this juncture, as all our mountaineers sat cross-legged round the fire, pipe in mouth, and with Indian gravity listened to the yarn of the old trapper, interrupting him only with an occasional wagh! or the assured exclamations of some participator in the events then under narration, who would every now and then put in a corroborative—"This child remembers that fix," or, "hyar's a niggur lifted hair that spree," &c.—that a whizzing noise was heard to whistle through the air, followed by a sharp but suppressed cry from one of the hunters.

In an instant the mountaineers had sprung from their seats, and, seizing the ever-ready rifle, each one had thrown himself on the ground a few paces beyond the light of the fire (for it was now nightfall); but not a word escaped them, as, lying close, with their keen eyes directed towards the gloom of the thicket, near which the camp was placed, with rifles cocked, they waited a renewal of the attack. Presently the leader of the band, no other than Killbuck,[28] who had so lately been recounting some of his experiences across the plains, and than whom no more crafty woodsman or more expert trapper ever tracked a deer or grained a beaverskin, raised his tall, leather-clad form, and, placing his hand over his mouth, made the prairie ring with the wild protracted note of an Indian war-whoop. This was instantly repeated from the direction where the animals belonging to the camp were grazing, under the charge of the horse-guard, and three shrill whoops answered the warning of the leader, and showed that the guard was on the alert, and understood the signal. However, with this manifestation of their presence, the Indians appeared to be satisfied; or, what is more probable, the act of aggression had been committed by some daring young warrior, who, being out on his first expedition, desired to strike the first *coup*, and thus signalise himself at the outset of the campaign. After waiting some few minutes, expecting a renewal of the attack, the mountaineers in a body rose from the ground and made towards the animals, with which they presently returned to the camp; and, after carefully hobbling and securing them to pickets firmly driven into the ground, and mounting an additional guard, they once more assembled round the fire, after examining the neighbouring thicket, relit their pipes, and puffed away the cheering weed as composedly as if no such being as a Redskin, thirsting for their lives, was within a thousand miles of their perilous encampment.

"If ever thar was bad Injuns on these plains," at last growled Killbuck, biting hard the pipe-stem between his teeth, "it's these Rapahos, and the meanest kind at that."

"Can't beat the Blackfeet anyhow," chimed in one La Bonté,[29] from the Yellow Stone country, and a fine, handsome specimen of a mountaineer.

[28] For a discussion of his identity see Appendix B, at the end of this volume.

[29] The question of the identity of La Bonté is considered below, in Appendix B.

"However, one of you quit this arrow out of my hump," he continued, bending forwards to the fire, and exhibiting an arrow sticking out under his right shoulder-blade, and a stream of blood trickling down his buckskin coat from the wound.

This his nearest neighbour essayed to do; but finding, after a tug, that it "would not come," expressed his opinion that the offending weapon would have to be "butchered" out. This was accordingly effected with the ready blade of a scalp-knife; and a handful of beaver-fur being placed on the wound, and secured by a strap of buckskin round the body, the wounded man donned his hunting-shirt once more, and coolly set about lighting his pipe, his rifle lying across his lap, cocked and ready for use.

It was now near midnight—dark and misty; and the clouds, rolling away to the eastward from the lofty ridges of the Rocky Mountains, were gradually obscuring the little light which was afforded by the dim stars. As the lighter vapours faded from the mountains, a thick black cloud succeeded them, and settled over the loftier peaks of the chain, which were faintly visible through the gloom of night, whilst a mass of fleecy scud soon overspread the whole sky. A hollow moaning sound crept through the valley, and the upper branches of the cottonwoods, with their withered leaves, began to rustle with the first breath of the coming storm. Huge drops of rain fell at intervals, hissing as they fell on the blazing fires, and pattered on the skins which the hunters were hurriedly laying on their exposed baggage. The mules near the camp cropped the grass with quick and greedy bites round the circuit of their pickets, as if conscious that the storm would soon prevent their feeding, and were already humping their backs as the chilling rain fell upon their flanks. The prairie wolves crept closer to the camp, and in the confusion that ensued from the hurry of the trappers to cover the perishable portions of their equipment, contrived more than once to dart off with a piece of meat, when their peculiar and mournful chiding would be heard as they fought for the possession of the ravished morsel.

As soon as every thing was duly protected, the men set to work to spread their beds, those who had not troubled themselves to erect a shelter getting under the lee of the piles of packs and saddles; while Killbuck, disdaining even such care of his carcass, threw his buffalo robe on the bare ground, declaring his intention to "take" what was coming at all hazards, and "any how." Selecting a high spot, he drew his knife and proceeded to cut drains round it, to prevent the water running into him as he lay; then taking a single robe he carefully spread it, placing under the end farthest from the fire a large stone brought from the creek. Having satisfactorily adjusted this pillow, he adds another robe to the one already laid, and places over all a Navajo blanket, supposed to be impervious to rain. Then he divests himself of his pouch and powder-horn, which, with his rifle, he places inside his bed, and quickly covers up lest the wet reach them. Having performed these operations to his satisfaction, he lighted his pipe by the hissing embers of the half-extinguished fire (for by this time the rain was pouring in torrents), and going the rounds of the picketed animals, and cautioning the guard round the camp to keep their "eyes skinned, for there would be 'powder burned' before morning," he returned to the fire, and kicking with his mocassined foot the slumbering ashes, squats down before it, and thus soliloquises:

"Thirty year have I been knocking about these mountains from Missoura's head as far sothe as the starving Gila. I've trapped a 'heap,'[30] and many a hundred pack of beaver I've traded in my time, wagh! What has come of it, and whar's the dollars as ought to be in my possibles? Whar's the ind of this, I say? Is a man to be hunted by Injuns all his days? Many's the time I've said I'd strike for Taos, and trap a squaw, for this child's getting old, and feels like wanting a woman's face about his lodge for the balance of his days; but when it comes to caching of the old traps, I've the smallest kind of heart, I have.

[30] An Indian is always a "heap" hungry or thirsty—loves a "heap"—is a "heap" brave—in fact, "heap" is tantamount to very much. Ruxton's note.

Certain, the old state comes across my mind now and again, but who's thar to remember my old body? But them diggings gets too over crowded now-a-days, and its hard to fetch breath amongst them big bands of corncrackers to Missoura. Beside, it goes against natur to leave bufler meat and feed on hog; and them white gals are too much like picturs, and a deal too 'fofar-raw' (fanfaron). No; darn the settlements, I say. It won't shine, and whar's the dollars? Howsever, beaver's 'bound to rise'; human natur can't go on selling beaver a dollar a pound;[31] no, no, that arn't a going to shine much longer, I know. Them was the times when this child first went to the mountains: six dollars the plew—old 'un or kitten. Wagh! but it's bound to rise, I says agin; and hyar's a coon knows whar to lay his hand on a dozen pack right handy, and then he'll take the Taos trail, wagh!"

Thus soliloquising, Killbuck knocked the ashes from his pipe, and placed it in the gaily ornamented case which hung round his neck, drew his knife-belt a couple of holes tighter, and once more donned his pouch and powder-horn, took his rifle, which he carefully covered with the folds of his Navajo blanket, and striding into the darkness, cautiously reconnoitred the vicinity of the camp. When he returned to the fire he sat himself down as before, but this time with his rifle across his lap; and at intervals his keen gray eye glanced piercingly around, particularly towards an old weatherbeaten, and grizzled mule, who now, old stager as she was, having filled her belly, was standing lazily over her picket pin, with head bent down and her long ears flapping over her face, her limbs gathered under her, and with back arched to throw off the rain, tottering from side to side as she rests and sleeps.

"Yep, old gal!" cried Killbuck to the animal, at the same time picking a piece of burnt wood from the fire and throwing it at her, at which the mule gathered itself up and cocked her ears as

---

[31] The old trapper was loath to leave his traps. Though the price of beaver was down, he was sure it would rise again. This was a faith often expressed by those who saw their occupation slipping from them.

she recognized her master's voice. "Yep, old gal! and keep your nose open; thar's brown skin about, I'm thinkin', and maybe you'll get 'roped' (lasso'd) by a Rapaho afore mornin."[32] Again the old trapper settled himself before the fire; and soon his head began to nod, as drowsiness stole over him. Already he was in the land of dreams; revelling amongst bands of "fat cow," or hunting along a stream well peopled with beaver; with no Indian "sign" to disturb him, and the merry rendezvous in close perspective, and his peltry selling briskly at six dollars the plew,[33] and galore of alcohol to ratify the trade. Or, perhaps, threading the back trail of his memory, he passed rapidly through the perilous vicissitudes of his hard, hard life—starving one day, revelling in abundance the next; now beset by whooping savages thirsting for his blood, baying his enemies like the hunted deer, but with the unflinching courage of a man; now, all care thrown aside, secure and forgetful of the past, a welcome guest in the hospitable trading fort; or back, as the trail gets fainter, to his childhood's home in the brown forests of old Kentuck, tended and cared for—no thought his, but to enjoy the homminy and johnny cakes of his thrifty mother. Once more, in warm and well remembered homespun, he sits on the snake fence round the old clearing, and munching his hoe-cake at set of sun, listens to the mournful note of the whip-poor-will, or the harsh cry of the noisy catbird, or watches the agile gambols of the squirrels as they chase each other, chattering the while, from branch to branch of the lofty tameracks, wondering how long it will be before he will be able to lift his father's heavy rifle, and use it against the tempting game. Sleep, however, sat lightly on the eyes of the wary mountaineer, and a snort from the old mule in an instant stretched his every nerve; and, without a movement of his body, the keen eye fixed itself upon the mule, which now was standing with head bent round, and eyes and ears pointed in one direction, snuffing the night

[32] The mule was an excellent detector of Indians and the trapper expected warning from his mule of the approach of Indians.

[33] "Plew" (*plus*) in trapper talk signified a prime beaver skin, and was a unit of exchange.

air and snorting with apparent fear. A low sound from the wake-ful hunter roused the others from their sleep; and raising their bodies from their well-soaked beds, a single word apprised them of their danger.

"Injuns!"

Scarcely was the word out of Killbuck's lips, when, above the howling of the furious wind, and the pattering of the rain, a hundred savage yells broke suddenly upon their ears from all directions round the camp; a score of rifle-shots rattled from the thicket, and a cloud of arrows whistled through the air, at the same time that a crowd of Indians charged upon the picketed animals. "Owgh, owgh—owgh—owgh—g-h-h." "A foot, by gor!" shouted Killbuck, "and the old mule gone at that. On 'em, boys, for old Kentuck!" and rushed towards his mule, which was jumping and snorting mad with fright, as a naked Indian strove to fasten a lariat round her nose, having already cut the rope which fastened her to the picket-pin.

"Quit that, you cussed devil!" roared the trapper, as he jumped upon the savage, and without raising his rifle to his shoulder, made a deliberate thrust with the muzzle at his naked breast, striking him full, and at the same time pulling the trigger, actually driving the Indian two paces backwards with the shock, when he fell in a heap and dead. But at the same moment, an Indian, sweeping his club round his head, brought it with fatal force down upon Killbuck's skull, and staggering for a moment, he threw out his arms wildly into the air, and fell headlong to the ground.

"Owgh! owgh, owgh-h-h!" cried the Rapaho as the white fell, and, striding over the prostrate body, seized with his left hand the middle lock of the trappers long hair, and drew his knife round the head to separate the scalp from the skull. As he bent over to his work, the trapper named La Bonté caught sight of the strait his companion was in, and quick as thought rushed at the Indian, burying his knife to the hilt between his shoulders, and with a gasping shudder, the Rapaho fell dead upon the prostrate body of his foe.

The attack, however, lasted but a few seconds. The dash at the animals had been entirely successful, and, driving them before them, with loud cries, the Indians disappeared quickly in the darkness. Without waiting for daylight, two of the three trappers who alone were to be seen, and who had been within the shanties at the time of attack, without a moment's delay commenced packing two horses, which having been fastened to the shanties had escaped the Indians, and placing their squaws upon them, showering curses and imprecations on their enemies, left the camp, fearful of another onset, and resolved to retreat and câche themselves until the danger was over. Not so La Bonté, who, stout and true, had done his best in the fight, and now sought the body of his old comrade, from which, before he could examine the wounds, he had first to remove the corpse of the Indian he had slain. Killbuck still breathed. He had been stunned; but, revived by the cold rain beating upon his face, he soon opened his eyes, recognising his trusty friend, who, sitting down, lifted his head into his lap, and wiped away the blood which streamed from the wounded scalp.

"Is the top-knot gone, boy?" asked Killbuck; "for my head feels queersome, I tell you."

"Thar's the Injun as felt like lifting it," answered the other, kicking the dead body with his foot.

"Wagh! boy, you've struck a coup; so scalp the nigger right off, and then fetch me a drink."

The morning broke clear and cold. With the exception of a light cloud which hung over Pike's Peak, the sky was spotless; and a perfect calm had succeeded the boisterous winds of the previous night. The creek was swollen and turbid with the rains; and as La Bonté proceeded a little distance down the bank to find a passage to the water, he suddenly stopped short, and an involuntary cry escaped him. Within a few feet of the bank lay the body of one of his companions who had formed the guard at the time of the Indians' attack. It was lying on the face, pierced through the chest with an arrow which was buried to the very feathers, and the scalp torn from the bloody skull.

Beyond, and all within a hundred yards, lay the three others, dead and similarly mutilated. So certain had been the aim, and so close the enemy, that each had died without a struggle, and consequently had been unable to alarm the camp. La Bonté, with a glance at the bank, saw at once that the wily Indians had crept along the creek, the noise of the storm facilitating their approach undiscovered, and crawling up the bank, had watched their opportunity to shoot simultaneously the four hunters who were standing guard.

Returning to Killbuck, he apprised him of the melancholy fate of their companions, and held a council of war as to their proceedings. The old hunter's mind was soon made up. "First," said he, "I get back my old mule; she's carried me and my traps these twelve years, and I ain't a goin' to lose her yet. Second, I feel like taking hair, and some Rapahos has to 'go under' for this night's work. Third, we have got to câche the beaver. Fourth, we take the Injun trail, wherever it leads."

No more daring mountaineer than La Bonté ever trapped a beaver, and no counsel could have more exactly tallied with his own inclination than the law laid down by old Killbuck.

"Agreed," was his answer, and forthwith he set about forming a câche. In this instance they had not sufficient time to construct a regular one, so contented themselves with securing their packs of beaver in buffalo robes, and tying them in the forks of several cottonwoods, under which the camp had been made. This done, they lit a fire, and cooked some buffalo meat; and, whilst smoking a pipe, carefully cleaned their rifles, and filled their horns and pouches with good store of ammunition.

A prominent feature in the character of the hunters of the far west is their quick determination and resolve in cases of extreme difficulty and peril, and their fixedness of purpose, when any plan of operations has been laid requiring bold and instant action in carrying out. It is here that they so infinitely surpass the savage Indian, in bringing to a successful issue their numerous hostile expeditions against the natural foe of the white man in the wild and barbarous regions of the west. Ready to resolve as they are prompt to execute, and with the advantage of far greater dash and daring with equal subtlety and caution, they possess great advantage over the vacillating Indian, whose superstitious mind in a great degree paralyses the physical energy of his active body; and in waiting for propitious signs and seasons before he undertakes an enterprise, he loses the opportunity which his white and more civilized enemy knows so well to profit by.

Killbuck and La Bonté were no exceptions to this characteristic rule, and, before the sun was a hand's-breadth above the eastern horizon, the two hunters were running on the trail of the victorious Indians. Striking from the creek where the night attack was made, they crossed to another known as Kioway, running parallel to Bijou, a few hours' journey westward, and likewise heading in the "divide." Following this to its forks, they struck into the upland prairies lying at the foot of the mountains; and crossing to the numerous water-courses which feed the creek called "Vermillion" or "Cherry,"[34] they pursued the trail over the mountain-spurs until it reached a fork of the Boiling Spring.[35] Here the war-party had halted and held a consultation, for from this point the trail turned at a tangent to the westward, and entered the rugged gorges of the mountains. It was now evident to the two trappers that their destination was the Bayou Salade—a mountain valley which is a favourite resort of the buffalo in the winter season, and also, and for this reason, often frequented by the Yuta Indians as their wintering ground. That the Rapahos were on a war expedition against the Yutas,[36] there was little doubt; and Killbuck, who knew every inch of the ground, saw at once, by the direction the trail had taken, that they were making for the Bayou in order to surprise their enemies, and, therefore, were not following the usual Indian trail up the cañon of the Boiling Spring River.

[34] Cherry Creek, that enters the South Platte at the site of Denver. Major S. H. Long called it Vermilion Creek.

[35] Fountain Creek of today.

[36] The Utes, mountain Indians and natural foes of the Arapahoes of the plains.

Having made up his mind to this, he at once struck across the broken ground lying at the foot of the mountains, steering a course a little to the eastward of north, or almost in the direction whence he had come: and then, pointing westward, about noon he crossed a mountain chain, and descending into a ravine through which a little rivulet tumbled over its rocky bed, he at once proved the correctness of his judgment by striking the Indian trail, now quite fresh, as it wound through the cañon along the bank of the stream. The route he had followed, which would have been impracticable to pack animals, had saved at least half-a-day's journey, and brought them within a short distance of the object of their pursuit; for, at the head of the gorge, a lofty bluff presenting itself, the hunters ascended to the summit, and, looking down, descried at their very feet the Indian camp, with their own stolen cavallada feeding quietly round.

"Wagh!" exclaimed both the hunters in a breath. "And thar's the old gal at that," chuckled Killbuck, as he recognised his old grizzled mule making good play at the rich buffalo grass with which these mountain valleys abound.

"If we don't make 'a raise' afore long, I wouldn't say so. Thar plans is plain to this child as beaver sign. They're after Yute hair, as certain as this gun has got hind-sights; but they ar'nt agoin' to pack them animals after 'em, and have crawled like 'rattlers' along this bottom to câche 'em till they come back from the Bayou—and maybe they'll leave half a dozen 'soldiers'[37] with 'em."

How right the wily trapper was in his conjectures will be shortly proved. Meanwhile, with his companion, he descended the bluff, and pushing his way into a thicket of dwarf pine and cedar, sat down on a log, and drew from an end of the blanket, which was strapped on his shoulder, a portion of a buffalo's liver, which they both discussed with infinite relish—and *raw;* eating in lieu of bread (an unknown luxury in these parts) sundry strips of dried fat. To have kindled a fire would have been

[37] The young untried warriors of the Indians are thus called. Ruxton's note.

dangerous, since it was not impossible that some of the Indians might leave their camp to hunt, when the smoke would at once have discovered the presence of enemies. A light was struck, however, for their pipes, and after enjoying this true consolation for some time, they laid a blanket on the ground, and, side by side, soon fell asleep.

If Killbuck had been a prophet, or the most prescient of "medicine men," he could not have more exactly predicted the movements in the Indian camp. About three hours before "sundown," he rose and shook himself, which movement was sufficient to awaken his companion. Telling La Bonté to lie down again and rest, he gave him to understand that he was about to reconnoitre the enemy's camp; and after examining carefully his rifle, and drawing his knife-belt a hole or two tighter, he proceeded on his dangerous errand. Ascending the same bluff from whence he had first discovered the Indian camp, he glanced rapidly round, and made himself master of the features of the ground—choosing a ravine by which he might approach the camp more closely, and without danger of being discovered. This was soon effected; and in half an hour the trapper was lying on his belly on the summit of a pine-covered bluff, which overlooked the Indians within easy rifle-shot, and so perfectly concealed by the low spreading branches of the cedar and arbor-vitæ, that not a particle of his person could be detected; unless, indeed, his sharp twinkling gray eye contrasted too strongly with the green boughs that covered the rest of his face. Moreover, there was no danger of their hitting upon his trail, for he had been careful to pick his steps on the rock-covered ground, so that not a track of his mocassin was visible. Here he lay, still as a carcagieu[38] in wait for a deer, only now and then shaking the boughs as his body quivered with a suppressed chuckle, when any movement in the Indian camp caused him to laugh inwardly at his (if they had known it) unwelcome propinquity. He was not a little surprised, however, to

[38] The carcajou, corruption of an Indian name for wolverine. The term was sometimes used in referring to the cougar.

25

discover that the party was much smaller than he had imagined, counting only forty warriors; and this assured him that the band had divided, one half taking the Yute trail by the Boiling Spring, the other (the one before him) taking a longer circuit in order to reach the Bayou, and make the attack on the Yutas, in a different direction.

At this moment the Indians were in deliberation. Seated in a large circle round a very small fire,[39] the smoke from which ascended in a thin straight column, they each in turn puffed a huge cloud of smoke from three or four long cherry-stemmed pipes, which went the round of the party; each warrior touching the ground with the heel of the pipe-bowl, and turning the stem upwards and away from him, as "medicine" to the Great Spirit, before he himself inhaled the fragrant kinnik-kinnik. The council, however, was not general, for no more than fifteen of the older warriors took part in it, the others sitting outside and at some little distance from the circle. Behind each were his arms—bow and quiver, and shield hanging from a spear stuck in the ground, and a few guns in ornamented covers of buckskin were added to some of the equipments.

Near the fire, and in the centre of the inner circle, a spear was fixed upright in the ground, and on this dangled the four scalps of the trappers killed the preceding night; and underneath them, affixed to the same spear, was the mystic "medicine bag," by which Killbuck knew that the band before him was under the command of the head chief of the tribe.

Towards the grim trophies on the spear, the warriors, who in turn addressed the council, frequently pointed—more than one, as he did so, making the gyratory motion of the right hand and arm, which the Indians use in describing that they have gained an advantage by skill or cunning. Then pointing westward, the speaker would thrust out his arm, extending his fingers at the same time, and closing and reopening them sev-

[39] There is a great difference between an Indian's fire and a white's. The former places the ends of logs to burn gradually; the latter, the centre, besides making such a bonfire that the Indians truly say, that "The white makes a fire so hot that he cannot approach to warm himself by it." Ruxton's note.

eral times, meaning, that although four scalps already ornamented the "medicine" pole, they were as nothing compared
to the numerous trophies they would bring from the Salt Valley,
where they expected to find their hereditary enemies the Yutes.
"That now was not the time to count their coups,"[40] (for at
this moment one of the warriors rose from his seat, and, swelling
with pride, advanced towards the spear, pointing to one of the
scalps, and then striking his open hand on his naked breast,
jumped into the air, as if about to go through the ceremony).
"That before many suns all their spears together would not
hold the scalps they had taken, and that then they would return
to their village, and spend a moon in relating their achievements,
and counting coups."

All this Killbuck learned: thanks to his knowledge of the
language of signs—a master of which, if even he have no ears
or tongue, never fails to understand, and be understood by,
any of the hundred tribes whose languages are perfectly distinct and different. He learned, moreover, that at sundown the
greater part of the band would resume the trail, in order to
reach the Bayou by the earliest dawn; and also, that no more
than four or five of the younger warriors would remain with
the captured animals. Still the hunter remained in his position
until the sun had disappeared behind the ridge; when, taking
up their arms, and throwing their buffalo robes on their shoulders, the war party of Rapahos, one behind the other, with
noiseless step, and silent as the dumb, moved away from the
camp; and, when the last dusky form had disappeared behind
a point of rocks which shut in the northern end of the little
valley or ravine, Killbuck withdrew his head from its screen,
crawled backwards on his stomach from the edge of the bluff,
and, rising from the ground, shook and stretched himself; then
gave one cautious look around, and immediately proceeded to
rejoin his companion.

[40] "Counting coups" was an Indian ceremony of relating the warrior's
achievements in "striking" an enemy. For a description of the Ute ceremony,
see below.

"*Lave* (get up), boy," said Killbuck, as soon as he reached him. "Hyar's grainin' to do afore long—and sun's about down, I'm thinking."

"Ready, old hos," answered La Bonté, giving himself a shake. "What's the sign like, and how many's the lodge?"

"Fresh, and five, boy. How do you feel?"

"*Half froze for hair.* Wagh!"

"We'll have moon to-night, and as soon as *she* gets up, we'll make 'em 'come.' "

Killbuck then described to his companion what he had seen, and detailed his plan—which was simply to wait until the moon afforded sufficient light, approach the Indian camp and charge into it—"lift" as much "hair" as they could, recover their animals, and start at once to the Bayou and join the friendly Yutes, warning them of the coming danger. The risk of falling in with either of the Rapaho bands was hardly considered; to avoid this, they trusted to their own foresight, and the legs of their mules, should they encounter them.

Between sundown and the rising of the moon, they had leisure to eat their supper, which, as before, consisted of raw buffalo-liver; after discussing which, Killbuck pronounced himself "a 'heap' better," and ready for "huggin."

In the short interval of almost perfect darkness which preceded the moonlight, and taking advantage of one of the frequent squalls of wind which howl down the narrow gorges of the mountains, these two determined men, with footsteps noiseless as the panther's, crawled to the edge of the little plateau of some hundred yards' square, where the five Indians in charge of the animals were seated round the fire, perfectly unconscious of the vicinity of danger. Several clumps of cedar bushes dotted the small prairie, and amongst these the well-hobbled mules and horses were feeding. These animals, accustomed to the presence of whites, would not notice the two hunters as they crept from clump to clump nearer to the fire, and also served, even if the Indians should be on the watch, to conceal their movements from them.

This the two men at once perceived; but old Killbuck knew that if he passed within sight or smell of his mule, he would be received with a hinny of recognition, which would at once alarm the enemy. He therefore first ascertained where his own animal was feeding, which luckily was at the farther side of the prairie, and would not interfere with his proceedings.

Threading their way amongst the feeding mules, they approached a clump of bushes about forty yards from the spot where the unconscious savages were seated smoking round the fire; and here they awaited, scarcely drawing breath the while, the moment when the moon rose above the mountain into the clear cold sky, and gave them light sufficient to make sure their work of bloody retribution. Not a pulsation in the hearts of these stern determined men beat higher than its wont; not the tremour of a nerve disturbed their frame. With lips compressed, they stood with ready rifles, the pistols loosened in their belts, and scalp-knives handy to their grip. The lurid glow of the coming moon already shot into the sky above the ridge, which stood out in bolder relief against the light; and the luminary herself was just peering over the mountain, illuminating its pine-clad summit, and throwing its beams on an opposite peak, when Killbuck touched his companion's arm, and whispered, "Wait for the full light, boy."

At this moment, however, unseen by the trapper, the old and grizzled mule had gradually approached, as it fed along the plateau; and, when within a few paces of their retreat, a gleam of moonshine revealed to the animal the erect forms of the two whites. Suddenly she stood still and pricked her ears, and stretching out her neck and nose, snuffed the air. Well she knew her old master.

Killbuck, with eyes fixed upon the Indians, was on the point of giving the signal of attack to his comrade, when the shrill hinny of his mule reverberated through the gorge. The next instant the Indians were jumping to their feet and seizing their arms, when, with a loud shout, Killbuck, crying, "At 'em boy; give the niggurs h——!" rushed from his concealment, and with

La Bonté by his side, yelling a fierce war-whoop, sprung upon the startled savages.

Panic-struck with the suddenness of the attack, the Indians scarcely knew where to run, and for a moment stood huddled together like sheep. Down dropped Killbuck on his knee, and stretching out his wiping stick, planted it on the ground to the extreme length of his arm. As methodically and as coolly as if about to aim at a deer, he raised his rifle to this rest and pulled the trigger. At the report an Indian fell forward on his face, at the same moment that La Bonté, with equal certainty of aim and like effect, discharged his own rifle.

The three surviving Indians, seeing that their assailants were but two, and knowing that their guns were empty, came on with loud yells. With the left hand grasping a bunch of arrows, and holding the bow already bent and arrow fixed, they steadily advanced, bending low to the ground to get their objects between them and the light, and thus render their aim more certain. The trappers, however, did not care to wait for them. Drawing their pistols, they charged at once; and although the bows twanged, and the three arrows struck their mark, on they rushed, discharging their pistols at close quarters; La Bonté throwing his empty one at the head of an Indian who was pulling his second arrow to its head at a yard distance, and drawing his knife at the same moment, made at him.

But the Indian broke and ran, followed by his living companion; and as soon as Killbuck could ram home another ball, he sent a shot flying after them as they scrambled up the mountain side, leaving in their fright and hurry their bows and shields on the ground.

The fight was over, and the two trappers confronted each other: "We've given 'em h——!" laughed Killbuck.

"*Well*, we have," answered the other, pulling an arrow out of his arm.—"Wagh!"

"We'll lift the hair, any how," continued the first, "afore the scalp's cold."

Taking his whetstone from the little sheath on his knife-belt, the trapper proceeded to "edge" his knife, and then stepping to the first prostrate body, he turned it over to examine if any symptom of vitality remained. "Thrown cold," he exclaimed, as he dropped the lifeless arm he had lifted. "I sighted him about the long ribs, but the light was bad, and I could'nt get a 'bead' 'off hand,' any how."

Seizing with his left hand the long and braided lock on the centre of the Indian's head, he passed the point edge of his keen butcher-knife round the parting, turning it at the same time under the skin to separate the scalp from the skull; then, with a quick and sudden jerk of his hand, he removed it entirely from the head, and giving the reeking trophy a wring upon the grass to free it from the blood, he coolly hitched it under his belt, and proceeded to the next; but seeing La Bonté operating upon this, he sought the third, who lay some little distance from the others. This one was still alive, a pistol-ball having passed through his body, without touching a vital spot.

"Gut-shot is this niggur," exclaimed the trapper; "them pistols never throws 'em in their tracks"; and thrusting his knife, for mercy's sake, into the bosom of the Indian, he likewise tore the scalp-lock from his head, and placed it with the other.

La Bonté had received two trivial wounds, and Killbuck till now had been walking about with an arrow sticking through the fleshy part of his thigh, the point being perceptible near the surface on the other side. To free his leg from the painful encumbrance, he thrust the weapon completely through, and then, cutting off the arrow-head below the barb, he drew it out, the blood flowing freely from the wound. A tourniquet of buckskin soon stopped this, and, heedless of the pain, the hardy mountaineer sought for his old mule, and quickly brought it to the fire (which La Bonté had rekindled), lavishing many a caress, and most comical terms of endearment, upon the faithful companion of his wanderings. They found all the animals safe and well, and after eating heartily of some venison which the Indians had been cooking at the moment of the attack, made instant preparations to quit the scene of their exploit, not wishing to trust to the chance of the Rapahos being too frightened to again molest them.

Having no saddles, they secured buffalo robes on the backs of two mules—Killbuck, of course, riding his own—and lost no time in proceeding on their way. They followed the course of the Indians up the stream, and found that it kept the cañons and gorges of the mountains where the road was better; but it was with no little difficulty that they made their way, the ground being much broken and covered with rocks. Killbuck's wound became very painful, and his leg stiffened and swelled distressingly, but he still pushed on all night, and, at daybreak, recognising their position, he left the Indian trail, and followed a little creek which rose in a mountain chain of moderate elevation, and above which, and to the south, Pike's Peak towered high into the clouds. With great difficulty they crossed this ridge, and ascending and descending several smaller ones which gradually smoothed away as they met the valley, about three hours after sunrise they found themselves in the southeast corner of the Bayou Salade.

The Bayou Salade, or Salt Valley, is the most southern of three very extensive valleys, forming a series of table-lands in the very centre of the main chain of the Rocky Mountains, known to the trappers by the name of the "Parks." The numerous streams by which they are watered abound in the valuable fur-bearing beaver, whilst every species of game common to the west is found here in great abundance. The Bayou Salade especially, owing to the salitrose nature of the soil and springs, is the favourite resort of all the larger animals common to the mountains; and, in the sheltered prairies of the Bayou, the buffalo, forsaking the barren and inclement regions of the exposed plains, frequent these upland valleys in the winter months; and feeding upon the rich and nutritious buffalo grass which, on the bare prairies, at that season, is either dry and rotten or entirely exhausted, not only are enabled to sustain life, but retain a great portion of the "condition" that the abundant fall and summer pasture of the lowlands has laid upon their bones.

Therefore is this valley sought by the Indians as a wintering ground; and its occupancy has been disputed by most of the mountain tribes, and long and bloody wars have been waged to make good the claims set forth by Yuta, Rapaho, Sioux, and Shians. However, to the first of these it may be said now to belong, since their "big village" has wintered there for many successive years; whilst the Rapahos seldom visit it unless on war expeditions against the Yutas.

Judging, from the direction the Rapahos were taking, that the friendly tribe of Yutas were there already, the trappers had resolved to join them as soon as possible; and therefore, without resting, pushed on through the uplands, and, towards the middle of the day, had the satisfaction of descrying the conical lodges of the village, situated on a large level plateau, through which ran a mountain stream. A numerous band of mules and horses was scattered over the pasture, and round them several mounted Indians were keeping guard. As the trappers descended the bluffs into the plain, some straggling Indians caught sight of them; and instantly one of them, lassoing a horse from the herd, mounted it, barebacked, and flew like the wind to the village to spread the news. Soon the lodges disgorged their inmates; first the women and children rushed to that side where the strangers were approaching; then the younger Indians, hardly able to restrain their curiosity, mounted their horses, and some galloped forth to meet them. The old chiefs, enveloped in buffalo robes (soft and delicately dressed as the Yutes alone know how), and with tomahawk held in one hand and resting in the hollow of the other arm, sallied last of all from their lodges, and, squatting in a row on a sunny bank outside the village, awaited, with dignified composure, the arrival of the whites. Killbuck was well known to most of them, having trapped in their country and traded with them years before at Roubideau's fort at the head waters of the Río Grande.[41]

[41] Robidoux Fort, or Fort Uncompahgre, was on the Gunnison River about three miles west of the present town of Delta, Colorado. Antoine Robidoux also had one or more forts in the Green River country. In early years the Colorado River was frequently called the Río Grande or Grand River.

After shaking hands with all who presented themselves, he at once gave them to understand that their enemies, the Rapahos, were at hand, with a hundred warriors at least, elated by the coup they had just struck the whites, bringing, moreover, four white scalps to incite them to brave deeds.

At this news the whole village was speedily in commotion: the war-shout was taken up from lodge to lodge; the squaws began to lament and tear their hair; the warriors to paint and arm themselves. The elder chiefs immediately met in council, and, over the medicine-pipe, debated as to the best course to pursue—whether to wait the attack, or sally out and meet the enemy. In the mean time, the braves collected together by the chiefs of their respective bands, and scouts, mounted on the fastest horses, despatched in every direction to procure intelligence of the enemy.

The two whites, after watering their mules and picketing them in some good grass near the village, drew near the council fire, without, however, joining in the "talk," until they were invited to take their seats by the eldest chief. Then Killbuck was called upon to give his opinion as to the direction in which he judged the Rapahos to be approaching, which he delivered in their own language, with which he was well acquainted. In a short time the council broke up, and, without noise or confusion, a band of one hundred chosen warriors left the village, immediately after one of the scouts had galloped in and communicated some intelligence to the chiefs. Killbuck and La Bonté volunteered to accompany the war-party, weak and exhausted as they were; but this was negatived by the chiefs, who left their white brothers to the care of the women, who tended their wounds, now stiff and painful; and spreading their buffalo robes in a warm and roomy lodge, left them to the repose they so much needed.

Trapping Beaver (Alfred Jacob Miller)

Making a *cache* (Alfred Jacob Miller)

Scenting the breeze (Alfred Jacob Miller)

"Vast herds of buffalo darkening the plains around them"

From the Porter collection

Approaching Buffalo (Alfred Jacob Miller)

A "Surround" of Buffalo by Indians (Alfred Jacob Miller)

Buffalo turning on his pursuers (Alfred Jacob Miller)

CHAPTER II

THE NEXT MORNING, Killbuck's leg was greatly inflamed, and he was unable to leave the lodge; but he made his companion bring the old mule to the door, when he gave her a couple of ears of Indian corn, the last remains of the slender store brought by the Indians from the Navajo country. The day passed, and with sundown came no tidings of the war-party, which caused no little wailing on the part of the squaws, but which the whites interpreted as a favourable augury. A little after sunrise, on the second morning, the long line of the returning warriors was discerned winding over the prairie, and a scout having galloped in to bring the news of a great victory, the whole village was soon in a ferment of paint and drumming. A short distance from the lodges, the warriors halted to await the approach of the people. Old men, children, and squaws, sitting astride their horses, sallied out to escort the victorious party in triumph to the village. With loud shouts and songs, and drums beating the monotonous Indian time, they advanced and encircled the returning braves, one of whom, with his face covered with black paint, carried a pole on which dangled thirteen scalps, the trophies of the expedition. As he lifted these on high, they were saluted with deafening whoops and cries of exultation and savage joy. In this manner they entered the village, almost before the friends of those fallen in the fight had ascertained their losses. Then the shouts of delight were converted into yells of grief; the mothers and wives of those braves who had been killed (and seven had "gone under"), presently returned with their faces, necks, and hands blackened, and danced and howled round the scalp pole, which had been deposited in the centre of the village, in front of the lodge of the great chief.

Killbuck now learned that a scout having brought intelligence that the two bands of Rapahos were hastening to form a junction, as soon as they learned that their approach was discovered, the Yutas had successfully prevented it; and attacking one party, had entirely defeated it, killing thirteen of the Rapaho braves. The other party had fled on seeing the issue of the fight, and a few of the Yuta warriors were now pursuing them.

To celebrate so signal a victory great preparations sounded their notes through the village. Paints—vermilion and ochres, red and yellow—were in great request; whilst the scrapings of charred wood, mixed with gunpowder, were used as substitute for black, the medicine colour.

The lodges of the village, numbering some two hundred or more, were erected in parallel lines, and covered a large space of the level prairie in shape of a parallelogram. In the centre, however, the space which half a dozen lodges in length would have taken up was left unoccupied, save by one large one, of red-painted buffalo skins, tatooed with the mystic totems of the "medicine" peculiar to the nation. In front of this stood the grim scalp-pole, like a decayed tree trunk, its bloody fruit tossing in the wind; and on another, at a few feet distance, was hung the "bag" with its mysterious contents. Before each lodge a tripod of spears supported the arms and shields of the Yuta chivalry, and on many of them, smoke-dried scalps rattled in the wind, former trophies of the dusky knights who were arming themselves within. Heraldic devices were not wanting— not, however, graved upon the shield, but hanging from the spear-head, the actual "totem" of the warrior it distinguished. The rattlesnake, the otter, the carcagieu, the mountain badger, the war-eagle, the kon-qua-kish, the porcupine, the fox, &c., dangled their well-stuffed skins, and displayed the guardian "medicine" of the warrior it pertained to, and represented the mental and corporeal qualities which were supposed to characterize the brave to whom it belonged.

From the centre lodge, two or three "medicine men," fantastically attired in the skins of wolves and bears, and bearing long peeled wands of cherry in their hands, occasionally emerged to tend a very small fire which they had kindled in the centre of the open space; and, when a thin column of smoke rose from it, one of them transferred the scalp-pole, planting it obliquely across the fire. Squaws in robes of whitely dressed buckskins, garnished with beads and porcupines' quills, and their faces painted bright red and black, then appeared. These ranged themselves round the outside of the square, the boys and children of all ages, mounted on bare-backed horses, galloping and screaming round and round, with all the eagerness of excitement and curiosity.

Presently the braves and warriors made their appearance, and squatted round the fire in two circles, those who had been engaged on the expedition being in the first or smaller one. One medicine man sat under the scalp-pole, having a drum between his knees, which he tapped at intervals with his hand, eliciting from the instrument a hollow monotonous sound. A bevy of women, shoulder to shoulder, then advanced from the four sides of the square, and some shaking a rattle-drum in time with their steps, commenced a jumping, jerking dance, now lifting one foot from the ground, and now rising with both, accompanying the dance with a low chant, which swelled from a low whisper to the utmost extent of their voices—now dying away, and again bursting into vociferous measure. Thus they advanced to the centre and retreated to their former positions; when six squaws, with their faces painted a deadened black, made their appearance from the crowd, and, in a soft and sweet measure, chanted a lament for the braves the nation had lost in the late battle: but soon as they drew near the scalp-pole, their melancholy note changed to the music (to them) of gratified revenge. In a succession of jumps, raising the feet alternately but a little distance from the ground, they made their way, through an interval left in the circle of warriors, to the grim pole, and encircling it, danced in perfect silence round it for a few moments. Then they burst forth with an extemporary song, laudatory of the achievements of their victorious braves. They addressed the scalps as "sisters" (to be called a squaw is the greatest insult that can be offered to an Indian), and, spitting at them, upbraided them with their rashness in leaving their lodges to seek for Yuta husbands; "that the Yuta warriors and young men despised them, and chastised them for their forwardness and presumption, bringing back their scalps to their own women."

After sufficiently proving that they had anything but lost the use of their tongues, but possessed as fair a length of that formidable weapon as any of their sex, they withdrew, and left the field in undisputed possession of the men: who, accompanied by taps of the drum, and the noise of many rattles, broke out into a war-song, in which the valour of themselves was not hidden in a bushel, nor modestly refused the light of day. After this came the more interesting ceremony of a warrior "counting his coups."

A young brave, with his face painted black, mounted on a white horse mysteriously marked with red clay, and naked to the breech clout, holding in his hand a long taper lance, rode into the circle, and paced slowly round it; then, flourishing his spear on high, he darted to the scalp-pole, round which the warriors were now sitting in a semicircle; and in a loud voice, and with furious gesticulations, related his exploits, the drums tapping at the conclusion of each. On his spear hung seven scalps, and holding it vertically above his head, and commencing with the top one, he narrated the feats in which he had raised the trophy hair. When he had run through these, the drums tapped loudly, and several of the old chiefs shook their rattles, in corroboration of the truth of his achievements. The brave, swelling with pride, then pointed to the fresh and bloody scalps hanging on the pole. Two of these had been torn from the heads of the Rapahos struck by his own hand, and this feat,

the exploit of the day, had entitled him to the honour of counting his coups. Then, sticking his spear into the ground by the
side of the pole, he struck his hand twice on his brawny and
naked chest, turned short round, and, swift as the antelope,
galloped into the plain: as if overcome by the shock his modesty
had received in being obliged to recount his own high-sound-
ing deeds.

"Wagh!" exclaimed old Killbuck, as he left the circle, and
pointed his pipe-stem towards the fast-fading figure of the
brave, "that Injun's heart's about as big as ever it will be, I'm
thinking."

With the Yutes, Killbuck and La Bonté remained during
the winter; and when the spring sun had opened the ice-bound
creeks, and melted the snow on the mountains; and its genial
warmth had expanded the earth and permitted the roots of the
grass to "live" once more, and throw out green and tender
shoots, the two trappers bade adieu to the hospitable Indians,
who were breaking up their village in order to start for the valleys of the Del Norte.[1] As they followed the trail from the
bayou, at sundown, just as they were thinking of camping,
they observed ahead of them a solitary horseman riding along,
followed by three mules.[2] His hunting-frock of fringed buckskin, and rifle resting across the horn of his saddle, at once proclaimed him white; but as he saw the mountaineers winding
through the cañon, driving before them half a dozen horses, *he*
judged they might possibly be Indians and enemies, the more
so as their dress was not the usual costume of the whites. The
trappers, therefore, saw the stranger raise the rifle in the hollow of his arm, and, gathering up his horse, ride steadily to
meet them, as soon as he observed they were but two; and two
to one in mountain calculation are scarcely considered odds, if
red skin to white.

However, on nearing them, the stranger discovered his mis-
take; and, throwing his rifle across the saddle once more, reined

---

[1] Río Grande del Norte, now usually called the Río Grande.
[2] Ruxton himself, in the spring of 1847.

in his horse and waited their approach; for the spot where he then stood presented an excellent camping-ground, with abundance of dry wood and convenient water.

"Where from, stranger?"

"The divide, and to the bayou for meat; and you are from there, I see. Any buffalo come in yet?"

"Heap, and seal-fat at that. What's the sign out on the plains?"

"War-party of Rapahos passed Squirrel at sundown yesterday, and nearly raised my animals. Sign, too, of more on left fork of Boiling Spring. No buffalo between this and Bijou. Do you feel like camping?"

"*Well*, we do. But whar's your companyeros?"

"I'm alone."

"Alone! Wagh! how do you get your animals along?"

"I go ahead, and they follow the horse."

"Well, that beats all! That's a smart-looking hos now; and runs some, I'm thinking."

"Well, it does."

"Whar's them mules from? They look like Californy."

"Mexican country—away down south."

"H——! Whar's yourself from?"

"There away, too."

"What's beaver worth in Taos?"

"Dollar."

"In Saint Louiy?"

"Same."

"H——! Any call for buckskin?"

"A heap! The soldiers in Santa Fé are half froze for leather; and mocassins fetch two dollars, easy."

"Wagh! How's trade on Arkansa, and what's doin to the Fort?"

"Shians at Big Timber, and Bent's people trading smart. On North Fork, Jim Waters got a hundred pack right off, and Sioux making more."

"Whar's Bill Williams?"

"Gone under they say: the Diggers took his hair."[3]

"How's powder goin?"

"Two dollars a pint."

"Bacca?"

"A plew a plug."

"Got any about you?"

"Have *so*."

"Give us a chaw; and now let's camp."

Whilst unpacking their own animals, the two trappers could not refrain from glancing, every now and then, with no little astonishment, at the solitary stranger they had so unexpectedly encountered. If truth be told, his appearance not a little perplexed them. His hunting frock of buckskin, shining with grease, and fringed pantaloons, over which the well-greased butcher-knife had evidently been often wiped after cutting his food, or butchering the carcass of deer and buffalo, were of genuine mountain make. His face, clean shaved, exhibited in its well-tanned and weather-beaten complexion, the effects of such natural cosmetics as sun and wind; and under the mountain hat of felt which covered his head, long uncut hair hung in Indian fashion on his shoulders. All this would have passed muster, had it not been for the most extraordinary equipment of a double-barreled rifle; which, when it had attracted the eyes of the mountaineers, elicited no little astonishment, not to say derision. But, perhaps, nothing excited their admiration so much as the perfect docility of the stranger's animals; which, almost like dogs, obeyed his voice and call; and albeit that one, in a small sharp head and pointed ears, expanded nostrils, and eye

[3] This is premature. Bill Williams was not killed until the spring of 1849, while in the San Juan Mountains recovering equipment of Frémont's disastrous expedition of the preceding winter.

Jim Waters, mentioned just above, was the noted trapper James W. Waters, born in Brainard's Bridge, New York, June 20, 1813. He came to the Rocky Mountains in 1835 and remained as trapper and trader until 1849, when he went to California, guiding a party of New Yorkers over the southern route via Cajon Pass. After settling in San Bernardino in 1856 he became a leading business man of this city, where he erected several buildings including an opera house. He died there on September 20, 1889. See J. Brown and J. Boyd, *History of San Bernardino and Riverside Counties* (Chicago, 1922), 676–77.

twinkling and malicious, exhibited the personification of a "lurking devil," yet they could not but admire the perfect ease which this one even, in common with the rest, permitted herself to be handled.

Dismounting from his horse, and unhitching from the horn of his saddle the coil of skin rope, one end of which was secured round the neck of the horse, he proceeded to unsaddle; and whilst so engaged, the three mules, two of which were packed, one with the unbutchered carcass of a deer, the other with a pack of skins, &c., followed leisurely into the space chosen for the camp, and, cropping the grass at their ease, waited until a whistle called them to be unpacked.

The horse was a strong square-built bay; and, although the severities of a prolonged winter, with scanty pasture and long and trying travel, had robbed his bones of fat and flesh, tucked up his flank, and "ewed" his neck; still his clean and well-set legs, oblique shoulder, and withers fine as a deer's, in spite of his gaunt half-starved appearance, bore ample testimony as to what he *had* been; while his clear cheerful eye, and the hearty appetite with which he fell to work on the coarse grass of the bottom, proved that he had something in him still, and was game as ever. His tail, ate by the mules in days of strait, attracted the observant mountaineers.[4]

"Hard doings when it come to that," remarked La Bonté.

Between the horse and two of the mules a mutual and great affection appeared to subsist, which was no more than natural, when their master observed to his companions that they had travelled together upwards of two thousand miles.

One of these mules was a short, thick-set, stumpy animal, with an enormous head surmounted by proportionable ears, and a pair of unusually large eyes, beaming the most perfect good temper and docility (most uncommon qualities in a mule). Her neck was thick, and rendered more so in appearance by reason of her mane not being roached (or in English, hogged),

[4] This horse was Ruxton's favorite, Panchito, which he had purchased in Mexico City. For the circumstances of his tail hair being chewed off by the mules, see *Ruxton of the Rockies*, 137.

which privilege she alone enjoyed of the trio; and her short, strong legs, ending in small, round, cat-like hoofs, were feathered with profusion of dark brown hair.

As she stood stock-still, while the stranger removed the awkwardly packed deer from her back, she flapped backward and forward her huge ears, occasionally turning her head, and laying her cold nose against her master's cheek. When the pack was removed, he advanced to her head, and, resting it on his shoulder, rubbed her broad and grizzled cheeks with both his hands for several minutes, the old mule laying her ears, like a rabbit, back upon her neck, and with half-closed eyes enjoyed mightily the manipulation. Then, giving her a smack upon the haunch, and a "hep-a" well-known to mule kind, the old favourite threw up her heels and cantered off to the horse, who was busily cropping the buffalo grass on the bluff above the stream.

Great was the contrast between the one just described and the next which came up to be divested of her pack. She, a tall beautifully shaped Mexican mule, of a light mouse colour, with a head like a deer's, and long springy legs, trotted up obedient to the call, but with ears bent back and curled up nose, and tail compressed between her legs. As her pack was being removed, she groaned and whined like a dog, as a thong or loosened strap touched her ticklish body, lifting her hind-quarters in a succession of jumps or preparatory kicks, and looking wicked as a panther. When nothing but the fore pack-saddle remained, she had worked herself into the last stage; and as the stranger cast loose the girth of buffalo hide, and was about to lift the saddle and draw the crupper from the tail, she drew her hind legs under her, more tightly compressed her tail, and almost shrieked with rage.

"Stand clear," he roared (knowing what was coming), and raised the saddle, when out went her hind legs, up went the pack into the air, and, with it dangling at her heels, away she tore, kicking the offending saddle as she ran. Her master, however, took this as a matter of course, followed her and brought back the saddle, which he piled on the others to windward of the fire one of the trappers was kindling. Fire-making is a simple process with the mountaineers. Their bullet-pouches always contain a flint and steel, and sundry pieces of "punk"[5] or tinder; and pulling a handful of dry grass, which they screw into a nest, they place the lighted punk in this, and, closing the grass over it, wave it in the air, when it soon ignites, and readily kindles the dry sticks forming the foundation of the fire.

The tit-bits of the deer the stranger had brought in were soon roasting over the fire; whilst, as soon as the burning logs had deposited a sufficiency of ashes, a hole was raked in them, and the head of the deer, skin, hair, and all, placed in this primitive oven, and carefully covered with the hot ashes.

A "heap" of "fat meat" in perspective, our mountaineers enjoyed their ante-prandial pipes, recounting the news of the respective regions whence they came; and so well did they like each other's company, so sweet the "honey-dew" tobacco of which the strange hunter had good store, so plentiful the game about the creek, and so abundant the pasture for their winter-starved animals, that before the carcass of the "two-year" buck had been more than four-fifths consumed; and although rib after rib had been picked and chucked over their shoulders to the wolves, and one fore leg and *the* "bit" of all, the head, still cooked before them, the three had come to the resolution to join company and hunt in their present locality for a few days at least—the owner of the "two-shoot" gun volunteering to fill their horns with powder, and find tobacco for their pipes.

Here, on plenty of meat, of venison, bear, and antelope, they merrily luxuriated; returning after their daily hunts to the brightly burning camp-fire, where one always remained to guard the animals, and unloading their packs of meat—all choicest portions, ate late into the night, and, smoking, wiled away the time in narrating scenes in their hard-spent lives, and fighting their battles o'er again.

The younger of the trappers, he who has figured under the

[5] A pithy substance found in dead pine-trees. Ruxton's note.

name of La Bonté in scraps and patches from his history, had
excited no little curiosity in the stranger's mind to learn the
ups and downs of his career; and one night, when they assembled earlier than usual at the fire, he prevailed upon the
modest trapper to "unpack" some passages in his wild adventurous life.

"Maybe," commenced the mountaineer, "you both remember
when old Ashley went out with the biggest kind of band to
trap the Columbia, and head-waters of Missoura and Yellow
Stone. Well, that was the time this niggur first felt like taking
to the mountains."

This brings us back to the year of our Lord 1825;[6] and perhaps it will be as well, to render La Bonté's mountain language
intelligible, to translate it at once to tolerable English, and tell
in the third person, but from his lips, the scrapes which him
befell in a sojourn of more than twenty years in the Far West,
and the causes which impelled him to quit the comfort and civilisation of his home, and seek the perilous but engaging life of
a trapper of the Rocky Mountains.

La Bonté was raised in the state of Mississippi, not far from
Memphis, on the left bank of that huge and snag-filled river.
His father was a Saint Louis Frenchman, his mother a native of
Tennessee. When a boy, our trapper was "some," he said, with
the rifle, and always had a hankering for the west; particularly
when, on accompanying his father to Saint Louis every spring,
he saw the different bands of traders and hunters start upon
their annual expeditions to the mountains; and envied the independent, *insouciant* trappers, as, in all the glory of beads and
buckskin, they shouldered their rifles at Jake Hawken's door
(the rifle-maker of St. Louis), and bade adieu to the cares and
trammels of civilised life.

However, like a thoughtless beaver-kitten, he put his foot
into a trap one fine day, set by Mary Brand,[7] a neighbour's
daughter, and esteemed "some punkins," or in other words

---

[6] Ashley's first fur trade venture up the Missouri was in 1822. In the winter
of 1824–25 he took a pack-horse company to the mountains.

[7] Ruxton said the real name was "Mary Chase," and to avoid possible diffi-

toasted as the beauty of Memphis County,[8] by the susceptible Mississippians. From that moment he was "gone beaver"; "he felt queer," he said, "all over, like a buffalo shot in the lights; he had no relish for mush and molasses; homminy and johnny cakes failed to excite his appetite. Deer and turkeys ran by him unscathed; he didn't know, he said, whether his rifle had hindsights or not. He felt bad, that was a fact; but what ailed him he didn't know."

Mary Brand—Mary Brand—Mary Brand! the old Dutch clock ticked it. Mary Brand! his head throbbed it when he lay down to sleep. Mary Brand! his rifle-lock spoke it plainly when he cocked it, to raise a shaking sight at a deer. Mary Brand, Mary Brand! the whip-poor-will sung it, instead of her own well-known note; the bull-frogs croaked it in the swamp, and mosquitos droned it in his ear as he tossed about his bed at night, wakeful, and striving to think what ailed him.

Who could that strapping young fellow, who passed the door just now, be going to see? Mary Brand: Mary Brand. And who can Big Pete Herring be dressing that silver fox-skin so carefully for? For whom but Mary Brand? And who is it that jokes, and laughs, and dances with all the "boys" but him; and why?

Who but Mary Brand: and because the love-sick booby carefully avoids her.

"And Mary Brand herself—what is she like?"

"She's 'some' now; that *is* a fact," "and the biggest kind of punkin at that," would have been the answer from any man, woman, or child, in Memphis County, and truly spoken too; always understanding that the pumpkin is *the* fruit to which the *ne-plus-ultra* of female perfection is compared by the figuratively speaking westerners.

Being an American woman, of course she was tall, and straight and slim as a hickory sapling, well formed withal, with

---

culties the publisher changed it to Mary Brand. See the sketch of Ruxton first published in *Blackwood's Edinburgh Magazine* for November of 1848, and reproduced in Appendix A at the end of this volume.

[8] There was no Memphis County in Mississippi or Tennessee.

rounded bust, and neck white and slender as the swan's. Her features were small, but finely chiselled; and in this, it may be remarked, the lower orders of the American women differ from, and far surpass the same class in England, or elsewhere, where the features, although far prettier, are more vulgar and commonplace. She had the bright blue eye, thin nose, and small but sweetly-formed mouth, the too fair complexion and dark brown hair, which characterise the beauty of the Anglo-American, the heavy masses (hardly curls) which fell over her face and neck contrasting with their polished whiteness. Such was Mary Brand: and to her good looks being added a sweet disposition, and all the good qualities of a thrifty housewife, it must be allowed that she fully justified the eulogiums of the good people of Memphis.

Well, to cut a love-story short, in the which not a little moral courage is shown, young La Bonté fell desperately in love with the pretty Mary, and she with him; and small blame to her, for he was a proper lad of twenty—six feet in his mocassins—the best hunter and rifle-shot in the country, with many other advantages too numerous to mention. But when did the course, &c. e'er run smooth? When the affair had become a recognised "courting" (and Americans alone know the horrors of such prolonged purgatory), they became, to use La Bonté's words, "awful fond," and consequently about once a-week had their tiffs and makes-up.

However, on one occasion, at a "husking," and during one of these tiffs, Mary, every inch a woman, to gratify some indescribable feeling, brought to her aid jealousy—that old serpent who has caused such mischief in this world; and by a flirtation over the corn-cobs with Big Pete, La Bonté's former and only rival, struck so hard a blow at the latter's heart, that on the moment his brain caught fire, blood danced before his eyes, and he became like one possessed. Pete observed and enjoyed his struggling emotion—better for him had he minded his corn-shelling alone; and the more to annoy his rival, paid the most sedulous attention to the pretty Mary.

Young La Bonté stood it as long as human nature, at boiling heat, could endure; but when Pete, in the exultation of his apparent triumph, crowned his success by encircling the slender waist of the girl with his arm, and snatched a sudden kiss, he jumped upright from his seat, and seizing a small whiskey-keg which stood in the centre of the corn-shellers, he hurled it at his rival, and crying to him, hoarse with passion, "to follow if he was a man," he left the house.

At that time, and even now, in the remoter states of the western country, rifles settled even the most trivial differences between the hot-blooded youths; and of such frequent occurrence and invariably bloody termination did they become, that they scarcely produced sufficient excitement to draw together half a dozen spectators of the duel.

In the present case, however, so public was the quarrel, and so well known the parties concerned, that not only the people who had witnessed the affair, but all the neighbourhood thronged to the scene of action, where, in a large field in front of the house, the preliminaries of a duel between Pete and La Bonté were being arranged by their respective friends.

Mary, when she discovered the mischief her thoughtlessness was likely to occasion, was almost beside herself with grief, but she knew how vain it would be to attempt to interfere. The poor girl, who was most ardently attached to La Bonté, was carried, swooning, into the house, where all the women congregated, and were locked in by old Brand, who, himself an old pioneer, thought but little of bloodshed, but refused to let the "women folk" witness the affray.

Preliminaries arranged, the combatants took up their respective positions at either end of a space marked for the purpose, at forty paces from each other. They were both armed with heavy rifles, and had the usual hunting-pouches, containing ammunition, hanging over the shoulder. Standing with the butts of their rifles on the ground, they confronted each other, and the crowd drawing away a few paces only on each side, left one man to give the word. This was the single word "fire"; and after this signal was given, the combatants were at liberty to fire away until one or the other dropped.

At the word both the men quickly raised their rifles to the shoulder, and as the sharp cracks rung instantaneously, they were seen to flinch, as either felt the pinging sensation of a bullet entering his flesh. Regarding each other steadily for a few moments, the blood running down La Bonté's neck from a wound under the left jaw, whilst his opponent was seen to place his hand once to his right breast, as if to feel the position of his wound, they commenced reloading their rifles. As, however, Pete was in the act of forcing down the ball with his long hickory wiping-stick, he suddenly dropped his right arm—the rifle slipped from his grasp—and, reeling for a moment like a drunken man—he fell dead to the ground.

Even here, however, there was law of some kind or another, and the consequences of the duel were, that the constables were soon on the trail of La Bonté to arrest him. He, however, easily avoided them, and taking to the woods, lived for several days in as wild a state as the beasts he hunted and killed for his support.

Tired of this, however, he resolved to quit the country, and betake himself to the mountains, for which life he had ever felt an inclination.

When, therefore, he thought the officers of justice had tired of seeking him, and the coast was comparatively clear, he determined to start on his distant expedition to the Far West.

Once more, before he carried his project into execution, he sought and had a last interview with Mary Brand.

"Mary," said he, "I'm about to break. They're hunting me like a fall buck, and I'm bound to quit. Don't think any more about me, for I shall never come back." Poor Mary burst into tears, and bent her head on the table near which she was sitting. When again she raised it, she saw La Bonté, with his long rifle on his shoulder, striding with rapid steps from the house; and year after year rolled on, and he never returned.

CHAPTER III

A FEW DAYS AFTER THIS he found himself at St. Louis, the emporium of the fur trade, and the fast rising metropolis of the precocious settlements of the West. Here, a prey to the agony of mind which jealousy, remorse, and blighted love mix into a very puchero of misery, La Bonté got into the company of certain "rowdies," a class which every western city particularly abounds in; and anxious to drown his sorrows in any way, and quite unscrupulous as to the means, he plunged into all the vicious excitements of drinking, gambling, and fighting, which form the every-day amusements of the rising generation of St. Louis.

Perhaps in no other part of the United States, where indeed humanity is frequently to be seen in many curious and unusual phases, is there a population so marked in its general character, and at the same time divided into such distinct classes, as in the above-named city. Dating, as it does, its foundation from yesterday—for what are thirty years in the growth of a metropolis?[1] —its founders are now scarcely passed middle life, regarding with astonishment the growing works of their hands; and whilst gazing upon its busy quays, piled with grain and other produce of the west, its fleets of huge steamboats lying tier upon tier alongside the wharves, its well-stored warehouses and all the bustling concomitants of a great commercial depot, they can scarcely realise the memory of a few short years, when on the same spot nothing was to be seen but the few miserable hovels of a French village—the only sign of commerce the un-

[1] St. Louis was started as a trading post in 1764, but its metropolitan growth was of a later date.

wieldy bateaux of the Indian traders, laden with peltries from the distant regions of the Platte and Upper Missouri. Where now intelligent and wealthy merchants walk erect, in conscious substantiality of purse and credit, and direct the commerce of a vast and numerously-populated region, but the other day stalked, in dress of buckskin, the Indian trader of the west; and all the evidences of life, mayhap, consisted of the eccentric vagaries of the different bands of trappers and hardy mountaineers, who accompanied, some for pleasure and some as escort, the periodically arriving bateaux, laden with the beaver skins and buffalo robes collected during the season at the different trading posts in the Far West.

These, nevertheless, were the men whose hardy enterprise opened to commerce and the plough the vast and fertile regions of the West. Rough and savage though they were, they alone were the pioneers of that extraordinary tide of civilisation which has poured its resistless current through tracts large enough for kings to govern; over a country now teeming with cultivation, where, a few short years ago, countless herds of buffalo roamed unmolested, the bear and deer abounded, and where the savage Indian skulked through the woods and prairies, lord of the unappreciated soil which now yields its prolific treasures to the spade and plough of civilised man. To the wild and half-savage trapper, who may be said to exhibit the energy, enterprise, and hardihood characteristic of the American people, divested of all the false and vicious glare with which a high state of civilization, too rapidly attained, has obscured their real and genuine character, in which the above traits are eminently prominent—to these men alone is due the empire of the West— destined in a few short years to become the most important of those confederate states which compose the mighty union of North America.

Sprung, then, out of the wild and adventurous fur trade, St. Louis, still the emporium of that species of commerce, preserves even now, in the character of its population, many of the marked peculiarities which distinguished its early founders, who were identified with the primitive Indian in hardiness and instinctive wisdom. Whilst the French portion of the population retain the thoughtless levity and frivolous disposition of their original source, the Americans of St. Louis, who may lay claim to be native, as it were, are as particularly distinguished for determination and energy of character as they are for physical strength and animal courage; and are remarkable, at the same time, for a singular aptitude in carrying out commercial enterprises to successful terminations, which would appear to be incompatible with love of adventure and excitement which forms so prominent a feature in their character. In St. Louis, nevertheless, and from her merchants, have emanated many commercial enterprises of gigantic speculation, not confined to its own locality or the distant Indian fur trade, but embracing all parts of the continent, and even a portion of the Old World. And here it must be remembered that St. Louis is situated inland, at a distance of upwards of one thousand miles from the sea, and three thousand from the capital of the United States.[2]

Besides her merchants and upper class, who form a little aristocracy even here, she has a large portion of her population still connected with the Indian and fur trade, who preserve all their characteristics unacted upon by the influence of advancing civilisation, and between whom and other classes there is a marked distinction. There is, moreover, a large floating population of foreigners of all nations, who must possess no little amount of enterprise to be tempted to this spot, from whence they spread over the remote western tracts, still invested by the savage; and, therefore, if any of their blood is infused into the native population, the characteristic energy and enterprise is increased, and not tempered down, by the foreign cross.

But perhaps the most singular of her casual population are the mountaineers, who, after several seasons spent in trapping, and with good store of dollars, arrive from the scene of their adventures, wild as savages, determined to enjoy themselves,

[2] St. Louis is about eight hundred miles from Washington, D. C.

for a time, in all the gaiety and dissipation of the western city. In one of the back streets of the town is a tavern well known as the "Rocky Mountain House," and here the trappers resort, drinking and fighting as long as their money lasts, which, as they are generous and lavish as Jack Tars, is for a few days only. Such scenes as are enacted in the Rocky Mountain House, both tragical and comical, are beyond the powers of pen to describe; and when a fandango is in progress, to which congregate the coquettish belles from "Vide Poche" ["Empty Pocket"], as the French portion of a suburb is nicknamed—the grotesque endeavours of the bear-like mountaineers to sport a figure on the light fantastic toe, and their insertions into the dance of the mystic jumps of Terpsichorean Indians when engaged in the "medicine" dances in honour of bear, of buffalo, or ravished scalp—are such startling innovations on the choreographic art as would cause the shade of Gallini to quake and gibber in his pumps.

Passing the open doors and windows of the Mountain House, the stranger stops short as the sounds of violin and banjo twang upon his ears, accompanied by extraordinary noises—which sound unearthly to the greenhorn listener, but which the initiated recognise as an Indian song roared out of the stentorian lungs of a mountaineer, who, patting his stomach with open hands, to improve the necessary shake, choruses the well-known Indian chant:

> Hi—Hi—Hi—Hi,
>   Hi-i—Hi-i—Hi-i—Hi-i
> Hi-ya—hi-ya—hi-ya—hi-ya
>   Hi-ya—hi-ya—hi-ya—hi-ya
> Hi-ya—hi-ya—hi—hi,
>   &c. &c. &c.

and polishing off the high notes with a whoop which makes the old wooden houses shake again, as it rattles and echoes down the street.

Here, over fiery "monaghahela," Jean Batiste, the sallow

half-breed voyageur from the north—and who, deserting the service of the "North-West" (the Hudson's Bay Company), has come down the Mississippi, from the "Falls," to try the sweets and liberty of "free" trapping—hobnobs with a stalwart leather-clad "boy," just returned from trapping on the waters of Grand River, on the western side the mountains, who interlards his mountain jargon with Spanish words picked up in Taos and California. In one corner a trapper, lean and gaunt from the starving regions of the Yellow Stone, has just recognized an old companyero, with whom he hunted years before in the perilous country of the Blackfeet.

"Why, John, old hos, how do you come on?"

"What! Meek, old 'coon! I thought you were under?"

One from Arkansa stalks into the centre of the room, with a pack of cards in his hand, and a handful of dollars in his hat. Squatting cross-legged on a buffalo robe, he smacks down the money, and cries out—"Ho, boys, hyar's a deck, and hyar's the beaver (rattling the coin), who dar set his hos? Wagh!"

Tough are the yarns of wondrous hunts and Indian perils, of hairbreadth 'scapes and curious "fixes." Transcendent are the qualities of sundry rifles, which call these hunters masters; "plum" is the "centre" each vaunted barrel shoots; sufficing for a hundred wigs if the "hair" each hunter has "lifted" from Indians' scalps; multitudinous the "coups" he has "struck." As they drink so do they brag, first of their guns, their horses, and their squaws, and lastly of themselves: and when it comes to that, "ware steel."

La Bonté, on his arrival at St. Louis, found himself one day in no less a place than this; and here he made acquaintance with an old trapper about to start for the mountains in a few days, to hunt on the head waters of Platte and Green River. With this man he resolved to start, and, having still some hundred dollars in cash, he immediately set about equipping himself for the expedition. To effect this, he first of all visited the gun-store of Hawken, whose rifles are renowned in the mountains, and exchanged his own piece, which was of very small bore, for a regular mountain rifle. This was of very heavy metal, carrying about thirty-two balls to the pound, stocked to the muzzle and mounted with brass, its only ornament being a buffalo bull, looking exceedingly ferocious, which was not very artistically engraved upon the trap in the stock. Here, too, he laid in a few pounds of powder and lead, and all the necessaries for a long hunt.

His next visit was to a smith's store, which smith was black by trade and black by nature, for he was a nigger, and, moreover, celebrated as being the best maker of beaver-traps in St. Louis, and of whom he purchased six new traps, paying for the same twenty dollars—procuring, at the same time, an old trap-sack, made of stout buffalo skin, in which to carry them.

We next find La Bonté and his companion—one Luke, better known as Grey-Eye, one of his eyes having been "gouged" in a mountain fray—at Independence, a little town situated on the Missouri, several hundred miles above St. Louis, and within a short distance of the Indian frontier.

Independence may be termed the "prairie port" of the western country. Here the caravans destined for Santa Fé and the interior of Mexico, assemble to complete their necessary equipment. Mules and oxen are purchased, teamsters hired, and all stores and outfit laid in here for the long journey over the wide expanse of prairie ocean. Here, too, the Indian traders and the Rocky Mountain trappers rendezvous, collecting in sufficient force to ensure their safe passage through the Indian country. At the seasons of departure and arrival of these bands, the little town presents a lively scene of bustle and confusion. The wild and dissipated mountaineers get rid of their last dollars in furious orgies, treating all comers to galore of drink, and pledging each other, in horns of potent whisky, to successful hunts and "heaps of beaver." When every cent has disappeared from their pouches, the free trapper often makes away with rifle, traps, and animals, to gratify his "dry" (for your mountaineer is never "thirsty"); and then, "hos and beaver" gone, is necessitated to hire himself to one of the leaders of big bands, and hypothecate his services for an equipment of traps and animals. Thus La Bonté picked up three excellent mules for a mere song, with their accompanying pack saddles, *apishamores*,[3] and lariats, and the next day, with Luke, "put out" for Platte.

As they passed through the rendezvous, which was encamped on a little stream beyond the town, even our young Mississippian was struck with the novelty of the scene. Upwards of forty huge waggons, of Conestoga and Pittsburg build, and covered with snow-white tilts, were ranged in a semicircle, or rather a horse-shoe form, on the flat open prairie, their long "tongues" (poles) pointing outwards; with the necessary harness for four pairs of mules, or eight yoke of oxen, lying on the ground beside them, spread in ready order for "hitching up." Round the waggons groups of teamsters, tall stalwart young Missourians, were engaged in busy preparation for the start, greasing the wheels, fitting or repairing harness, smoothing ox-bows, or overhauling their own moderate kits or "possibles." They were all dressed in the same fashion: a pair of "homespun" pantaloons, tucked into thick boots reaching nearly to the knee, and confined round the waist by a broad leathern belt, which supported a strong butcher knife in a sheath. A coarse checked shirt was their only other covering, with a fur cap on the head.

Numerous camp-fires surrounded the waggons, and by them lounged wild-looking mountaineers, easily distinguished from the "greenhorn" teamsters by their dresses of buckskin, and their weather-beaten faces. Without an exception, these were under the influence of the rosy god; and one, who sat, the picture of misery, at a fire by himself—staring into the blaze with vacant countenance, his long matted hair hanging in unkempt masses over his face, begrimed with the dirt of a week, and pallid with the effects of ardent drink—was suffering from the usual consequences of having "kept it up" beyond the usual point, and now was paying the penalty in a fit of "horrors"—as *delirium tremens* is most aptly termed by sailors and the unprofessional.

In another part, the merchants of the caravan and Indian

[3] Saddle-blanket made of buffalo-calf skin. Ruxton's note.

traders were superintending the lading of the waggons, or mule packs. These were dressed in civilised attire, and some be-dizened in St. Louis or Eastern City dandyism, to the infinite disgust of the mountain men, who look upon a bourge-way (bourgeois) with most undisguied contempt, despising the very simplest forms of civilisation. The picturesque appear-ance of the encampment was not a little heightened by the addition of several Indians from the neighbouring Shawnee settlement, who, mounted on their small active horses, on which they reclined, rather than sat, in negligent attitudes, quietly looked on at the novel scene, indifferent to the "chaff" which the thoughtless teamsters indulged in at their expense. Numbers of mules and horses were picketed at hand, while a large herd of noble oxen were being driven towards the camp—the wo-ha of the teamsters sounding far and near, as they collected the scattered beasts in order to yoke up.

As most of the mountain men were utterly unable to move from camp, Luke and La Bonté, with three or four of the most sober, started in company, intending to wait on "Blue," a stream which runs into the Caw or Kanzas River, until the "bal-ance" of the band came up. Mounting their mules, and leading the loose animals, they struck at once into the park-like prairie, and were out of sight of civilisation in an instant.[4]

It was the latter end of May, towards the close of the season of heavy rains, which in early spring render the climate of this country almost intolerable, at the same time that they serve to fertilise and thaw the soil, so long bound up by the winter's frosts. The grass was every where luxuriously green, and gaudy flowers dotted the surface of the prairie. This term, however, should hardly be applied to the beautiful undulating scenery of this park-like country. Unlike the flat monotony of the Grand Plains, here well wooded uplands clothed with forest trees of every species, and picturesque dells through which run clear and bubbling streams belted with gay-blossomed

[4] They are to travel northwest to the Platte and up that stream, on a route that became famous as the Oregon Trail.

shrubs, every where present themselves; whilst on the level meadowland, topes of trees with spreading foliage afforded a shelter to the game and cattle, and well-timbered knolls rise at intervals from the plain.

Many clear streams dashing over their pebbly beds intersect the country, from which, in the noonday's heat, the red-deer jump, shaking their wet sides, as the noise of approaching man disturbs them; and booming grouse rise from the tall luxuriant herbage at every step. Where the deep escarpments of the river banks exhibit the section of the earth, a rich alluvial soil of surprising depth appears to court the cultivation of civilised man; and in every feature it is evident that here nature has worked with kindliest and most bountiful hand.

For hundreds of miles along the western or right bank of the Missouri does such a country as this extend, to which, for fertility and natural resources, no part of Europe can offer even feeble comparison. Sufficiently large to contain an enormous population, it has, besides, every advantage of position, and all the natural capabilities which should make it the happy abode of civilized man. Through this unpeopled country the United States pours her greedy thousands, to seize upon the barren territories of her feeble neighbour.

Camping the first night on "Black Jack," our mountaineers here cut each man a spare hickory wiping-stick for his rifle, and La Bonté, who was the only greenhorn of the party, witnessed a savage ebullition of rage on the part of one of his companions, exhibiting the perfect unrestraint which these men impose upon their passions, and the barbarous anger which the slightest opposition to the will excites. One of the trappers, on arriving at the camping-place, dismounted from his horse, and, after divesting it of the saddle, endeavoured to lead his mule by the rope up to spot where he wished to deposit his pack. Mule-like, however, the more he pulled the more stubbornly she remained in her tracks, planting her fore-legs firmly, and stretching out her neck with provoking obstinacy. If truth be told, it does require the temper of a thousand Jobs to manage a mule; and in no case does the wilful mulishness of the animal stir up one's choler more than in the very trick which this one was playing, and which is a daily occurrence. After tugging ineffectually for several minutes, winding the rope round his body, and throwing himself forward and suddenly with all his strength, the trapper actually foamed with passion; and although he might have subdued the animal at once by fastening the rope with a half-hitch round its nose, with an obstinacy equal to that of the mule he refused to attempt it, preferring to vanquish her by main strength. However, this failed, and with a volley of blasphemous imprecations the mountaineer suddenly seized his rifle, and, levelling it at the mule's head, shot her dead.

Passing the Wa-ka-rasha [Wakarusa], a well-timbered stream, they met a band of Osages going "to buffalo." These Indians, in common with some tribes of the Pawnees, shave the head, with the exception of a ridge from the forehead to the centre of the scalp, which is "roached" or hogged like the mane of a mule, and stands erect, plastered with unguents, and ornamented by feathers of the hawk and turkey. The naked scalp is often painted in mosaic with black and red, the face with shining vermilion. They were all naked to the breech-clout, the warmth of the sun having caused them to throw their dirty blankets from their shoulders. These Indians not unfrequently levy contributions on strangers whom they may accidentally meet; but they easily distinguish the determined mountaineer from the incautious greenhorn, and think it better to let the former alone.

Crossing Vermilion, they arrived on the fifth day at "Blue," where they encamped in the broad timber which belts the creek, and there awaited the arrival of the remainder of the party.

It was two days before they came up; but the day after, fourteen in number, they started for the mountains, striking a trail which follows the "Big Blue" in its course through the prairies, which, as they advance to the westward, are gradually smoothing away into a vast unbroken expanse of rolling plain. Herds of antelope began to show themselves, and some of the hunters, leaving the trail, soon returned with plenty of their tender meat. The luxuriant but coarse grass they had hitherto seen now changed into the nutritious and curly buffalo grass, and their animals soon improved in appearance on the excellent pasture. In a few days, without any adventure, they struck the Platte River, its shallow waters (from which it derives its name)[5] spreading over a wide and sandy bed, numerous sand bars obstructing the sluggish current, and with nowhere sufficient water to wet the forder's knee.

By this time, but few antelope having been seen, the party became entirely out of meat; and, one whole day and part of another having passed without so much as a sage rabbit having presented itself, not a few objurgations on the buffalo grumbled from the lips of the hunters, who expected ere this to have reached the land of plenty. La Bonté killed a fine deer, however, in the river bottom, after they encamped, not one particle of which remained after supper that night, but which hardly took the rough edge off their keen appetites. Although already in the buffalo range, no traces of these animals had yet been seen; and as the country afforded but little game, and the party did not care to halt and lose time in hunting for it, they moved along hungry and sulky, the theme of conversation being the well remembered merits of good buffalo meat—of "fat fleece," "hump rib," and "tender loin"; of delicious "boudins," and marrow bones too good to think of. La Bonté had never seen the lordly animal, and consequently but half believed the accounts of the mountaineers, who described their countless bands as covering the prairie far as the eye could reach, and requiring days of travel to pass through; but the visions of such dainty and abundant feeding as they descanted on set his mouth watering, and danced before his eyes as he slept supperless, night after night, on the banks of the hungry Platte.

One morning he had packed his animals before the rest, and was riding a mile in advance of the party, when he saw on one

[5] Peter and Paul Mallet, first Frenchmen to penetrate from the Illinois country to Santa Fé (in 1739), applied the French name to the Platte River.

side of the trail, looming in the refracted glare which mirages the plains, three large dark objects without shape or form, which rose and fell in the exaggerated light like ships at sea. Doubting what it could be, he approached the strange objects; and as the refraction disappeared before him, the dark masses assumed a more distinct form, and clearly moved with life. A little nearer, and he made them out—they were buffalo. Thinking to distinguish himself, the greenhorn dismounted from his mule, and quickly hobbled her, throwing his lasso on the ground to trail behind when he wished to catch her. Then, rifle in hand, he approached the huge animals, and, being a good hunter, knew well to take advantage of the inequalities of the ground and face the wind; by which means he crawled at length to within forty yards of the buffalo, who were quietly cropping the grass, unconscious of danger. Now, for the first time, he gazed upon the noble beast of which he had so often heard, and longed to see. With coal-black beard sweeping the ground as he fed, an enormous bull was in advance of the others, his wild brilliant eyes peering from an immense mass of shaggy hair, which covered his neck and shoulder. From this point his skin was bare as one's hand, a sleek and shining dun, and his ribs well covered with shaking flesh. As he leisurely cropped the short curly grass he occasionally lifted his tail into the air, and stamped his foot as a fly or mosquito annoyed him—flapping the intruder with his tail, or snatching at the itching part with his ponderous head.

When La Bonté had sufficiently admired the animal, he lifted his rifle, and, taking steady aim, and certain of his mark, pulled the trigger, expecting to see the huge beast fall over at the report. What was his surprise and consternation, however, to see the animal flinch as the ball struck him, but gallop off, followed by the others, and apparently unhurt. As is generally the case with greenhorns, he had fired too high, not understanding that the only certain spot to strike a buffalo is but a few inches above the brisket, and that above this a shot is rarely fatal. When he rose from the ground, he saw all the party halting in full view of his discomfiture; and when he joined them, loud were the laughs, and deep the regrets of the hungry at his first attempt.

However, they now knew that they were in the country of meat; and a few miles farther, another band of stragglers presenting themselves, three of the hunters went in pursuit, La Bonté taking a mule to pack in the meat. He soon saw them crawling towards the band, and shortly two puffs of smoke, and the sharp cracks of their rifles showed that they had got within shot; and when he had ridden up, two fine buffaloes were stretched upon the ground. Now, for the first time, he was initiated into the mysteries of "butchering," and watched the hunters as they turned the carcass on the belly, stretching out the legs to support it on each side. A transverse cut was then made at the nape of the neck, and, gathering the long hair of the boss in one hand, the skin was separated from the shoulder. It was then laid open from this point to the tail, along the spine, and the skin was freed from the sides and pulled down to the brisket, but, still attached to it, was stretched upon the ground to receive the dissected portions. Then the shoulder was severed, the fleece removed from along the backbone, and the hump-ribs cut off with a tomahawk. All this was placed upon the skin; and after the "boudins" had been withdrawn from the stomach, and the tongue—a great dainty—taken from the head, the meat was packed upon the mule, and the whole party hurried to camp rejoicing.

There was merry-making in the camp that night, and the way they indulged their appetites—or, in their own language, "throw'd" the meat "cold"—would have made the heart of a dyspeptic leap for joy or burst with envy. Far into the "still watches of the tranquil night" the fat-clad *"depouille"* saw its fleshy mass grow small by degrees and beautifully less, before the trenchant blades of the hungry mountaineers; appetising yards of well-browned "boudin" slipped glibly down their throats; rib after rib of tender hump was picked and flung to the wolves; and when human nature, with helpless gratitude, and confident that nothing of superexcellent comestibility remained, was lazily wiping the greasy knife that had done such good service—a skilful hunter was seen to chuckle to himself as he raked the deep ashes of the fire, and drew therefrom a pair of tongues so admirably baked, so soft, so sweet, and of such exquisite flavour, that a veil is considerably drawn over the effects their discussion produced in the mind of our green-horn La Bonté, and the raptures they excited in the bosom of that, as yet, most ignorant mountaineer. Still, as he ate he wondered, and wondering admired, that nature, in giving him such profound gastronomic powers, and such transcendent capabilities of digestion, had yet bountifully provided an edible so peculiarly adapted to his ostrich-like appetite, that after consuming nearly his own weight in rich and fat buffalo meat, he felt as easy and as incommoded as if he had been lightly supping on strawberries and cream.

Sweet was the digestive pipe after such a feast, and soft the sleep and deep, which sealed the eyes of the contented trappers that night. It felt like the old thing, they said, to be once more amongst the "meat"; and, as they were drawing near the dangerous portion of the trail, they felt at home; although not a night now passed but, when they lay down on their buffalo robes to sleep, they could not be confident that that sleep was not their last—knowing full well that savage men were hovering near, thirsting for their lives.

However, no enemies showed themselves as yet, and they proceeded quietly up the river, vast herds of buffaloes darkening the plains around them, affording them more than abundance of the choicest meat; but, to their credit be it spoken, no more was killed than absolutely required—unlike the cruel slaughter made by most of the white travellers across the plains, who wantonly destroy these noble animals, not even for the excitement of sport, but in cold-blooded and insane butchery. La Bonté had practice enough to perfect him in the art, and, before the buffalo range was passed, he was ranked at a first-rate hunter. One evening he had left the camp for meat, and was approaching a band of cows for that purpose, crawling towards them along the bed of a dry hollow in the prairie, when he observed them suddenly jump away towards him, and immediately after a score of mounted Indians appeared in sight, whom, by their dress, he at once knew to be Pawnees and enemies. Thinking they might not discover him, he crouched down in the ravine; but a noise behind causing him to turn his head, he saw some five or six advancing up the bed of the dry creek, whilst several more were riding on the bluffs. The cunning savages had cut off his retreat to his mule, which he saw in the possession of one of the Indians. His presence of mind, however, did not desert him; and seeing at once that to remain where he was would be like being caught in a trap (as the Indians could advance to the edge of the bluff and shoot him from above), he made for the open prairie, determined at least to sell his scalp dearly, and make "a good fight." With a yell the Indians charged, but halted when they saw the sturdy trapper deliberately kneel, and, resting his rifle on the wiping-stick, take a steady aim as they advanced. Full well the Pawnees know, to their cost, that a mountaineer seldom pulls his trigger without sending a bullet to the mark; and, certain that one at least must fall, they hesitated to make the onslaught. Steadily the white retreated with his face to the foe, bringing the rifle to his shoulder the instant that one advanced within shot, the Indians galloping round, firing the few guns they had amongst them at long distances, but without effect. One young "brave," more daring than the rest, rode out of the crowd, and dashed at the hunter, throwing himself, as he passed within a few yards, from the saddle, and hanging over the opposite side of his horse —presenting no other mark than his left foot—discharged his bow from under the animal's neck, and with such good aim, that the arrow, whizzing through the air, struck the stock of La Bonté's rifle, which was at his shoulder, and, glancing off, pierced his arm, inflicting, luckily, but a slight wound. Again the Indian turned in his course, the others encouraging him with loud war-whoops, and once more passing at still less distance, drew his arrow to the head. This time, however, the eagle

eye of the white caught sight of the action, and suddenly rising
from his knee as the Indian was approaching, hanging by his
foot alone over the opposite side of the horse, he jumped towards the animal with outstretched arms and a loud yell, causing it to start so suddenly, and swerve from its course, that the
Indian lost his foot-hold, and, after in vain struggling to regain
his position, fell to the ground; but instantly rose upon his feet
and gallantly confronted the mountaineer, striking his hand
upon his brawny chest and shouting a loud whoop of defiance.
In another instant the rifle of La Bonté had poured forth its
contents; and the brave Indian, springing into the air, fell dead
to the ground, just as the other trappers, who had heard the firing, galloped up to the spot, at sight of whom the Pawnees,
with yells of disappointed vengeance, hastily retreated.

That night La Bonté first lifted hair!

A few days after they reached the point where the Platte
divides into two great forks: the northern one, stretching to
the northwest, skirts the eastern base of the Black Hills,[6] and
sweeping round to the south rises in the vicinity of the mountain
valley called the New Park,[7] receiving the Laramie, Medicine
Bow, and Sweet-Water creeks. The other, or "South Fork,"
strikes towards the mountains in a southwesterly direction,
hugging the base of the main chain of the Rocky Mountains,
and, fed by several small creeks, rises in the uplands of the
Bayou Salade, near which is also the source of the Arkansa.
To the forks of the Platte the valley of that river extends from
three to five miles on each side, being enclosed by steep sandy
bluffs, from the summits of which the prairies stretch away in
broad undulating expanse to the north and south. The "bottom," as it is termed, is but thinly covered with timber, the
cottonwoods being scattered only here and there; but some of
the islands in the broad bed of the stream are well wooded,
which leads to the inference that the trees on the banks have

---

[6] These were the Black Hills in the vicinity of Fort Laramie; not the Black
Hills of South Dakota.

[7] New Park was the present North Park, Colorado.

been felled by Indians who formerly frequented this river as a chosen hunting-ground. As during the long winters the pasture in the vicinity is scarce and withered, the Indians feed their horses on the bark of the sweet cottonwood, upon which they subsist, and even fatten. Thus, wherever a village has been encamped, the trunks of these trees strew the ground, with their upper limbs and smaller branches peeled of their bark, and looking as white and smooth as if scraped with a knife.

On the forks, however, the timber is heavier and of greater variety, some of the creeks being well wooded with ash and cherry, which break the monotony of the everlasting cottonwood.

Dense masses of buffalo still continued to darken the plains, and numerous bands of wolves hovered round the outskirts of the vast herds, singling out the sick and wounded animals, and preying upon the calves whom the rifles and arrows of the hunters had bereaved of their mothers. The white wolf is the invariable attendant upon the buffalo; and when one of these persevering animals is seen, it is certain sign that buffalo are not far distant. Besides the buffalo wolf, there are four distinct varieties common to the plains, and all more or less attendant upon the buffalo. These are, the black, the gray, the brown, and last and least the *coyote*, or *cayeute* of the mountaineers, the "wach-unkamnet," or "medicine wolf" of the Indians, who hold the latter animal in reverential awe. This little wolf, whose fur is of great thickness and beauty, although of diminutive size, is wonderfully sagacious, and makes up by cunning what it wants in physical strength. In bands of from three to thirty they will not unfrequently station themselves along the "runs" of the deer and the antelope, extending their line for many miles—and the quarry being started, each wolf will follow in pursuit until tired, when it relinquishes the chase to another relay, following slowly after until the animal is fairly run down, when all hurry to the spot and speedily consume the carcass. The cayeute, however, is often made a tool of by his larger brethren, unless, indeed, he acts from motives of spontaneous charity. When a hunter has slaughtered game, and is in the act of butchering it, these little wolves sit patiently at a short distance from the scene of operations, while at a more respectful one the larger wolves (the white or gray) lope hungrily around, licking their chops in hungry expectation. Not unfrequently the hunter throws a piece of meat towards the smaller one, who seizes it immediately, and runs off with the morsel in his mouth. Before he gets many yards with his prize, the large wolf pounces with a growl upon him, and the cayeute, dropping the meat, returns to his former position, and will continue his charitable act as long as the hunter pleases to supply him.

Wolves are so common on the plains and in the mountains, that the hunter never cares to throw away a charge of ammunition upon them, although the ravenous animals are a constant source of annoyance to him, creeping to the camp-fire at night, and gnawing his saddles and *apishamores*, eating the skin ropes which secure the horses and mules to their pickets, and even their very hobbles, and not unfrequently killing or entirely disabling the animals themselves.

Round the camp, during the night, the cayeute keeps unremitting watch, and the traveller not unfrequently starts from his bed with affright, as the mournful and unearthly chiding of the wolf breaks suddenly upon his ear: the long-drawn howl being taken up by others of the band, until it dies away in the distance, as some straggler passing within hearing answers to the note, and howls as he lopes away.

Our party crossed the south fork about ten miles from its juncture with the main stream, and then, passing the prairie, struck the north fork a day's travel from the other. At the mouth of an ash-timbered creek they came upon Indian "sign," and, as now they were in the vicinity of the treacherous Sioux, they moved along with additional caution, Frapp[8] and Gonne-

[8] Henry Fraeb, usually pronounced "Frapp," was a well-known trapper of the eighteen forties and was co-owner with Peter Sarpy of Fort Jackson on the South Platte. He was killed in an Indian fight on Battle Creek, in northwestern Colorado, in 1841. See LeRoy R. Hafen, "Fraeb's Last Fight and How Battle Creek got Its Name," in the *Colorado Magazine*, Vol. VII, No. 3 (May, 1930), 97–101.

ville, two experienced mountaineers, always heading the advance.

About noon they had crossed over to the left bank of the fork, intending to camp on a large creek where some fresh beaver "sign" had attracted the attention of some of the trappers; and as, on further examination, it appeared that two or three lodges of that animal were not far distant, it was determined to remain here a day or two, and set their traps.

Gonneville, old Luke, and La Bonté, had started up the creek, and were carefully examining the banks for "sign," when the former, who was in front, suddenly paused, and looking intently up the stream, held up his hand to his companions to signal them to stop.

Luke and La Bonté both followed the direction of the trapper's intent and fixed gaze. The former uttered in a suppressed tone the expressive exclamation, Wagh!—the latter saw nothing but a wood-duck swimming swiftly down the stream, followed by her downy progeny.

Gonneville turned his head, and extending his arm twice with a forward motion up the creek, whispered—"*Les sauvages.*"

"Injuns, sure, and Sioux at that," answered Luke.

Still La Bonté looked, but nothing met his view but the duck with her brood, now rapidly approaching; and as he gazed, the bird suddenly took wing, and, flapping on the water, flew a short distance down the stream and once more settled on it.

"Injuns?" he asked; "where are they?"

"Whar?" repeated old Luke, striking the flint of his rifle, and opening the pan to examine the priming. "What brings a duck a-streakin it down stream, if humans aint behint her? and who's thar in these diggins but Injuns, and the worst kind; and we'd better push to camp, I'm thinking, if we mean to save our hair."

"Sign" sufficient, indeed, it was to all the trappers, who, on being apprised of it, instantly drove in their animals, and picketed them; and hardly had they done so when a band of Indians made their appearance on the banks of the creek, from

whence they galloped to the bluff which overlooked the camp
at the distance of about six hundred yards; and crowning this,
in number some forty or more, commenced brandishing their
spears and guns, and whooping loud yells of defiance. The
trappers had formed a little breast-work of their packs, forming
a semicircle, the chord of which was made by the animals
standing in a line, side by side, closely picketed and hobbled.
Behind this defence stood the mountaineers, rifle in hand, and
silent and determined. The Indians presently descended the
bluff on foot, leaving their animals in charge of a few of the
party, and, scattering, advanced under cover of the sage bushes
which dotted the bottom, to about two hundred yards of the
whites. Then a chief advanced before the rest, and made the
sign for a talk with the Long-knives, which led to a consultation amongst the latter, as to the policy of acceding to it. They
were in doubts as to the nation these Indians belonged to, some
bands of the Sioux being friendly, and others bitterly hostile
to the whites.

Gonneville, who spoke the Sioux language, and was well acquainted with the nation, affirmed they belonged to a band
called the Yanka-taus [Yanktons], well known to be the most
evil-disposed of that treacherous nation; another of the party
maintaining that they were Brulés, and that the chief advancing towards them was the well-known Tah-sha-tunga or Bull
Tail, a most friendly chief of that tribe. The majority, however, trusted to Gonneville, and he volunteered to go out to
meet the Indian, and hear what he had to say. Divesting himself of all arms save his butcher-knife, he advanced towards the
savage, who awaited his approach, enveloped in the folds of
his blanket. At a glance he knew him to be a Yanka-tau, from
the peculiar make of his mocassins, and the way in which his
face was daubed with paint.

"Howgh!" exclaimed both as they met; and, after a silence
of a few moments, the Indian spoke, asking—"Why the Long-
knives hid behind their packs, when his band approached?
Were they afraid, or were they preparing a dog-feast to en-

tertain their friends? That the whites were passing through his country, burning his wood, drinking his water, and killing his game; but he knew that they had now come to pay for the mischief they had done, and that the mules and horses they had brought with them were intended as a present to their red friends.

"He was Mah-to-ga-shane," he said, "the Brave Bear: his tongue was short, but his arm long; and he loved rather to speak with his bow and his lance, than with the weapon of a squaw. He had said it: the Long-knives had horses with them and mules; and these were for him, he knew, and for his 'braves.' Let the White-face go back to his people and return with the animals, or he, the 'Brave Bear,' would have to come and take them; and his young men would get mad and would feel blood in their eyes; and then he would have no power over them; and the whites would have to 'go under.' "

The trapper answered shortly—"The Long-knives," he said, "had brought the horses for themselves—their hearts were big, but not towards the Yanka-taus: and if they had to give up their animals, it would be to *men* and not *squaws*. They were not '*wah-keitcha*'[9] (French *engagés*), but Long-knives; and, however short were the tongues of the Yanka-taus, theirs were still shorter, and their rifles longer. The Yanka-taus were dogs and squaws, and the Long-knives spat upon them."

Saying this, the trapper turned his back and rejoined his companions; whilst the Indian slowly proceeded to his people, who, on learning the contemptuous way in which their threats had been treated, testified their anger with loud yells; and, seeking whatever cover was afforded, commenced a scattering volley upon the camp of the mountaineers. The latter reserved their fire, treating with cool indifference the balls which began to rattle about them; but as the Indians, emboldened by this apparent inaction, rushed for a closer position, and exposed their

[9] The French Canadians are called *wah-keitcha*—"bad medicine"—by the Indians, who account them treacherous and vindictive, and at the same time less daring than the American hunters. Ruxton's note.

bodies within a long range, half-a-dozen rifles rang from the assailed, and two Indians fell dead, one or two more being wounded. As yet, not one of the whites had been touched, but several of the animals had received wounds from the enemy's fire of balls and arrows. Indeed, the Indians remained at too great a distance to render the volleys from their crazy fusees anything like effectual, and had to raise their pieces considerably to make their bullets reach as far as the camp. After having lost three of their band killed outright, and many more being wounded, their fire began to slacken, and they drew off to a greater distance, evidently resolved to beat a retreat; and retiring to the bluff, discharged their pieces in a last volley, mounted their horses and galloped off, carrying their wounded with them. This last volley, however, although intended as a mere bravado, unfortunately proved fatal to one of the whites. Gonneville, at the moment, was standing on one of the packs, in order to get an uninterrupted sight for a last shot, when one of the random bullets struck him in the breast. La Bonté caught him in his arms as he was about to fall, and, laying the wounded trapper gently on the ground, they proceeded to strip him of his buckskin hunting-frock, to examine the wound. A glance was sufficient to convince his companions that the blow was mortal. The ball had passed through the lungs; and in a few moments the throat of the wounded man began to swell, as the choking blood ascended, and turned a livid blue colour. But a few drops of purple blood trickled from the wound—a fatal sign—and the eyes of the mountaineer were already glazing with death's icy touch. His hand still grasped the barrel of his rifle, which had gone good service in the fray. Anon he essayed to speak, but, choked with blood, only a few inarticulate words reached the ears of his companions, who were bending over him.

"Rubbed—out—at—last," they heard him say, the words gurgling in his blood-filled throat; and opening his eyes once more, and looking upwards to take a last look at the bright sun, the trapper turned gently on his side and breathed his last sigh.

With no other tools than their scalp-knives, the hunters dug a grave on the banks of the creek; and whilst some were engaged in this work, others sought the bodies of the Indians they had slain in the attack, and presently returned with three reeking scalps, the trophies of the fight. The body of the mountaineer was then wrapped in a buffalo robe, the scalps being placed on the dead man's breast, laid in the shallow grave, and quickly covered—without a word of prayer, or sigh of grief; for, however much his companions may have felt, not a word escaped them; although the bitten lip and frowning brow told tale of anger more than sorrow, and vowed—what they thought would better please the spirit of the dead man than sorrow—lasting revenge.

Trampling down the earth which filled the grave, they placed upon it a pile of heavy stones; and packing their mules once more, and taking a last look of their comrade's lonely resting-place, they turned their backs upon the stream, which has ever since been known as "Gonneville's Creek."[10]

If the reader casts his eye over any of the recent maps of the western country, which detail the features of the regions embracing the Rocky Mountains, and the vast prairies at their bases, he will not fail to observe that many of the creeks or smaller streams which feed the larger rivers—as the Missouri, Platte, and Arkansa—are called by familiar proper names, both English and French. These are invariably christened after some unfortunate trapper, killed there in Indian fight; or treacherously slaughtered by the lurking savages, while engaged in trapping beaver on the stream. Thus alone is the memory of these hardy men perpetuated, at least of those whose fate is ascertained: for many, in every season, never return from their hunting expeditions, having met a sudden death from Indians, or a more lingering fate from accident or disease in some of the lonely gorges of the mountains, where no footfall save their own, or the heavy tread of grizzly bear, disturbs the unbroken silence of these awful solitudes. Then, as many winters pass without some old familiar faces making their appearance at the merry

[10] Later called Pumpkinseed and now Pumpkin Creek, in western Nebraska.

rendezvous, their long protracted absence may perhaps occasion such remarks, as to where such and such a mountain worthy can have betaken himself, to which the casual rejoinder of "Gone under, maybe," too often gives a short but certain answer.

In all the philosophy of hardened hearts, our hunters turned from the spot where the unmourned trapper met his death. La Bonté, however, not yet entirely steeled by mountain life to a perfect indifference to human feeling, drew his hard hand across his eye, as the unbidden tear rose from his rough but kindly heart. He could not forget so soon the comrade they had lost, the companionship in the hunt or over the cheerful campfire, the narrator of many a tale of dangers past, of sufferings from hunger, cold, and thirst, and from untended wounds, of Indian perils, and of a life spent in such vicissitudes. One tear dropped from the young hunter's eye, and rolled down his cheek—the last for many a long year.

In the forks of the northern branch of the Platte, formed by the junction of the Laramie, they found a big village of the Sioux encamped near the station of one of the fur companies.[11] Here the party broke up; many, finding the alcohol of the traders an impediment to their further progress, remained some time in the vicinity, while La Bonté, Luke, and a trapper named Marcelline,[12] started in a few days to the mountains, to trap on Sweet Water and Medicine Bow. They had leisure, however, to observe all the rascalities connected with the Indian trade, although at this season (August) hardly commenced. However, a band of Indians having come in with several packs of last year's robes, and being anxious to start speedily on their return, a trader from one of the forts had erected his lodge in the village.

[11] The first fur-trade post near the junction of the North Platte and Laramie rivers was Fort William, later known as Fort Laramie, and built by Sublette and Campbell in 1834. See LeRoy R. Hafen and Francis M. Young, *Fort Laramie and the Pageant of the West, 1834–1890* (Glendale, California, 1938).

[12] Probably Marcelline St. Vrain.

Here he set to work immediately, to induce the Indians to trade. First, a chief appointed three "soldiers" to guard the trader's lodge from intrusion; and who, amongst the thieving fraternity, can be invariably trusted. Then the Indians were invited to have a drink—a taste of the fire-water being given to all to incite them to trade. As the crowd presses upon the entrance to the lodge, and those in rear become impatient, some large-mouthed possessor of many friends, who has received a portion of the spirit, makes his way, with his mouth full of the liquor and cheeks distended, through the throng, and is instantly surrounded by his particular friends. Drawing the face of each, by turns, near his own, he squirts a small quantity into his open mouth, until the supply is exhausted, when he returns for more, and repeats the generous distribution.

When paying for the robes, the traders, in measuring out the liquor in a tin half-pint cup, thrust their thumbs or the four fingers of the hand into the measure, in order that it may contain the less, or not unfrequently fill the bottom with melted buffalo fat, with the same object. So greedy are the Indians, that they never discover the cheat, and once under the influence of the liquor, cannot distinguish between the first cup of comparatively strong spirit, and the following ones diluted five hundred per cent, and poisonously drugged to boot.

Scenes of drunkenness, riot, and bloodshed last until the trade is over, which in the winter occupies several weeks, during which period the Indians present the appearance, under the demoralizing influence of the liquor, of demons rather than men.

Trappers and horses around a fire (Alfred Jacob Miller)

*"Away to the head waters of the Platte . . . were camped a band
of trappers on a creek called Bijou"*

Scene at "Rendezvous" (Alfred Jacob Miller)

Trappers' Encampment on the "Big Sandy" River
(Alfred Jacob Miller)

War ground (Alfred Jacob Miller)

"Still, the near neighbourhood of these Indians was hardly desirable"

From the Porter collection

Escape from Blackfeet (Alfred Jacob Miller)

"Sauve-qui-peut *was the order of the day*"

Trappers without ammunition and in a starving condition near
Independence Rock (Alfred Jacob Miller)

*"They were gaunt and lantern-jawed, and clothed in
tattered buckskin"*

The trapper's bride (Alfred Jacob Miller)

*"Here he . . . took unto himself another bride, as by
mountain law allowed"*

From the Porter collection

Indian hospitality (Alfred Jacob Miller)

"The chiefs left their white brothers to the care of the women, who tended their wounds"

Courtesy Walters Art Gallery

CHAPTER IV

La BONTÉ AND HIS COMPANIONS proceeded up the river, the Black Hills on their left hand, from which several small creeks or feeders swell the waters of the North Fork. Along these they hunted unsuccessfully for beaver "sign," and it was evident that the spring hunt had almost entirely exterminated the animal from this vicinity. Following Deer Creek to the ridge of the Black Hills, they crossed the mountain on to the waters of the Medicine Bow, and here they discovered a few lodges, and La Bonté set his first trap. He and old Luke finding "cuttings" near the camp, followed the "sign" along the bank until the practised eye of the latter discovered a "slide," where the beaver had ascended the bank to chop the trunk of a cottonwood, and convey the bark to its lodge. Taking a trap from "sack," the old hunter after "setting" the "trigger," placed it carefully under the water, where the "slide" entered the stream, securing the chain to the stem of a sapling on the bank; while a stick, also attached to the trap by a thong, floated down the stream, to mark the position of the trap, should the animal carry it away. A little farther on, and near another "run," three traps were set; and over these Luke placed a little stick, which he first dipped into a mysterious-looking phial which contained his "medicine."[1]

The next morning they visited the traps, and had the satisfaction of finding three fine beaver secured in the first three they visited, and the fourth, which had been carried away, they dis-

[1] A substance obtained from a gland in the scrotum of the beaver, and used to attract that animal to the trap. Ruxton's note. Modern beaver trappers still use this musk gland in making their bait.

covered by the floatstick, a little distance down the stream, with a large drowned beaver between its teeth.

The animals being carefully skinned, they returned to camp with the choicest portions of the meat, and the tails, on which they most luxuriously supped; and La Bonté was fain to confess that all his ideas of the superexcellence of buffalo were thrown in the shade by the delicious beaver tail, the rich meat of which he was compelled to allow was "great eating," unsurpassed by "tender loin" or "boudin," or other meat of whatever kind he had eaten of before.

The country where La Bonté and his companions were trapping, is very curiously situated in the extensive bend of the Platte which encloses the Black Hill range on the north, and which bounds the large expanse of broken tract known as the Laramie Plains, their southern limit being the base of the Medicine Bow Mountains. From the northwestern corner of the bend, an inconsiderable range extends to the westward, gradually decreasing in height until they reach an elevated plain, which forms a break in the stupendous chain of the Rocky Mountains, and affords their easy passage, now known as the Great, or South Pass. So gradual is the ascent of this portion of the mountain, that the traveller can scarcely believe that he is crossing the dividing ridge between the waters which flow into the Atlantic and Pacific Oceans, and in a few minutes can fling a stick into two neighbouring streams, one of which would be carried thousands of miles, which the eastern waters traverse in their course to the Gulf of Mexico, the other, borne a lesser distance, to the Gulf of California.

The country is frequented by the Crows and Snakes, who are at perpetual war with the Shians and Sioux, following them often far down the Platte, where many bloody battles have taken place. The Crows are esteemed friendly to the whites; but when on war expeditions, and "hair" their object, it is always dangerous to fall in with Indian war-parties, and particularly in the remote regions of the mountains, where they do not anticipate retaliation.

Trapping with tolerable success in this vicinity, as soon as the premonitory storms of approaching winter warned them to leave the mountains, they crossed over to the waters of Green River, one of the affluents of the Colorado, intending to winter at a rendezvous to be held in "Brown's Hole"[2]—an enclosed valley so called, which, abounding in game, and sheltered on every side by lofty mountains, is a favourite winteringground of the mountaineers. Here they found several trapping bands already arrived; and a trader from the Uintah country, with store of powder, lead, and tobacco, prepared to ease them of their hardly earned peltries.

In bands numbering from two to ten, and singly, the trappers dropped into the rendezvous; some with many pack-loads of beaver, others with greater or less quantity, and more than one came in on foot, having lost his animals and peltry by Indian thieving. Here were soon congregated many mountaineers, whose names are famous in the history of the Far West. Fitzpatrick[3] and Hatcher, and old Bill Williams, with their bands, well-known leaders of trapping parties, soon arrived. Sublette came in with his men from Yellow Stone, and many of Wyeth's New Englanders[4] were there. Chábonard with his half-breeds, *Wah-keitchas* all, brought his peltries from the lower country; and half-a-dozen Shawanee and Delaware Indians, with a Mexican from Taos, one Marcellin,[5] a fine strapping fellow, the best trapper and hunter in the mountains, and ever first in the fight. Here, too, arrived the "Bourgeois" traders of the "North

[2] Brown's Hole, a mountain-walled valley that crosses the northwest border of Colorado and extends into Utah, was a favorite winter resort of trappers. Here in the late eighteen forties Fort Davy Crockett was operated by Thompson, Craig, and Sinclair.

[3] Thomas Fitzpatrick was an outstanding fur man who later became guide for official explorers and emigrants and in 1847 became the first Indian agent for the tribes of the upper Platte and Arkansas. See LeRoy R. Hafen and W. J. Ghent, *Broken Hand, the Life Story of Thomas Fitzpatrick, Chief of the Mountain Men* (Denver, 1931).

[4] Nathaniel J. Wyeth, ice merchant from Cambridge, Massachusetts, brought his first trapper band into the West in 1832.

[5] This is probably the Mexican guide, "Massalino," whom Gunnison and Beckwith hired at the Greenhorn settlement in 1853. See *Reports of Explorations and Surveys for the Pacific Railroad*, 33 Cong., 2 sess., *Ex. Doc. 91*, 35, 39.

West"[6] Company, with their superior equipments, ready to meet their trappers, and purchase the beaver at an equitable value; and soon the encampment began to assume a busy appearance when the trade opened.

A curious assemblage did the rendezvous present, and representatives of many a land met there. A son of *La belle France* here lit his pipe from one proffered by a native of New Mexico. An Englishman and a Sandwich islander cut a quid from the same plug of tobacco. A Swede and an "old Virginian" puffed together. A Shawanee blew a peaceful cloud with a scion of the "Six Nations." One from the Land of Cakes—a canny chiel—sought to "get round" (in trade) a right "smart" Yankee, but couldn't "shine."

The beaver went briskly, six dollars being the price paid per lb. in goods—for money is seldom given in the mountain market, where "beaver" is cash for which the articles supplied by the traders are bartered. In a very short time peltries of every description had changed hands, either by trade, or gambling with cards and betting. With the mountain men bets decide every question that is raised, even the most trivial; and if the Editor of *Bell's Life* was to pay one of these rendezvous a winter visit, he would find the broad sheet of his paper hardly capacious enough to answer all the questions which would be referred to his decision.

Before the winter was over, La Bonté had lost all traces of civilised humanity, and might justly claim to be considered as "hard a case" as any of the mountaineers then present. Long before the spring opened, he had lost all the produce of his hunt and both his animals, which, however, by a stroke of luck, he recovered, and wisely "held on to" for the future. Right glad when spring appeared, he started from Brown's Hole, with four companions, to hunt the Uintah or Snake country, and the affluents of the larger streams which rise in that region and fall into the Gulf of California.

[6] The Hudson's Bay Company is so called by the American trapper. Ruxton's note.

In the valley of the Bear River they found beaver abundant, and trapped their way westward until they came upon the famed locality of the Beer and Soda Springs[7]—natural fountains of mineral water, renowned amongst the trappers as being "medicine" of the first order.

Arriving one evening, about sundown, at the Beer Spring, they found a solitary trapper sitting over the rocky basin, intently regarding, and with no little awe, the curious phenomenon of the bubbling gas. Behind him were piled his saddles and a pack of skins, and at a little distance a hobbled Indian pony was feeding amongst the cedars which formed a little grove round the spring. As the three hunters dismounted from their animals, the lone trapper scarcely noticed their arrival, his eyes being still intently fixed upon the water. Looking round at last, he was instantly recognized by one of La Bonté's companions, and saluted as "Old Rube."[8] Dressed from head to foot in buckskin, his face, neck, and hands appeared to be of the same leathery texture, so nearly did they assimilate in colour to the materials of his dress. He was at least six feet two or three in his mocassins, straight-limbed and wiry, with long arms ending in hands of tremendous grasp, and a quantity of straight black hair hanging on his shoulders. His features, which were undeniably good, wore an expression of comical gravity, never relaxing into a smile, which a broad good-humored mouth could have grinned from ear to ear.

"What, boys," he said, "will you be simple enough to camp here, alongside these springs? Nothing good ever came of sleeping here, I tell you, and the worst kind of devils are in those dancing waters."

"Why, old hos," cried La Bonté, "what brings you hyar then, and camp at that?"

"This niggur," answered Rube solemnly, "has been down'd upon a sight too often to be skeared by what can come out from

---

[7] The town of Soda Springs, Idaho, is beside these famous springs on the bank of Bear River.

[8] Valentine J. Herring, whom we shall meet again.

them waters; and thar arn't a devil as hisses thar, as can 'shine' with this child, I tell you. I've tried him onest, an' fout him to clawin' away to Eustis,[9] and if I draws my knife agin on such varmint, I'll raise his hair, as sure as shootin'."

Spite of the reputed dangers of the locality, the trappers camped on the spot, and many a draught of the delicious sparkling water they quaffed in honour of the "medicine" of the fount. Rube, however, sat sulky and silent, his huge form bending over his legs, which were crossed, Indian fashion, under him, and his long bony fingers spread over the fire, which had been made handy to the spring. At last they elicited from him that he had sought this spot for the purpose of *"making medicine,"* having been persecuted by extraordinary ill luck, even at this early period of his hunt—the Indians having stolen two out of his three animals, and three of his half-dozen traps. He had, therefore, sought the springs for the purpose of invoking the fountain spirits, which, a perfect Indian in his simple heart, he implicitly believed to inhabit their mysterious waters. When the others had, as he thought, fallen asleep, La Bonté observed the ill-starred trapper take from his pouch a curiously carved red stone pipe, which he carefully charged with tobacco and kinnik-kinnik. Then approaching the spring, he walked three times round it, and gravely sat himself down. Striking fire with his flint and steel, he lit his pipe, and, bending the stem there several times towards the water, he inhaled a vast quantity of smoke, and, bending back his neck and looping upwards, puffed it into the air. He then blew another puff towards the four points of the compass, and emptying the pipe into his hand, cast the consecrated contents into the spring, saying a few Indian "medicine" words of cabalistic import. Having performed the ceremony to his satisfaction, he returned to the fire, smoked a pipe on his own hook, and turned into his buffalo robe, conscious of having done a most important duty.[10]

[9] A small lake near the head waters of the Yellow Stone, near which are some curious thermal springs of ink-black water. Ruxton's note.

[10] Ruxton met Rube Herring at Pueblo in the late winter of 1847.

In the course of their trapping expedition, and accompanied by Rube, who knew the country well, they passed near the vicinity of the Great Salt Lake, a vast inland sea, whose salitrose waters cover an extent of upwards of one hundred and forty miles in length, by eighty in breadth. Fed by several streams, of which the Big Bear River is the most considerable, this lake presents the curious phenomenon of a vast body of water without any known outlet. According to the trappers, an island, from which rises a chain of lofty mountains, nearly divides the northwestern portion of the lake, whilst a smaller one, within twelve miles of the northern shore, rises six hundred feet from the level of the water. Rube declared to his companions that the larger island was known by the Indians to be inhabited by a race of giants, with whom no communication had ever been held by mortal man; and but for the casual wafting to the shores of the lake of logs of gigantic trees, cut by axes of extraordinary size, the world would never have known that such a people existed. They were, moreover, white as themselves, and lived upon corn and fruits, and rode on elephants, &c.[11]

Whilst following a small creek at the southwest extremity of the lake, they came upon a band of miserable Indians, who, from the fact of their subsisting chiefly on roots, are called the Diggers. At first sight of the whites, they immediately fled from their wretched huts, and made towards the mountain; but one of the trappers, galloping up on his horse, cut off their retreat, and drove them like sheep before him back to their village. A few of these wretched creatures came into camp at sundown, and were regaled with such meat as the larder afforded. They appeared to have no other food in their village but bags of dried ants and their larvæ, and a few roots of the yampah. Their huts were constructed of a few bushes of greasewood, piled up as a sort of breakwind, in which they huddled

[11] This is quite fantastic, as the islands are mostly barren. See Dale L. Morgan, *The Great Salt Lake* (Indianapolis, 1947), 25.

in their filthy skins.[12] During the night, they crawled up to the camp and stole two of the horses, and the next morning not a sign of them was visible. Now La Bonté witnessed a case of mountain law, and the practical effects of the *"lex talionis"* of the Far West.

The trail of the runaway Diggers bore to the northwest, or along the skirt of a barren waterless desert, which stretches far away from the southern shores of the Salt Lake to the borders of Upper California. La Bonté, with three others, determined to follow the thieves, recover their animals, and then rejoin the other two (Luke and Rube) on a creek two days' journey from their present camp. Starting at sunrise, they rode on at a rapid pace all day, closely following the trail, which led directly to the northwest, through a wretched sandy country, without game or water. From the appearance of the track, the Indians must still have been several hours ahead of them, when the fatigue of their horses, suffering from want of grass and water, compelled them to camp near the head of a small water-course, where they luckily found a hole containing a little water, and whence a broad Indian trail passed, apparently frequently used. Long before daylight they were again in the saddle, and, after proceeding a few miles, saw the lights of several fires a short distance ahead of them. Halting here, one of the party advanced on foot to reconnoitre, and presently returned with the intelligence that the party they were in pursuit of had joined a village numbering thirty or forty huts.

Loosening their girths, they permitted their tired animals to feed on the scanty herbage which presented itself, whilst they refreshed themselves with a pipe of tobacco—for they had no meat of any description with them, and the country afforded no game. As the first streak of dawn appeared in the east, they mounted their horses, after first examining their rifles, and moved cautiously towards the Indian village. As it was scarcely light enough for their operations, they waited behind a sandhill

[12] The Diggers were the lowest order of the Ute nation and lived principally in the Nevada desert region.

in the vicinity, until objects became more distinct, and then, emerging from their cover with loud war-whoops, they charged abreast into the midst of the village.

As the frightened Indians were scarcely risen from their beds, no opposition was given to the daring mountaineers, who, rushing upon the flying crowd, discharged their rifles at close quarters, and then, springing from their horses, attacked them knife in hand, and only ceased the work of butchery when nine Indians lay dead upon the ground. All this time the women, half dead with fright, were huddled together on the ground, howling piteously; and the mountaineers advancing to them, whirled their lassos round their heads, and throwing the open nooses into the midst, hauled out three of them, and securing their arms in the rope, bound them to a tree, and then proceeded to scalp the dead bodies. Whilst they were engaged in this work, an old Indian, withered and grisly, and hardly bigger than an ape, suddenly emerged from a rock, holding in his left hand a bow and a handful of arrows, whilst one was already drawn to the head. Running towards them, and almost before the hunters were aware of his presence, he discharged an arrow at a few yards' distance, which buried itself in the ground not a foot from La Bonté's head as he bent over the body of the Indian he was scalping; and hardly had the whiz ceased, when whirr flew another, striking him in his right shoulder. Before the Indian could fit a third arrow to his bow, La Bonté sprang upon him, seized him by the middle, and spinning the pigmy form of the Indian round his head, as easily as he would have twirled a tomahawk, he threw him with tremendous force on the ground at the feet of one of his companions, who, stooping down, coolly thrust his knife into the Indian's breast, and quickly tore off his scalp.

The slaughter over, without casting an eye to the captive squaws, the trappers proceeded to search the village for food, of which they stood much in need. Nothing, however, was found but a few bags of dried ants, which, after eating voraciously of, but with wry mouths, they threw aside, saying the food was worse than "poor bull." They found, however, the animals they had been robbed of, and two more besides— wretched half-starved creatures; and on these mounting their captives, they hurried away on their journey back to their companions, the distance being computed at three days' travel from their present position. However, they thought, by taking a more direct course, they might find better pasture for their animals, and water, besides saving at least half a day by the short cut. To their cost, they proved the truth of the old saying, that "a short cut is always a long road," as will be presently shown.

It has been said that from the southwestern extremity of the Great Salt Lake a vast desert extends for hundreds of miles, unbroken by the slightest vegetation, destitute of game and water, and presenting a cheerless expanse of sandy plain, or rugged mountain, thinly covered with dwarf pine or cedar, the only evidence of vegetable life. Into this desert, ignorant of the country, the trappers struck, intending to make their short cut; and, travelling on all day, were compelled to camp at night, without water or pasture for their exhausted animals, and themselves ravenous with hunger and parched with thirst. The next day three of their animals "gave out," and they were fain to leave them behind; but imagining that they must soon strike a creek, they pushed on until noon, but still no water presented itself, nor a sign of game of any descriptoin. The animals were nearly exhausted, and a horse which could scarcely keep up with the slow pace of the others was killed, and its blood greedily drunk; a portion of the flesh being eaten raw, and a supply carried with them for future emergencies.

The next morning two of the horses lay dead at their pickets, and one only remained, and this in such a miserable state that it could not possibly have travelled six miles further. It was, therefore, killed, and its blood drunk, of which, however, the captive squaws refused to partake. The men began to feel the effects of their consuming thirst, which the hot horse's blood only served to increase; their lips became parched and swollen,

their eyes bloodshot, and a giddy sickness seized them at intervals. About mid-day they came in sight of a mountain on their
right hand, which appeared to be more thickly clothed with
vegetation; and arguing from this that water would be found
there, they left their course and made towards it, although some
eight or ten miles distant. On arriving at the base, the most
minute search failed to discover the slightest traces of water,
and the vegetation merely consisted of dwarf piñon and cedar.
With their sufferings increased by the exertions they had used
in reaching the mountain, they once more sought the trail, but
every step told on their exhausted frames. The sun was very
powerful, the sand over which they were floundering deep
and heavy, and, to complete their sufferings, a high wind was
blowing it in their faces, filling their mouths and noses with its
searching particles.

Still they struggled onwards manfully, and not a murmur
was heard until their hunger had entered the *second stage* attendant upon starvation. They had now been three days without food, and three without water; under which privation nature can hardly sustain herself for a much longer period. On the
fourth morning, the men looked wolfish, their captives following behind in sullen and perfect indifference, occasionally
stooping down to catch a beetle if one presented itself, and
greedily devouring it. A man named Forey, a Canadian half-
breed, was the first to complain. "If this lasted another sundown," he said, "some of them would be 'rubbed out'; that meat
had to be 'raised' anyhow; and for his part, he knew where to
look for a feed, if no game was seen before they put out of
camp on the morrow; and meat was meat, anyhow they fixed it."

No answer was made to this, though his companions well
understood him: their natures as yet revolted against the last
expedient. As for the three squaws, all of them young girls,
they followed behind their captors without a word of com-
plaint, and with the stoical indifference to pain and suffering,
which alike characterises the haughty Delaware of the north and
the miserable stunted Digger of the deserts of the Far West.

On the morning of the fifth day, the party were sitting round a small fire of piñon, hardly able to rise and commence their journey, the squaws squatting over another at a little distance, when Forey commenced again to suggest that, if nothing offered, they must either take the alternative of starving to death, for they could not hope to last another day, or have recourse to the revolting extremity of sacrificing one of the party to save the lives of all. To this, however, there was a murmur of dissent, and it was finally resolved that all should sally out and hunt; for a deer-track had been discovered near the camp, which, although it was not a fresh one, proved that there must be game in the vicinity. Weak and exhausted as they were, they took their rifles and started for the neighbouring uplands, each taking a different direction.

It was nearly sunset when La Bonté returned to the camp, where he already espied one of his companions engaged in cooking something over it. Hurrying to the spot, overjoyed with the anticipations of a feast, he observed that the squaws were gone; but, at the same time, thought it was not improbable they had escaped during their absence. Approaching the fire, he observed Forey broiling some meat on the embers, whilst at a little distance lay what he fancied was the carcass of a deer.

"Hurrah, boy!" he exclaimed, as he drew near the fire. "You've 'made' a 'raise,' I see."

"*Well*, I have," rejoined the other, turning his meat with the point of his butcher knife. "There's the meat, hos—help yourself."

La Bonté drew the knife from his scabbard, and approached the spot his companion was pointing to; but what was his horror to see the yet quivering body of one of the Indian squaws, with a large portion of the flesh butchered from it, and part of which Forey was already greedily devouring. The knife dropped from his hand, and his heart rose to his throat.[13]

[13] There were several instances where cannibalism was resorted to—in the Donner party of 1846, imprisoned in the snows of the high Sierras; during Frémont's attempt to cross the San Juan Mountains in the winter of 1848–49;

The next day he and his companion struck the creek where Rube and the other trapper had agreed to await them, and whom they found in camp with plenty of meat, and about to start again on their hunt, having given up the others for lost. From the day they parted, nothing was ever heard of La Bonté's two companions, who doubtless fell a prey to utter exhaustion, and were unable to return to the camp. And thus ended the Digger expedition.[14]

It may appear almost incredible that men having civilised blood in their veins could perpetrate such wanton and cold-blooded acts of aggression on the wretched Indians, as that detailed above; but it is fact that the mountaineers never lose an opportunity of slaughtering these miserable Diggers, and attacking their villages, often for the purpose of capturing women, whom they carry off, and not unfrequently sell to other tribes, or to each other.[15] In these attacks neither sex nor age is spared; and your mountaineer has as little compunction in taking the life of an Indian woman, as he would have in sending his rifle-ball through the brain of a Crow or Blackfoot warrior.

La Bonté now found himself without animals, and fairly "afoot"; consequently nothing remained for him but to seek some of the trapping bands, and hire himself for the hunt. Luckily for him, he soon fell in with Roubideau, on his way to Uintah,[16] and was supplied by him with a couple of animals; and thus equipped, started again with a large band of trappers,

in the Pikes Peak gold rush of 1859, by a party of gold-seekers traveling the "Starvation Route" between the source of the Smoky Hill River and the mountains; and others. Regarding one early trapper who won an unsavory reputation, see LeRoy R. Hafen, "Big Phil, the Cannibal," in the *Colorado Magazine*, Vol. XIII, No. 2 (March, 1936), 53–58.

[14] Ewing Young is reported to have made an unsuccessful attempt to cross the desert from Utah Lake to upper California and to have lost five of his twenty men in the effort. T. J. Farnham, *Life, Adventures, and Travels in California* (Pictorial edition, New York, 1849), 324.

[15] The trade in Indian captives was a long established business in New Mexico and was conducted in the Utah country as late as the eighteen fifties. See W. J. Snow, "Utah Indians and Spanish Slave Trade," and accompanying articles in the *Utah Historical Quarterly*, Vol. II, No. 3 (July, 1929), 67–80.

[16] Antoine Robidoux had a trading post on the Uintah fork of Green River.

who were going to hunt on the waters of Grand River and the Gila. Here they fell in with another nation of Indians, from which branch out the innumerable tribes inhabiting Northern Mexico and part of California. They were in general friendly, but lost no opportunity of stealing horses or any articles left lying about the camp. On one occasion, being camped on a northern affluent of the Gila, as they sat round the camp-fires, a volley of arrows was discharged amongst them, severely wounding one or two of the party. The attack, however, was not renewed, and the next day the camp was moved further down the stream, where beaver was tolerably abundant. Before sundown a number of Indians made their appearance, and making signs of peace, were admitted into the camp.

The trappers were all sitting at their suppers over the fires, the Indians looking gravely on, when it was remarked that now would be a good opportunity to retaliate upon them for the trouble their incessant attacks had entailed upon the camp. The suggestion was highly approved of, and instantly acted upon. Springing to their feet, the trappers seized their rifles, and commenced the slaughter. The Indians, panic-struck, fled without resistance, and numbers fell before the death-dealing rifles of the mountaineers. A chief, who had been sitting on a rock near the fire where the leader of the trappers sat, had been singled out by the latter as the first mark for his rifle.

Placing the muzzle to his heart, he pulled the trigger, but the Indian, with extraordinary tenacity of life, rose and grappled with his assailant. The white was a tall powerful man, but, notwithstanding the deadly wound the Indian had received, he had his equal in strength to contend against. The naked form of the Indian twisted and writhed in his grasp, as he sought to avoid the trapper's uplifted knife. Many of the latter's companions advanced to administer the *coup-de-grâce* to the savage, but the trapper cried to them to keep off: "If he couldn't whip the Injun," he said, "he'd go under."

At length he succeeded in throwing him, and, plunging his knife no less than seven times into his body, tore off his scalp, and went in pursuit of the flying savages. In the course of an hour or two, all the party returned, and sitting by the fires, resumed their suppers, which had been interrupted in the manner just described.[17] Walker, the captain of the band, sat down by the fire where he had been engaged in the struggle with the Indian chief, whose body was lying within a few paces of it. He was in the act of fighting the battle over again to one of his companions, and was saying that the Indian had as much life in him as a buffalo bull, when, to the horror of all present, the savage, who had received wounds sufficient for twenty deaths, suddenly rose to a sitting posture, the fire shedding a glowing light upon the horrid spectacle. The face was a mass of clotted blood, which flowed from the lacerated and naked scalp, whilst gouts of blood streamed from eight gaping wounds in the naked breast.

Slowly this frightful figure rose to a sitting posture, and, bending slowly forward to the fire, the mouth was seen to open wide, and a hollow gurgling—owg-h-h—broke from it.

"H——!" exclaimed the trapper—and jumping up, he placed a pistol to the ghastly head, the eyes of which sternly fixed themselves on his, and pulling the trigger, blew the poor wretch's head to atoms.

The Gila passes through a barren, sandy country, with but little game, and sparsely inhabited by several different tribes of the great nation of the Apache. Unlike the rivers of this western region, this stream is, in most parts of its course, particularly towards its upper waters, entirely bare of timber, and the bottom, through which it runs, affords but little of the coarsest grass. Whilst on this stream, the trapping party lost several animals from the want of pasture, and many more from the predatory attacks of the cunning Indians. These losses, however, they invariably made good whenever they encountered a native village—taking care, moreover, to repay themselves with interest whenever occasion offered.

[17] We have not found detailed corroboration of this particular attack, but accounts of several similar ones are found in the records.

Notwithstanding the sterile nature of the country, the trappers, during their passage up the Gila, saw with astonishment that the arid and barren valley had once been peopled by a race of men far superior to the present nomad tribes who roam over it. With no little awe they gazed upon the ruined walls of large cities, and the remains of houses, with their ponderous beams and joists, still testifying to the skill and industry with which they were constructed: huge ditches and irrigating canals, now filled with rank vegetation, furrowed the plains in the vicinity, marking the spot where once the green waving maize and smiling gardens covered what now was a bare and sandy desert.[18] Pieces of broken pottery, of domestic utensils, stained with bright colours, every where strewed the ground; and spear and arrow-heads of stone, and quaintly carved idols, and women's ornaments of agate and obsidian, were picked up often by the wondering trappers, examined with child-like curiosity, and thrown carelessly aside.[19]

A Taos Indian, who was amongst the band, was evidently impressed with a melancholy awe, as he regarded these ancient monuments of his fallen people. At midnight he rose from his blanket and left the camp, which was in the vicinity of the ruined city, stealthily picking his way through the line of slumbering forms which lay around; and the watchful sentinel observed him approach the ruins with a slow and reverential gait. Entering the mouldering walls, he gazed silently around, where in ages past his ancestors trod proudly, a civilised race, the tradition of which, well known to his people, served but to make their present degraded position more galling and apparent. Cowering under the shadow of a crumbling wall, the Indian drew his blanket over his head, and conjured to his mind's eye the former power and grandeur of his race—that warlike

[18] Archaeologists have found ruins of big communal houses and of irrigation systems that indicate the existence of large populations in the Gila Valley of Arizona.

[19] The Aztecs are supposed to have built this city during their migration to the south; there is little doubt, however, but that the region extending from the Gila to the Great Salt Lake, and embracing the province of New Mexico, was the locality from which they emigrated. Ruxton's note.

people who, forsaking their own country for causes of which not the most dim tradition affords a trace, sought in the fruitful and teeming valleys of the south for a soil and climate which their own lands did not afford; and displacing the wild and barbarous hordes which inhabited the land, raised there a mighty empire, great in riches and civilisation, of which but the vague tradition now remains.

The Indian bowed his head and mourned the fallen greatness of his tribe. Rising, he slowly drew his tattered blanket round his body, and was preparing to leave the spot, when the shadow of a moving figure, creeping past a gap in the ruined wall, through which the moonbeams were playing, suddenly arrested his attention. Rigid as a statue, he stood transfixed to the spot, thinking a former inhabitant of the city was visiting, in a ghostly form, the scenes his body once knew so well. The bow in his right hand shook with fear as he saw the shadow approach, but was as tightly and steadily grasped when, on the figure emerging from the shade of the wall, he distinguished the form of a naked Apache, armed with bow and arrow, crawling stealthily through the gloomy ruins.

Standing undiscovered within the shadow of the wall, the Taos raised his bow, and drew an arrow to the head, until the other, who was bending low to keep under cover of the wall, and thus approach the sentinel standing at a short distance, seeing suddenly the well-defined shadow on the ground, rose upright on his legs, and, knowing escape was impossible, threw his arms down his sides, and, drawing himself erect, exclaimed, in a suppressed tone, "Wa-g-h!"

"Wagh!" exclaimed the Taos likewise, but quickly dropped his arrow point, and eased the bow.

"What does my brother want," he asked, "that he lopes like a wolf round the fires of the white hunters?"

"Is my brother's skin not red?" returned the Apache, "and yet he asks a question that needs no answer. Why does the 'medicine wolf' follow the buffalo and deer! For blood—and for blood the Indian follows the treacherous white from camp to camp, to strike blow for blow, until the deaths of those so basely killed are fully avenged."

"My brother speaks with a big heart, and his words are true; and though the Taos and Pimo (Apache) black their faces towards each other (are at war), here, on the graves of their common fathers, there is peace between them. Let my brother go."

The Apache moved quickly away, and the Taos once more sought the camp-fires of his white companions.

Following the course of the Gila to the eastward, they crossed a range of the Sierra Madre, which is a continuation of the Rocky Mountains, and struck the waters of the Río del Norte, below the settlements of New Mexico. On this stream they fared well; besides trapping a great quantity of beaver, game of all kinds abounded, and the bluffs near the well-timbered banks of the river were covered with rich gramma grass, on which their half-starved animals speedily improved in condition.

They remained for some weeks encamped on the right bank of the stream, during which period they lost one of their number, who was shot with an arrow whilst lying asleep within a few feet of the camp-fire.

The Navajos continually prowl along that portion of the river which runs through the settlements of New Mexico, preying upon the cowardly inhabitants, and running off with their cattle whenever they are exposed in sufficient numbers to tempt them. Whilst ascending the river, they met a party of these Indians returning to their mountain homes with a large band of mules and horses which they had taken from one of the Mexican towns, besides several women and children, whom they had captured, as slaves. The main body of the trappers halting, ten of the band followed and charged upon the Indians, who numbered at least sixty, killed seven of them, and retook the prisoners and the whole cavallada of horses and mules. Great were the rejoicings when they entered Socorro, the town from whence the women and children had been taken, and as loud the remonstrances, when, handing them over to their families, the trappers rode on, driving fifty of the best of the rescued animals before them, which they retained as payment for their services. Messengers were sent on to Albuquerque with intelligence of the proceeding; and as there were some troops stationed there, the commandant was applied to to chastise the insolent whites.

That warrior, on learning that the trappers numbered less than fifteen, became alarmingly brave, and ordering out the whole of his disposable force, some two hundred dragoons, sallied out to intercept the audacious mountaineers. About noon one day, just as the latter had emerged from a little town between Socorro and Albuquerque, they descried the imposing force of the dragoons winding along a plain ahead. As the trappers advanced, the officer in command halted his men, and sent out a trumpeter to order the former to await his coming. Treating the herald to a roar of laughter, on they went, and, as they approached the soldiers, broke into a trot, ten of the number forming line in front of the packed and loose animals, and, rifle in hand, charging with loud whoops. This was enough for the New Mexicans. Before the enemy were within shooting distance, the gallant fellows turned tail, and splashed into the river, dragging themselves up the opposite bank like half-drowned rats, and saluted with loud peals of laughter by the victorious mountaineers, who, firing a volley into the air, in token of supreme contempt, quietly continued their route up the stream.

Before reaching the capital of the province, they struck again to the westward, and following a small creek to its junction with the Green River, ascended that stream, trapping *en route* to the Uintah or Snake Fork, and arrived at Roubideau's rendezvous early in the fall, where they quickly disposed of their peltries, and were once more on "the loose."

Here La Bonté married a Snake squaw, with whom he crossed the mountains and proceeded to the Platte through the Bayou Salade, where he purchased of the Yutes a commodious lodge, with the necessary poles, &c.; and being now "rich" in mules and horses, and all things necessary for *otium cum dignitate*, he took unto himself another wife, as by mountain law allowed; and thus equipped, with both his better halves attired in all the glory of fofarraw, he went his way rejoicing.

In a snug little valley lying under the shadow of the mountains, watered by Vermilion Creek, and in which abundance of buffalo, elk, deer, and antelope fed and fattened on the rich grass, La Bonté raised his lodge, employing himself in hunting, and fully occupying his wives' time in dressing the skins of the many animals he killed. Here he enjoyed himself amazingly until the commencement of winter, when he determined to cross to the North Fork and trade his skins, of which he had now as many packs as his animals could carry. It happened that he had left his camp one day, to spend a couple of days hunting buffalo in the mountains, whither the bulls were now resorting, intending to "put out" for Platte on his return. His hunt, however, had led him farther into the mountains than he anticipated, and it was only on the third day that sundown saw him enter the little valley where his camp was situated.

Crossing the creek, he was not a little disturbed at seeing fresh Indian sign on the opposite side, which led in the direction of his lodge; and his worst fears were realised when, on coming within sight of the little plateau where the conical top of his white lodge had always before met his view, he saw nothing but a blackened mass strewing the ground, and the burnt ends of the poles which had once supported it.

Squaws, animals, and peltry, all were gone—an Arapaho mocassin lying on the ground told him where. He neither fumed nor fretted, but throwing the meat off his pack animal, and the saddle from his horse, he collected the blackened ends of the lodge poles and made a fire—led his beasts to water and hobbled them, threw a piece of buffalo meat upon the coals, squatted down before the fire, and lit his pipe. La Bonté was a true philosopher. Notwithstanding that his house, his squaws, his peltries, were gone "at one fell swoop," the loss scarcely disturbed his equanimity; and before the tobacco of his pipe was half smoked out, he had ceased to think of his misfortune. Certes, as he turned his apolla of tender loin, he sighed as he thought of the delicate manipulations with which his Shosshone squaw, Sah-qua-manish, was wont to beat to tenderness the toughest bull meat—and missed the tending care of Yute Chil-co-the, or the "reed that bends," in patching the holes worn in his neatly fitting mocassin, the work of her nimble fingers. However, he ate and smoked, and smoked and ate, and slept none the worse for his mishap; thought, before he closed his eyes, a little of his lost wives, and more perhaps of the "Bending Reed" than Sah-qua-manish, or "she who runs with the stream," drew his blanket tightly round him, felt his rifle handy to his grasp, and was speedily asleep.

As the tired mountaineer breathes heavily in his dream, careless and unconscious that a living soul is near, his mule on a sudden pricks her ears and stares into the gloom, from whence a figure soon emerges, and with noiseless steps draws near the sleeping hunter. Taking one look at the slumbering form, the same figure approaches the fire and adds a log to the pile; which done, it quietly seats itself at the feet of the sleeper, and remains motionless as a statue. Towards morning the hunter awoke, and, rubbing his eyes, was astonished to feel the glowing warmth of the fire striking on his naked feet, which, in Indian fashion, were stretched towards it; as by this time, he knew, the fire he left burning must long since have expired. Lazily raising himself on his elbow, he saw a figure sitting near it with the back turned to him, which, although his exclamatory wagh was loud enough in all conscience, remained perfectly motionless, until the trapper rising, placed his hand upon the shoulder: then, turning up its face, the features displayed to his wondering eyes were those of Chilcothe, his Yuta wife. Yes, indeed, the "reed that bends" had escaped from her Arapaho captors, and made her way back to her white husband, fasting and alone.

The Indian women who follow the fortunes of the white hunters are remarkable for their affection and fidelity to their husbands, the which virtues, it must be remarked, are all on their own side; for, with very few exceptions, the mountaineers seldom scruple to abandon their Indian wives, whenever the fancy takes them to change their harems; and on such occasions the squaws, thus cast aside, wild with jealousy and despair, have been not unfrequently known to take signal vengeance both on their faithless husbands and the successful beauties who have supplanted them in their affections. There are some honourable exceptions, however, to such cruelty, and many of the mountaineers stick to their red-skinned wives for better and for worse, often suffering them to gain the upper hand in the domestic economy of the lodges, and being ruled by their better halves in all things pertaining to family affairs; and it may be remarked, when once the lady dons the unmentionables, she becomes the veriest termagant that ever henpecked an unfortunate husband.

Your refined trappers, however, who, after many years of bachelor life, incline to take to themselves a better half, often undertake an expedition into the settlements of New Mexico, where not unfrequently they adopt a very "Young Lochinvar" system in procuring the required rib; and have been known to carry off, *vi et armis*, from the midst of a fandango in Fernandez, or El Rancho of Taos, some dark-skinned beauty—with or without her own consent is a matter of unconcern—and bear the ravished fair one across the mountains, where she soon becomes inured to the free and roving life which fate has assigned her.

American women are valued at a low figure in the mountains. They are too fine and "fofarraw." Neither can they make moccassins, or dress skins; nor are they so schooled to perfect obedience to their lords and masters as to stand a "lodge poleing," which the western lords of the creation not unfrequently deem it their bounden duty to inflict upon their squaws for some dereliction of domestic duty.

To return, however, to La Bonté. That worthy thought himself a lucky man to have lost but one of his wives, and the worst at that. "Here's the beauty," he philosophised, "of having two 'wiping sticks' to your rifle; if the one break whilst ramming down a ball, still there's hickory left to supply its place." Although, with animals and peltry, he had lost several hundred dollars' worth of "possibles," he never groaned or grumbled. "There's red-skin will pay for this," he once muttered, and was done.

Packing all that was left on the mule, and mounting Chilco-the on his buffalo horse, he shouldered his rifle and struck the Indian trail for Platte. On Horse Creek they came upon a party of French[20] trappers and hunters, who were encamped with their lodges and Indian squaws, and formed quite a village. Several old companions were amongst them; and, to celebrate the arrival of a "camarade," a splendid dog-feast was prepared in honour of the event. To effect this, the squaws sallied out of their lodges to seize upon sundry of the younger and plumper of the pack, to fill the kettles for the approaching feast. With a presentiment of the fate in store for them, the curs slunk away with tails between their legs, and declined the pressing invitations of the anxious squaws. These shouldered their tomahawks and gave chase; but the cunning pups outstripped them, and would have fairly beaten the kettles, if some of the mountaineers had not stepped out with their rifles and quickly laid half-a-dozen ready to the knife. A cayeute, attracted by the scent of blood, drew near, unwitting of the canine feast in progress, and was likewise soon made *dog* of, and thrust into the boiling kettle with the rest.

The feast that night was long protracted; and so savoury was the stew, and so agreeable to the palates of the hungry hunters, that at the moment when the last morsel was being drawn from the pot, and all were regretting that a few more dogs had not been slaughtered, a wolfish-looking cur incautiously poked his long nose and head under the lodge skin, and was instantly pounced upon by the nearest hunter, who in a moment drew his knife across the animal's throat, and threw it

20 Creoles of St. Louis, and French Canadians. Ruxton's note.

to a squaw to skin and prepare it for the pot. The wolf had long since been vigorously discussed, and voted by all hands to be "good as dog."

"Meat's meat," is a common saying in the mountains, and from the buffalo down to the rattlesnake, including every quadruped that runs, every fowl that flies, and every reptile that creeps, nothing comes amiss to the mountaineer. Throwing aside all the qualms and conscientious scruples of a fastidious stomach, it must be confessed that *dog-meat* takes a high rank in the wonderful variety of cuisine afforded to the gourmand and the gourmet by the prolific "mountains." Now, when the bill of fare offers such tempting viands as buffalo beef, venison, mountain mutton, turkey, grouse, wildfowl, hares, rabbits, beaver and their tails, &c. &c., the station assigned to "dog" as No. 2 in the list can be well appreciated—No. 1, in delicacy of flavour, richness of meat, and other good qualities, being the flesh of *panthers*,[21] which surpasses every other, and all put together.

"Painter meat can't 'shine' with this," says a hunter, to express the delicious flavour of an extraordinary cut of "tender loin," or delicate fleece.

La Bonté started with his squaw for the North Fork early in November, and arrived at the Laramie at the moment that the big village of the Sioux came up for their winter trade. Two other villages were encamped lower down the Platte, including the Brulés and the Yanka-taus, who were now on more friendly terms with the whites. The first band numbered several hundred lodges, and presented quite an imposing appearance, the village being laid out in parallel lines, the lodge of each chief being marked with his particular totem. The traders had a particular portion of the village allotted to them, and a line was marked out which was strictly kept by the soldiers appointed for the protection of the whites. As there were many rival traders, and numerous *coureurs des bois*,[22] or peddling ones, the market promised to be brisk, the more so as a large quantity

21 Panthers, or "painters," were cougars, or mountain lions.

of ardent spirits was in their possession, which would be dealt with no unsparing hand to put down the opposition of so many competing traders.

In opening a trade a quantity of liquor is first given "on the prairie,"[23] as the Indians express it in words, or by signs in rubbing the palm of one hand quickly across the other, holding both flat. Having once tasted the pernicious liquid, there is no fear but they will quickly come to terms; and not unfrequently the spirit is drugged, to render the unfortunate Indians still more helpless. Sometimes, maddened and infuriated by drink, they commit the most horrid atrocities on each other, murdering and mutilating in a barbarous manner, and often attempting the lives of the traders themselves. On one occasion a band of Sioux, whilst under the influence of liquor, attacked and took possession of a trading fort of the American Fur Company, stripping it of every thing it contained, and roasting the trader himself over his own fire during the process.

The principle on which the nefarious trade is conducted is this, that the Indians, possessing a certain quantity of buffalo robes, have to be cheated out of them, and the sooner the better. Although it is explicitly prohibited by the laws of the United States to convey spirits across the Indian frontier, and its introduction amongst the Indian tribes subjects the offender to a heavy penalty; yet the infraction of this law is of daily occurrence, and perpetrated almost in the very presence of the government officers, who are stationed along the frontier for the very purpose of enforcing the laws for the protection of the Indians.[24]

The misery entailed upon these unhappy people by the illicit traffic must be seen to be fully appreciated. Before the effects of the poisonous "fire-water," they disappear from the earth

[22] *Coureurs des bois* (rangers of the wood) were the independent French traders.

[23] "On the prairie," is the Indian term for free gift. Ruxton's note.

[24] The larger trading companies generally supported the government officers and tried to suppress the liquor trade, for they soon noted its degenerating effect upon the Indians. But the competition of unscrupulous traffickers often forced the higher class traders to employ liquor also.

like "snow before the sun"; and knowing the destruction it entails upon them, the poor wretches have not moral courage to shun the fatal allurement it holds out to them, of wild excitement and a temporary oblivion of their many sufferings and privations. With such palpable effects, it appears only likely that the illegal trade is connived at by those whose policy it has ever been gradually but surely to exterminate the Indians, and by any means extinguish their title to the few lands they now own on the outskirts of civilisation. Certain it is that large quantities of liquor find their way annually into the Indian country, and as certain are the fatal results of the pernicious system, and that the American government takes no steps to prevent it.[25] There are some tribes who have as yet withstood the great temptation, and have resolutely refused to permit liquor to be brought into their villages. The marked difference between the improved condition of these, and the moral and physical abasement of those tribes which give way to the fatal passion for drinking, sufficiently proves the pernicious effects of the liquor trade on the unfortunate and abused aborigines; and it is matter of regret that no philanthropist has sprung up in the United States to do battle for the rights of the Red man, and call attention to the wrongs they endure at the hands of their supplanters in the lands of their fathers.

Robbed of their homes and hunting-grounds, and driven by the encroachments of the whites to distant regions, which hardly support their bare existence, the Indians, day by day, are gradually decreasing before the accumulating evils, of body and soul, which their civilised persecutors entail upon them. With every man's hand against them, they drag on to their final destiny; and the day is not far distant when the American Indian will exist only in the traditions of his pale-faced conquerors.[26]

The Indians who were trading at this time on the Platte were

[25] It was hardly true to say that the United States government took no steps to suppress the liquor traffic in the Indian country. But in such a large territory and with many conniving individuals, it must be admitted that the government efforts were not especially successful.

mostly of the Sioux nation, including the tribes of Burnt-woods [Burnt Thighs, or Brulés], Yanka-taus, Pian-Kashas, Assina-boins, Oglallahs, Broken Arrows, all of which belong to the great Sioux nation, or La-cotahs [Da-cotahs], as they call them-selves, and which means cut-throats. There were also some Cheyennes allied to the Sioux, as well as a small band of Re-publican Pawnees.

Horse-racing, gambling, and ball-play, served to pass away the time until the trade commenced, and many packs of dressed robes changed hands amongst themselves. When playing at the usual game of "*hand*," the stakes, comprising all the valuables the players possess, are piled in two heaps close at hand, the winner at the conclusion of the game sweeping the goods to-wards him, and often returning a small portion "on the prairie," with which the loser may again commence operations with an-other player.

The game of "hand" is played by two persons. One, who commences, places a plum or cherry-stone in the hollow formed by joining the concaved palms of the hands together, then shaking the stone for a few moments, the hands are suddenly separated, and the other player must guess which hand now contains the stone.

Large bets are often wagered on the result of this favourite game, which is also often played by the squaws, the men stand-ing round encouraging them to bet, and laughing loudly at their grotesque excitement. ·

A Burnt-wood Sioux, Tah-tunga-nisha, and one of the bravest chiefs of his tribe, when a young man, was out on a solitary war expedition against the Crows. One evening he drew near a certain "medicine" spring, where, to his astonishment, he encountered a Crow warrior in the act of quenching his thirst. He was on the point of drawing his bow upon him, when he remembered the sacred nature of the spot, and making the sign of peace, he fearlessly drew near his foe, and proceeded like-

[26] Recent census reports show a slight increase in the population of In-dian blood.

wise to slake his thirst. A pipe of kinnik-kinnik being produced, it was proposed to pass away the early part of the night in a game of "hand." They accordingly sat down beside the spring, and commenced the game.

Fortune favoured the Crow. He won arrow after arrow from the Burnt-wood brave; then his bow, his club, his knife, his robe, all followed, and the Sioux sat naked on the plain. Still he proposed another stake against the other's winnings—his scalp. He played, and lost; and bending forward his head, the Crow warrior drew his knife and quickly removed the bleeding prize. Without a murmur the luckless warrior rose to depart, but first exacted a promise from his antagonist, that he would meet him once more at the same spot, and engage in another trial of skill.

On the day appointed, the Burnt-wood sought the spot, with a new equipment, and again the Crow made his appearance, and they sat down to play. This time fortune changed sides, and the Sioux won back his former losses, and in his turn the Crow was stripped to his skin.

Scalp against scalp was now the stake, and this time the Crow submitted his head to the victorious Burnt-wood's knife; and both the warriors stood scalpless on the plain.

And now the Crow had but one single stake of value to offer, and the offer of it he did not hesitate to make. He staked his life against the other's winnings. They played; and fortune still being adverse, he lost. He offered his breast to his adversary. The Burnt-wood plunged his knife into his heart to the very hilt; and, laden with his spoils, returned to his village, and to this day wears suspended from his ears his own and enemy's scalp.

The village presented the usual scene of confusion as long as the trade lasted. Fighting, brawling, yelling, dancing, and all the concomitants of intoxication, continued to the last drop of the liquor-keg, when the reaction after such excitement was almost worse than the evil itself. During this time, all the work devolved upon the squaws, who, in tending the horses, packing wood and water from a long distance, had their time sufficiently occupied. As there was little or no grass in the vicinity, the animals were supported entirely on the bark of the cottonwood; and to procure this, the women were daily engaged in felling huge trees, or climbing them fearlessly, chopping off the upper limbs—springing like squirrels from branch to branch, which, in their confined costume, appeared matter of considerable difficulty.

The most laughter-provoking scenes, however, were, when a number of squaws sallied out to the grove, with their long-nosed, wolfish-looking dogs harnessed to their *travées*[27] or trabogans, on which loads of cottonwood were piled. The dogs, knowing full well the duty required of them, refuse to approach the coaxing squaws, and, at the same time, are fearful of provoking their anger by escaping and running off. They, therefore, squat on their haunches, with tongues hanging out of their long mouths, the picture of indecision, removing a short distance as the irate squaw approaches. When once harnessed to the travée, however, which is simply a couple of lodge-poles lashed on either side of the dog, with a couple of cross-bars near the ends to support the freight, they follow quietly enough, urged by bevies of children, who invariably accompany the women. When arrived at the scene of their labours, the reluctance of the curs to draw near the piles of cottonwood is most comical. They will lie down stubbornly at a little distance, whining their uneasiness, or sometimes scamper off bodily, with their long poles trailing after them, pursued by the yelling and half frantic squaws.

When the travées are laden, the squaws take the lead, bent double under loads of wood sufficient to break a porter's back, and calling to the dogs, which are urged on by the buffalo-fed urchins in rear, take up the line of march. The curs, taking advantage of the helpless state of their mistresses, turn a deaf

---

[27] The term is usually rendered "travois." After the Indian obtained the horse from the white man, horse-drawn travois were the chief reliance for transportation.

ear to their coaxing, lying down every few yards to rest, growling and fighting with each other, in which encounters every cur joins the *mêlée*, charging pell-mell into the yelping throng, upsetting the squalling children, and making confusion worse confounded. Then, armed with lodge-poles, the squaws, throwing down their loads, rush to the rescue, dealing stalwart blows on the pugnacious curs, and finally restoring something like order to the march.

"*Tszoo—tszoo!*" they cry, "*wah- kashne, ceitcha*—get on, you devilish beasts—*tszoo—tszoo!*" and belabouring them without mercy, start them into a gallop, which, once effected, they generally continue till they reach their destination.

The Indian dogs are, however, invariably well treated by the squaws, since they assist materially the everyday labours of these patient overworked creatures, in hauling firewood to the lodge, and, on the line of march, carrying many of the household goods and chattels which otherwise the squaw herself would have to carry on her back. Every lodge possesses from half-a-dozen to a score—some for draught and others for eating—for dog meat forms part and parcel of an Indian feast. The former are stout, wiry animals, half wolf half sheep-dog, and are regularly trained to draught; the latter are of a smaller kind, more inclined to fat, and embrace every variety of the genus cur. Many of the southern tribes possess a breed of dogs entirely divested of hair, which evidently have come from South America, and are esteemed highly for the kettle. Their meat, in appearance and flavour, resembles young pork, but far surpasses it in richness and delicacy of flavour.

The Sioux are very expert in making their lodges comfortable, taking more pains in their construction than most Indians. They are all of conical form: a framework of straight slender poles, resembling hop-poles, and from twenty to twenty-five feet long, is first erected, round which is stretched a sheeting of buffalo robes, softly dressed, and smoked to render them watertight. The apex, through which the ends of the poles protrude, is left open to allow the smoke to escape. A small opening, sufficient to permit the entrance of a man, is made on one side, over which is hung a door of buffalo hide. A lodge of the common size contains about twelve or fourteen skins, and contains comfortably a family of twelve in number. The fire is made in the centre immediately under the aperture in the roof, and a flap of the upper skins is closed or extended at pleasure, serving as a cowl or chimney-top to regulate the draught and permit the smoke to escape freely. Round the fire, with their feet towards it, the inmates sleep on skins and buffalo rugs, which are rolled up during the day, and stowed at the back of the lodge.

In travelling, the lodge-poles are secured half on each side a horse, and the skins placed on transversal bars near the ends, which trail along the ground—two or three squaws or children mounted on the same horse, or the smallest of the latter borne in the dog travées. A set of lodge-poles will last from three to seven years, unless the village is constantly on the move, when they are soon worn out in trailing over the gravelly prairie. They are usually of ash, which grows on many of the mountain creeks, and regular expeditions are undertaken when a supply is required, either for their own lodges, or for trading with those tribes who inhabit the prairies at a great distance from the locality where the poles are procured.

There are also certain creeks where the Indians resort to lay in a store of kinnik-kinnik (the inner bark of the red willow), which they use as a substitute for tobacco, and which has an aromatic and very pungent flavour. It is prepared for smoking by being scraped in thin curly flakes from the slender saplings, and crisped before the fire, after which it is rubbed between the hands into a form resembling leaf-tobacco, and stored in skin bags for use. It has a highly narcotic effect on those not habituated to its use, and produces a heaviness sometimes approaching stupefaction, altogether different from the soothing effects of tobacco.

Every year, owing to the disappearance of the buffalo from their former haunts, the Indians are necessitated to encroach upon each other's hunting-grounds, which is a fruitful cause of war between the different tribes. It is a curious fact, that the buffalo retire before the whites, while the presence of Indians in their pastures appears in no degree to disturb them. Wherever a few white hunters are congregated in a trading port, or elsewhere, so sure it is that, if they remain in the same locality, the buffalo will desert the vicinity and seek pasture elsewhere; and in this, the Indians affirm the *wah-keitcha*, or "bad medicine," of the pale-faces is very apparent; and ground their well-founded complaints of the encroachments made upon their hunting-grounds by the white hunters.

In the winter, many of the tribes are reduced to the very verge of starvation—the buffalo having passed from their country into that of their enemies, when no other alternative is offered them, but to remain where they are and starve, or follow the game into a hostile region, entailing a war and all its horrors upon them.

Reckless, moreover, of the future, in order to prepare robes for the traders, and procure the pernicious fire-water, they wantonly slaughter vast numbers of buffalo cows every year (the skins of which sex only are dressed), and thus add to the evils in store for them. When questioned on this subject, and such want of foresight being pointed out to them, they answer, that however quickly the buffalo disappears, the Red man "goes under" in greater proportion; and that the Great Spirit has ordained that both shall be "rubbed out" from the face of nature at one and the same time—"that arrows and bullets are not more fatal to the buffalo than the small-pox and fire-water to them, and that before many winters' snows have disappeared, the buffalo and the Red man will only be remembered by their bones, which will strew the plains."—"They look forward, however, to a future state, when, after a long journey, they will reach the happy hunting-grounds, where buffalo will once more blacken the prairies; where the pale-faces daren't come to disturb them; where no winter snows cover the ground, and the buffalo are always plentiful and fat."

As soon as the streams opened, La Bonté, now reduced to but two animals and four traps, sallied forth again, this time seeking the dangerous country of the Blackfeet, on the head waters of the Yellow Stone and Upper Missouri. He was accompanied by three others, a man named Wheeler, and one Cross-Eagle, a Swede, who had been many years in the western country. Reaching the fork of a small creek, on both of which appeared plenty of beaver sign, La Bonté followed the left-hand one alone, whilst the others trapped the right in company, the former leaving his squaw in the company of a Sioux woman, who followed the fortunes of Cross-Eagle, the party agreeing to rendezvous at the junction of the two forks as soon as they had trapped to their heads and again descended them. The larger party were the first to reach the rendezvous, and camped on the banks of the main stream to await the arrival of La Bonté.

The morning after their return, they had just risen from their blankets, and were lazily stretching themselves before the fire, when a volley of fire-arms rattled from the bank of the creek, and two of their number fell dead to the ground, at the same moment that the deafening yells of Indians broke upon the ears of the frightened squaws. Cross-Eagle seized his rifle, and, though severely wounded, rushed to the cover of a hollow tree which stood near, and crawling into it, defended himself the whole day with the greatest obstinacy, killing five Indians outright, and wounding several more. Unable to drive the gallant trapper from his retreat, the savages took advantage of a favourable wind which sprang up suddenly, and fired the long and dried-up grass which surrounded the tree. The rotten log catching fire at length compelled the hunter to leave his retreat, and, clubbing his rifle, he charged amongst the Indians, and fell at last pierced through and through with wounds, but not before two more of his assailants had fallen by his hand.

The two squaws were carried off, and, shortly after, one was sold to some white men at the trading ports on the Platte; but La Bonté never recovered the "Bending Reed," nor even heard of her existence from that day. So once more was the mountaineer bereft of his better half; and when he returned to the rendezvous, a troop of wolves were feasting on the bodies of his late companions, and of the Indians killed in the affray, of which he only heard the particulars a long time after from a trapper, who had been present when one of the squaws was offered at the trading post for sale, and who had recounted the miserable fate of her husband and his companions on the forks of the creek, which, from the fact of that trapper being the leader of the party, is still called La Bonté's Creek.[28]

Nevertheless, he continued his solitary hunt, passing through the midst of the Crow and the Blackfeet country; encountering many perils, often hunted by the Indians, but escaping all; and speedily loading both his animals with beaver, he thought of bending his steps to some of the trading rendezvous on the other side of the mountains, where employés of the Great Northwest Fur Company meet the trappers with the produce of their hunts, on Lewis's fork[29] of the Columbia, or one of its numerous affluents, and intending to pass the winter at some of the company's trading posts in Oregon, into which country he had never yet penetrated.

[28] There is in Wyoming a branch of the North Platte called La Bonté Creek, but whether or not it has any relation to Ruxton's hero it is impossible to say. There was a trapper called Davis La Bonté at Fort Jackson on the South Platte in 1839. Uncle Dick Wootton reports a trapper called Le Bonte being killed by Indians between 1838 and 1840. See Howard L. Conard, *"Uncle Dick" Wootton, the Pioneer Frontiersman of the Rocky Mountain Region* (Chicago, 1890), 80.

[29] Unfortunately, the name was later changed to Snake River.

A young woman of the Flat Head tribe (Alfred Jacob Miller)

"The Indian women . . . are remarkable for their affection and fidelity to their husbands"

Old age with dignity (Alfred Jacob Miller)

*"The old chiefs, enveloped in buffalo robes . . . sallied
last of all from their lodges"*

Joseph Walker—the Bourgeois (Alfred Jacob Miller)

"For California, ho!"

From the Porter collection

Taking the Hump Rib (Alfred Jacob Miller)

Trappers and Indians communicating by signs
(Alfred Jacob Miller)

A Herd of Antelopes (Alfred Jacob Miller)

Conversing by signs (Alfred Jacob Miller)

Moonlight—camp scene (Alfred Jacob Miller)

CHAPTER V

WE HAVE SAID that La Bonté was a philosopher: he took the streaks of ill luck which checkered his mountain life in a vein of perfect carelessness, if not of stoical indifference. Nothing ruffled his danger-steeled equanimity of temper; no sudden emotion disturbed his mind. We have seen how wives were torn from him without eliciting a groan or grumble (but such *contretemps*, it may be said, can scarcely find a place in the category of ills); how the loss of mules and mustangs, harried by horse-stealing Indians, left him in the *ne-plus-ultra* of mountain misery—"afoot"; how packs and peltries, the hard-earned "beaver" of his perilous hunts, were "raised" at one fell swoop by free-booting bands of savages. Hunger and thirst, we know, were commonplace sensations to the mountaineer. His storm-hardened flesh scarce felt the pinging wounds of arrow-point or bullet; and when in the midst of Indian fight, it is not probable that any tender qualms of feeling would allay the itching of his fingers for his enemy's scalp-lock, nor would any remains of civilised fastidiousness prevent his burying his knife again and again in the life-blood of an Indian savage.

Still, in one dark corner of his heart, there shone at intervals a faint spark of what was once a fiercely-burning fire. Neither time, that corroder of all things, nor change, that ready abettor of oblivion, nor scenes of peril and excitement, which act as dampers to more quiet memory, could smother this little smouldering spark, which now and again—when rarely-coming calm succeeded some stirring passage in the hunter's life, and left him, for a brief time, devoid of care and victim to his thoughts

—would flicker suddenly, and light up all the nooks and corners of his rugged breast, and discover to his mind's eye that one deep-rooted memory clung there still, though long neglected; proving that, spite of time and change, of life and fortune,

"*On revient toujours à ses premiers amours.*"

Often and often, as La Bonté sat cross-legged before his solitary camp-fire, and, pipe in mouth, watched the blue smoke curling upwards in the clear cold sky, a well-remembered form appeared to gaze upon him from the vapoury wreaths. Then would old recollections crowd before him, and old emotions, long a stranger to his breast, shape themselves, as it were, into long-forgotten but now familiar pulsations. Again he felt the soft subduing influence which once, in days gone by, a certain passion exercised over his mind and body; and often a trembling seized him, the same he used to experience at the sudden sight of one Mary Brand, whose dim and dreamy apparition so often watched his lonely bed, or, unconsciously conjured up, cheered him in the dreary watches of the long and stormy winter nights.

At first he only knew that one face haunted his dreams by night, and the few moments by day when he thought of any thing, and this face smiled lovingly upon him, and cheered him mightily. Name he had quite forgotten, or recalled it vaguely, and, setting small store by it, had thought of it no more.

For many years after he had deserted his home, La Bonté had cherished the idea of again returning to his country. During this period he had never forgotten his old flame, and many a choice fur he had carefully laid by, intended as a present for Mary Brand; and many a *gâge d'amour* of cunning shape and device, worked in stained quills of porcupine and bright-colored beads—the handiwork of the nimble-fingered squaws—he had packed in his possible sack for the same destination, hoping a time would come when he might lay them at her feet.

Year after year wore on, however, and still found him, with traps and rifle, following his perilous avocation; and each succeeding one saw him more and more wedded to the wild mountain-life. He was conscious how unfitted he had become again to enter the galling harness of conventionality and civilisation. He thought, too, how changed in manners and appearance he now must be, and could not believe that he would again find favour in the eyes of his quondam love, who, he judged, had long since forgotten him; and inexperienced as he was in such matters, yet he knew enough of womankind to feel assured that time and absence had long since done the work, if even the natural fickleness of woman's nature had lain dormant. Thus it was that he came to forget Mary Brand, but still remembered the all-absorbing feeling she had once created in his breast, the shadow of which still remained, and often took form and feature in the smoke-wreaths of his solitary camp-fire.

If truth be told, La Bonté had his failings as a mountaineer, and—sin unpardonable in hunter law—still possessed, in holes and corners of his breast seldom explored by his inward eye, much of the leaven of kindly human nature, which now and again involuntarily peeped out, as greatly to the contempt of his comrade trappers as it was blushingly repressed by the mountaineer himself. Thus, in his various matrimonial episodes, he treated his dusky *sposas* with all the consideration the sex could possibly demand from hand of man. No squaw of his ever humped shoulder to receive a castigatory and marital "lodge-poling" for offence domestic; but often has his helpmate blushed to see her pale-face lord and master devote himself to the feminine labour of packing huge piles of fire-wood on his back, felling trees, butchering unwieldy buffalo—all which are included in the Indian category of female duties. Thus he was esteemed an excellent *parti* by all the marriageable young squaws of Blackfoot, Crow, and Shoshone, of Yutah, Shian, and Arapaho; but after his last connubial catastrophe, he steeled his heart against all the charms and coquetry of Indian belles, and persevered in unblessed widowhood for many a long day.

From the point where we left him on his way to the waters of the Columbia, we must jump with him over a space of nearly two years, during which time he had a most uninterrupted run of good luck; trapping with great success on the head streams of the Columbia and Yellow Stone—the most dangerous of trapping ground—and finding good market for his peltries at the "North-west" posts—beaver fetching as high a price as five and six dollars a "plew"—the "golden age" of trappers, now, alas, never to return, and existing only in the fond memory of the mountaineers. This glorious time, however, was too good to last. In mountain language, "such heap of fat meat was not going to 'shine' much longer."

La Bonté was at this time one of a band of eight trappers, whose hunting ground was about the head waters of the Yellow Stone, which we have before said is in the country of the Blackfeet. With him were Killbuck, Meek,[1] Marcelline, and three others; and the leader of the party was Bill Williams, that old "hard case" who had spent forty years and more in the mountains, until he had become as tough as the parflêche soles of his mocassins. They were all good men and true, expert hunters, and well-trained mountaineers. After having trapped all the streams they were acquainted with, it was determined to strike into the mountains, at a point where old Williams affirmed, from the "run" of the hills, there must be plenty of water, although not one of the party had before explored the country, or knew any thing of its nature, or of the likelihood of its affording game for themselves or pasture for their animals. However, they packed their peltry, and put out for the land in view —a lofty peak, dimly seen above the more regular summit of the chain, being their landmark.

For the first day or two their route lay between two ridges of mountains, and by following the little valley which skirted a creek, they kept on level ground, and saved their animals considerable labour and fatigue. Williams always rode ahead, his body bent over his saddle-horn, across which rested a long heavy rifle, his keen gray eyes peering from under the slouched brim of a flexible felt-hat, black and shining with grease. His

---

[1] This was doubtless Joe Meek, who first came to the mountains in 1829. For an account of his life, see Frances F. Victor, *River of the West* (San Francisco, 1870), and Harvey E. Tobie, *No Man Like Joe: the Life and Times of Joseph L. Meek* (Portland, [1949]).

buckskin hunting-shirt, bedaubed until it had the appearance of polished leather, hung in folds over his bony carcass; his nether extremities being clothed in pantaloons of the same material (with scattered fringes down the outside of the leg—which ornaments, however, had been pretty well thinned to supply "whangs" for mending mocassins or pack-saddles), which, shrunk with wet, clung tightly to his long, spare, sinewy legs. His feet were thrust into a pair of Mexican stirrups, made of wood, and as big as coal-scuttles; and iron spurs of incredible proportions, with tinkling drops attached to the rowels, were fastened to his heel—a bead-worked strap, four inches broad, securing them over the instep. In the shoulder-belt which sustained his powder-horn and bullet-pouch, were fastened the various instruments essential to one pursuing his mode of life. An awl, with deer-horn handle, and the point defended by a case of cherry-wood carved by his own hand, hung at the back of the belt, side by side with a worm for cleaning the rifle; and under this was a squat and quaint-looking bullet mould, the handles guarded by strips of buckskin to save his fingers from burning when running balls, having for its companion a little bottle made from the point of an antelope's horn, scraped transparent, which contained the "medicine" used in baiting the traps. The old coon's face was sharp and thin, a long nose and chin hob-nobbing each other; and his head was always bent forward, giving him the appearance of being hump-backed. He *appeared* to look neither to the right nor left, but, in fact, his little twinkling eye was everywhere. He looked at no one he was addressing, always seeming to be thinking of something else than the subject of his discourse, speaking in a whining, thin, cracked voice, and in a tone that left the hearer in doubt whether he was laughing or crying. On the present occasion he had joined this band, and naturally assumed the leadership (for Bill ever refused to go in harness), in opposition to his usual practice, which was to hunt alone. His character was well known. Acquainted with every inch of the Far West, and with all the Indian tribes who inhabited it, he never failed to outwit his Red enemies, and generally made his appearance at the rendezvous, from his solitary expeditions, with galore of beaver, when numerous bands of trappers dropped in on foot, having been despoiled of their packs and animals by the very Indians through the midst of whom old Williams had contrived to pass unseen and unmolested. On occasions when he had been in company with others, and attacked by Indians, Bill invariably fought manfully, and with all the coolness that perfect indifference to death or danger could give, but always "on his own hook." His rifle cracked away merrily, and never spoke in vain; and in a charge—if ever it came to that—his keen-edged butcher-knife tickled the fleece of many a Blackfoot. But at the same time, if he saw that discretion was the better part of valour, and affairs wore so cloudy an aspect as to render retreat advisable, he would first express his opinion in curt terms, and decisively, and, charging up his rifle, would take himself off, and "câche"[2] so effectually that to search for him was utterly useless. Thus, when with a large party of trappers, when any thing occurred which gave him a hint that trouble was coming, or more Indians were about than he considered good for his animals, Bill was wont to exclaim—

"Do 'ee hyar now, boys, thar's sign about? this hos feels like câching"; and, without more words, and stoically deaf to all remonstrances, he would forthwith proceed to pack his animals, talking the while to an old, crop-eared, raw-boned Nez-percé pony, his own particular saddle-horse, who, in dogged temper and iron hardiness, was a worthy companion of his self-willed master. This beast, as Bill seized his apishamore to lay upon its galled back, would express displeasure by humping its back and shaking its withers with a wincing motion, that always excited the ire of the old trapper; and no sooner had he laid the apishamore smoothly on the chafed skin, than a wriggle of the animal shook it off.

"Do 'ee hyar now, you darned crittur!" he would whine out, "can't 'ee keep quiet your old fleece now? Isn't this old coon

2 Hide—from câcher. Ruxton's note.

putting out to save 'ee from the darned Injuns now, do 'ee hyar?" And then, continuing his work, and taking no notice of his comrades, who stood by bantering the eccentric trapper, he would soliloquise—"Do 'ee hyar now? This niggur sees sign ahead—he does; he'll be afoot afore long, if he don't keep his eye skinned—*he* will. *Injuns* is all about, they ar': Blackfoot at that. Can't come round this child—they can't, wagh!" And at last, his pack animals securely tied to the tail of his horse, he would mount, and throwing the rifle across the horn of his saddle, and without noticing his companions, would drive the jingling spurs into his horse's gaunt sides, and muttering, "Can't come round this child—they can't!" would ride away; and nothing more would be seen or heard of him perhaps for months, when they would not unfrequently, themselves bereft of animals in the scrape he had foreseen, find him located in some solitary valley, in his lonely camp, with his animals securely picketed around, and his peltries safe.

However, if he took it into his head to keep company with a party, all felt perfectly secure under his charge. His iron frame defied fatigue, and, at night, his love for himself and his own animals was sufficient guarantee that the camp would be well guarded. As he rode ahead, his spurs jingling, and thumping the sides of his old horse at every step, he managed, with admirable dexterity, to take advantage of the best line of country to follow—avoiding the gullies and cañons and broken ground, which would otherwise have impeded his advance. This tact appeared instinctive, for he looked neither right nor left, whilst continuing a course as straight as possible at the foot of the mountains. In selecting a camping site, he displayed equal skill: wood, water, and grass began to fill his thoughts towards sundown, and when these three requisites for a camping ground presented themselves, old Bill sprang from his saddle, unpacked his animals in a twinkling, and hobbled them, struck fire and ignited a few chips (leaving the rest to pack in the wood), lit his pipe, and enjoyed himself. On one occasion, when passing through the valley, they had come upon a band of fine buffalo cows, and, shortly after camping, two of the party rode in with a good supply of fat fleece. One of the party was a "greenhorn" on his first hunt, and, fresh from a fort on Platte, was as yet uninitiated in the mysteries of mountain cooking. Bill, lazily smoking his pipe, called to him, as he happened to be nearest, to butcher off a piece of meat and put it in his pot. Markhead[3] seized the fleece, and commenced innocently carving off a huge ration, when a gasping roar from the old trapper caused him to drop his knife.

"Ti-yah," growled Bill, "do 'ee hyar, now, you darned greenhorn, do 'ee spile fat cow like that whar you was raised? Them doin's won't shine in this crowd, boy, do 'ee hyar, darn you? What! butcher meat across the grain! why, whar'll the blood be goin' to, you precious Spaniard? Down the grain I say," he continued in a severe tone of rebuke, "and let your flaps be long, or out the juice'll run slick—do 'ee hyar, now?" But this heretical error nearly cost the old trapper his appetite, and all night long he grumbled his horror at seeing "fat cow spiled in that fashion."

When two or three days' journey brought them to the end of the valley, and they commenced the passage of the mountain, their march was obstructed by all kinds of obstacles; although they had chosen what appeared to be a gap in the chain, and what was in fact the only practicable passage in that vicinity. They followed the cañon of a branch of the Yellow Stone, where it entered the mountain; but from this point it became a torrent, and it was only by dint of incredible exertions that they reached the summit of the ridge. Game was exceedingly scarce in the vicinity, and they suffered extremely from hunger, having, on more than one occasion, recourse to the parflêche soles of their mocassins to allay its pangs. Old Bill, however, never grumbled; he chewed away at his shoes with relish even, and as long as he had a pipeful of tobacco in his pouch, was a

[3] Markhead appears frequently in the fur trade literature. For an account of his death, see *Ruxton of the Rockies*, 220.

happy man. Starvation was as yet far off, for all their animals were in existence; but as they were in a country where it was difficult to procure a remount, each trapper hesitated to sacrifice one of his horses to his appetite.

From the summit of the ridge, Bill recognised the country on the opposite side to that whence they had just ascended as familiar to him, and pronounced it to be full of beaver, as well as abounding in the less desirable commodity of Indians. This was the valley lying about the lakes now called Eustis and Biddle, in which are many thermal and mineral springs, well known to the trappers by the names of the Soda, Beer, and Brimstone Springs, and regarded by them with no little awe and curiosity, as being the breathing places of his Satanic majesty—considered, moreover, to be the "biggest kind" of "Medicine" to be found in the mountains. If truth be told, old Bill hardly relished the idea of entering this country, which he pronounced to be of "bad medicine" notoriety, but nevertheless agreed to guide them to the best trapping ground.

One day they reached a creek full of beaver sign, and determined to halt here and establish their headquarters, while they trapped in the neighbourhood. We must here observe, that at this period—which was one of considerable rivalry amongst the various trading companies in the Indian country—the Indians, having become possessed of arms and ammunition in great quantities, had grown unusually daring and persevering in their attacks on the white hunters who passed through their country, and consequently the trappers were compelled to roam about in larger bands for mutual protection, which, although it made them less liable to open attack, yet rendered it more difficult for them to pursue their calling without being discovered; for, where one or two men might pass unseen, the broad trail of a large party, with its animals, was not likely to escape the sharp eyes of the cunning savages.

They had scarcely encamped when the old leader, who had sallied out a short distance from camp to reconnoitre the neighbourhood, returned with an Indian mocassin in his hand, and informed his companions that its late owner and others were about.

"Do 'ee hyar now, boys, thar's *Injuns* knocking round, and Blackfoot at that; but thar's plenty of beaver, too, and this child means trapping any how."

His companions were anxious to leave such dangerous vicinity; but the old fellow, contrary to his usual caution, determined to remain where he was—saying that there were Indians all over the country for that matter; and as they had determined to hunt here, he had made up his mind too—which was conclusive, and all agreed to stop where they were, in spite of the Indians. La Bonté killed a couple of mountain sheep close to camp, and they feasted rarely on the fat mutton that night, and were unmolested by marauding Blackfeet.

The next morning, leaving two of their number in camp, they started in parties of two, to hunt for beaver sign and set their traps. Markhead paired with one Batiste, Killbuck and La Bonté formed another couple, Meek and Marcelline another; two Canadians trapped together, and Bill Williams and another remained to guard the camp: but this last, leaving Bill mending his mocassins, started off to kill a mountain sheep, a band of which animals was visible.

Markhead and his companion, the first couple on the list, followed a creek, which entered that on which they had encamped, about ten miles distant. Beaver sign was abundant, and they had set eight traps, when Markhead came suddenly upon fresh Indian sign, where squaws had passed through the shrubbery on the banks of the stream to procure water, as he knew from observing a large stone placed by them in the stream, on which to stand to enable them to dip their kettles in the deepest water. Beckoning to his companion to follow, and cocking his rifle, he carefully pushed aside the bushes and noiselessly proceeded up the bank, when, creeping on hands and knees, he gained the top, and, looking from his hiding-place, descried three Indian huts standing on a little plateau near the creek. Smoke curled from the roofs of branches, but the skin doors were carefully closed, so that he was unable to distinguish the number of the inmates. At a little distance, however, he observed two or three squaws gathering wood, with the usual attendance of curs, whose acuteness in detecting the scent of strangers was much to be dreaded.

Markhead was a rash and daring young fellow, caring no more for Indians than he did for prairie dogs, and acting ever on the spur of the moment, and as his inclination dictated, regardless of consequences. He at once determined to enter the lodges, and attack the enemy, should any be there; and the other trapper was fain to join him in the enterprise. The lodges proved empty, but the fires were still burning and meat cooking upon them, to which the hungry hunters did ample justice, besides helping themselves to whatever goods and chattels, in the shape of leather and mocassins, took their fancy.

Gathering their spoil into a bundle, they sought their horses, which they had left tied under cover of the timber on the banks of the creek; and, mounting, took the back trail, to pick up their traps and remove from so dangerous a neighbourhood. They were approaching the spot where the first trap was set, a thick growth of ash and quaking-ash concealing the stream, when Markhead, who was riding ahead, observed the bushes agitated, as if some animal was making its way through them. He instantly stopped his horse, and his companion rode to his side, to inquire the cause of this abrupt halt. They were within a few yards of the belt of shrubs which skirted the stream; and before Markhead had time to reply, a dozen swarthy heads and shoulders suddenly protruded from the leafy screen, and as many rifle-barrels and arrows were pointing at their breasts. Before the trappers had time to turn their horses and fly, a cloud of smoke burst from the thicket almost in their faces. Batiste, pierced with several balls, fell dead from his horse, and Markhead felt himself severely wounded. However, he struck the spurs into his horse; and as some half-score Blackfeet jumped with loud cries from their cover, he discharged his rifle amongst them, and galloped off, a volley of balls and arrows whistling after him. He drew no bit until he reined up at the camp-fire, where he found Bill quietly dressing a deer-skin. That worthy looked up from his work; and seeing Markhead's face streaming with blood, and the very unequivocal evidence of an Indian rencontre in the shape of an arrow sticking in his back, he asked—"Do 'ee feel bad now, boy? Whar away you see them darned Blackfoot?"

"Well, pull this arrow out of my back, and may be I'll feel like telling," answered Markhead.

"Do 'ee hyar now! hold on till I've grained this cussed skin, will 'ee! Did 'ee ever see sich a darned pelt, now? it won't take the smoke any how I fix it." And Markhead was fain to wait the leisure of the imperturbable old trapper, before he was eased of his annoying companion.

Old Bill expressed no surprise or grief when informed of the fate of poor Batiste. He said it was "just like greenhorns, runnin' into them cussed Blackfoot"; and observed that the defunct trapper, being only a Vide-pôche, was "no account anyhow." Presently Killbuck and La Bonté galloped into camp, with another alarm of Indians. They had also been attacked suddenly by a band of Blackfeet, but, being in a more open country, had got clear off, after killing two of their assailants, whose scalps hung at the horns of their saddles. They had been in a different direction to that where Markhead and his companion had proceeded, and, from the signs they had observed, expressed their belief that the country was alive with Indians. Neither of these men had been wounded. Presently the two Canadians made their appearance on the bluff, galloping with might and main to camp, and shouting "Indians, Indians," as they came. All being assembled, and a council held, it was determined to abandon the camp and neighbourhood immediately. Old Bill was already packing his animals, and as he pounded the saddle down on the withers of his old Rosinate, he muttered, "Do 'ee hyar, now! this coon 'ull câche, *he* will." So mounting his horse, and leading his pack mule by a lariat, he bent over his saddle-horn, dug his ponderous rowels into the lank sides of his beast, and, without a word, struck up the bluff and disappeared.

The others, hastily gathering up their packs, and most of them having lost their traps, quickly followed his example, and "put out." On cresting the high ground which rose from the creek, they observed thin columns of smoke mounting into the air from many different points, the meaning of which they were at no loss to guess. However, they were careful not to show themselves on elevated ground, keeping as much as possible under the banks of the creek, when such a course was practicable; but, the bluffs sometimes rising precipitously from the water, they were more than once compelled to ascend the banks, and continue their course along the uplands, whence they might easily be discovered by the Indians. It was nearly sundown when they left their camp, but they proceeded during the greater part of the night at as rapid a rate as possible; their progress, however, being greatly retarded as they advanced into the mountain, their route lying up stream. Towards morning they halted for a brief space, but started again as soon as daylight permitted them to see their way over the broken ground.

The creek now forced its way through a narrow cañon, the banks being thickly clothed with a shrubbery of cottonwood and quaking-ash. The mountain rose on each side, but not abruptly, being here and there broken into plateaus and shelving prairies. In a very thick bottom, sprinkled with coarse grass, they halted about noon, and removed the saddles and packs from their wearied animals, piqueting them in the best spots of grass.

La Bonté and Killbuck, after securing their animals, left the camp to hunt, for they had no provisions of any kind; and a short distance beyond it, the former came suddenly upon a recent mocassin track in the timber. After examining it for a moment, he raised his head with a broad grin, and, turning to his companion, pointed into the cover, where, in the thickest part, they discerned the well-known figure of old Bill's horse, browsing upon the cherry bushes. Pushing through the thicket in search of the brute's master, La Bonté suddenly stopped short as the muzzle of a rifle-barrel gaped before his eyes at the distance of a few inches, whilst the thin voice of Bill muttered—

"Do 'ee hyar now, I was nigh giving 'ee h——: I *was* now. If I didn't think 'ee was Blackfoot, I'm dogged now." And not a little indignant was the old fellow that his câche had been so easily, though accidentally, discovered. However, he presently made his appearance in camp, leading his animals, and once more joined his late companions, not deigning to give any explanation as to why or wherefore he had deserted them the day before, merely muttering, "do 'ee hyar now, thar's trouble comin'."

The two hunters returned after sundown with a black-tailed deer; and after eating the better part of the meat, and setting a guard, the party were glad to roll in their blankets and enjoy the rest they so much needed. They were undisturbed during the night; but at dawn of day the sleepers were roused by a hundred fierce yells, from the mountains enclosing the creek on which they had encamped. The yells were instantly followed by a ringing volley, the bullets thudding into the trees, and cutting the branches near them, but without causing any mischief. Old Bill rose from his blanket and shook himself, and exclaimed "Wagh!" as at that moment a ball plumped into the fire over which he was standing, and knocked the ashes about in a cloud. All the mountaineers seized their rifles and sprang to cover; but as yet it was not sufficiently light to show them their enemy, the bright flashes from the guns alone indicating their position. As morning dawned, however, they saw that both sides of the cañon were occupied by the Indians; and, from the firing, judged there must be at least a hundred warriors engaged in the attack. Not a shot had yet been fired by the trappers, but as the light increased, they eagerly watched for an Indian to expose himself, and offer a mark to their trusty rifles. La Bonté, Killbuck, and old Bill, lay a few yards distant from each other, flat on their faces, near the edge of the thicket, their rifles raised before them, and the barrels resting in the forks of convenient bushes. From their place of concealment to the position of the Indians—who, however, were scattered here and there, wherever a rock afforded them cover—was a distance of about a hundred and fifty yards, or within fair rifle-shot. The trappers were obliged to divide their force, since both sides of the creek were occupied; but such was the nature of the ground, and the excellent cover afforded by the rocks and boulders, and clumps of dwarf pine and hemlock, that not a hand's-breadth of an Indian's body had yet been seen. Nearly opposite La Bonté, a shelving glade in the mountain side ended in an abrupt precipice, and at the very edge, and almost toppling over it, were several boulders, just of sufficient size to afford cover to a man's body. As this bluff overlooked the trapper's position, it was occupied by the Indians, and every rock covered an assailant. At one point, just over where La Bonté and Killbuck were lying, two boulders lay together, with just sufficient interval to admit a rifle-barrel between them, and from this breastwork an Indian kept up a most annoying fire. All his shots fell in dangerous propinquity to one or other of the trappers, and already Killbuck had been grazed by one better directed than the others. La Bonté watched for some time in vain for a chance to answer this persevering marksman, and at length an opportunity offered, by which he was not long in profiting.

The Indian, as the light increased, was better able to discern his mark, and fired, and yelled every time he did so, with re-doubled vigor. In his eagerness, and probably whilst in the act of taking aim, he leaned too heavily against the rock which covered him, and, detaching it from its position, down it rolled into the cañon, exposing his body by its fall. At the same instant, a wreath of smoke puffed from the bushes which concealed the trappers, and the crack of La Bonté's rifle spoke the first word of reply to the Indian challenge. But a few feet behind the rock, fell the dead body of the Indian, rolling down the steep sides of the cañon, and only stopped by a bush at the very bottom, within a few yards of the spot where Markhead lay concealed in some high grass.

That daring fellow instantly jumped from his cover, and, drawing his knife, rushed to the body, and in another moment held aloft the Indian's scalp, giving, at the same time, a triumphant whoop. A score of rifles were levelled and discharged at the intrepid mountaineer; but in the act many Indians incautiously exposed themselves, every rifle in the timber cracked simultaneously, and for each report an Indian bit the dust.

But now they changed their tactics. Finding they were unable to drive the trappers from their position, they retired from the mountain, and the firing suddenly ceased. In their retreat, however, they were forced to expose themselves, and again the whites dealt destruction amongst them. As the Indians retired, yelling loudly, the hunters thought they had given up the contest; but presently a cloud of smoke rising from the bottom immediately below them, at once discovered the nature of their plans. A brisk wind was blowing up the cañon, and, favoured by it, they fired the brush on the banks of the stream, knowing that before this the hunters must speedily retreat.

Against such a result, but for the gale of wind which drove the fire roaring before it, they could have provided—for your mountaineer never fails to find resources on a pinch. They would have fired the brush to leeward of their position, and also carefully ignited that to windward, or between them and the advancing flame, extinguishing it immediately when a sufficient space had thus been cleared, and over which the fire-flame could not leap, and thus cutting themselves off from it both above and below their position. In the present instance, they could not profit by such a course, as the wind was so strong that, if once the bottom caught fire, they would not be able to extinguish it; besides which, in the attempt they would so expose themselves that they would be picked off by the Indians without difficulty. As it was, the fire came roaring before the wind with the speed of a race-horse, and, spreading from the bottom, licked the mountain sides, the dry grass burning like tinder.

Huge volumes of stifling smoke rolled before it, and, in a very few minutes, the trappers were hastily mounting their animals, driving the packed ones before them. The dense clouds of smoke concealed every thing from their view, and, to avoid this, they broke from the creek and galloped up the sides of the cañon on to the more level plateau. As they attained this, a band of mounted Indians charged them. One, waving a red blanket, dashed through the cavallada, and was instantly followed by all the loose animals of the trappers, the rest of the Indians following with loud shouts. So sudden was the charge, that the whites had not power to prevent the stampede. Old Bill, as usual, led his pack mules by the lariat; but the animals, mad with terror at the shouts of the Indians, broke from him, nearly pulling him out of his seat at the same time.

To cover the retreat of the others with their prey, a band of mounted Indians now appeared, threatening an attack in front, whilst their first assailants, rushing from the bottom, at least a hundred strong, assaulted in rear. "Do 'ee hyar, boys!" shouted old Bill, "break, or you'll go under. This child's goin' to câche!" and saying the word, off he went. *Sauve-qui-peut* was the order of the day, and not a moment too soon, for overwhelming numbers were charging upon them, and the mountain resounded with savage yells. La Bonté and Killbuck stuck together: they saw old Bill, bending over his saddle, dive right into the cloud of smoke, and apparently make for the creek bottom—their other companions scattering each on his own hook, and saw no more of them for many a month; and thus was one of the most daring and successful bands broken up that ever trapped in the mountains of the Far West.

It is painful to follow the steps of the poor fellows who, thus despoiled of the hardly-earned produce of their hunt, saw all their wealth torn from them at one swoop. The two Canadians were killed upon the night succeeding that of the attack. Worn with fatigue, hungry and cold, they had built a fire in what they thought was a secure retreat, and, rolled in their blankets, were soon buried in a sleep from which they never awoke. An Indian boy tracked them, and watched their camp. Burning with the idea of signalising himself thus early, he awaited his opportunity, and noiselessly approaching their resting-place, shot them both with arrows, and returned in triumph to his people with their horses and scalps.

La Bonté and Killbuck sought a passage in the mountain by which to cross over to the head waters of the Columbia, and there fall in with some of the traders or trappers of the Northwest. They became involved in the mountains, in a part where there was no game of any description, and no pasture for their miserable animals. One of these they killed for food; the other, a bag of bones, died from sheer starvation. They had very little ammunition, their mocassins were worn out, and they were unable to procure skins to supply themselves with fresh ones. Winter was fast approaching, the snow already covered the mountains, and storms of sleet and hail poured incessantly through the valleys, benumbing their exhausted limbs, hardly protected by scanty and ragged covering. To add to their miseries, poor Killbuck was taken ill. He had been wounded in the groin by a bullet some time before, and the ball still remained. The wound, aggravated by walking and the excessive cold, assumed an ugly appearance, and soon rendered him incapable of sustained exertion, all motion even being attended with intolerable pain. La Bonté had made a shanty for his suffering companion, and spread a soft bed of pine branches for him, by the side of a small creek at the point where it came out of the mountain and followed its course through a little prairie. They had been three days without other food than a piece of parflêche, which had formed the back of La Bonté's bullet-pouch, and which, after soaking in the creek, they eagerly devoured. Killbuck was unable to move, and sinking fast from exhaustion. His companion had hunted from morning till night, as well as his failing strength would allow him, but had not seen the traces of any kind of game, with the exception of some old buffalo tracks, made apparently months before by a band of bulls crossing the mountain.

The morning of the fourth day La Bonté, as usual, rose at daybreak from his blanket, and was proceeding to collect wood for the fire during his absence while hunting, when Killbuck called to him, and in an almost inarticulate voice desired him to seat himself by his side.

"Boy," he said, "this old hos feels like goin' under, and that afore long. You're stout yet, and if thar was meat handy, you'd come round slick. Now, boy, I'll be under, as I said, afore many hours, and if you don't raise meat you'll be in the same fix. I never eat dead meat[4] myself, and wouldn't ask no one to do it neither; but meat fair killed is meat any way; so, boy, put your knife in this old niggur's lights, and help yourself. It's 'poor bull,' I know, but maybe it'll do to keep life in; and along the fleece thar's meat yet, and maybe my old hump ribs has picking on 'em."

"You're a good old hos," answered La Bonté, "but this child ain't turned niggur yet."

Killbuck then begged his companion to leave him to his fate, and strive himself to reach game; but this alternative La Bonté likewise generously refused, and faintly endeavouring to cheer the sick man, left him once again to look for game. He was so weak that he felt difficulty in supporting himself, and knowing how futile would be his attempts to hunt, he sallied from the camp convinced that a few hours more would see the last of him.

He had scarcely raised his eyes, when, hardly crediting his senses, he saw within a few hundred yards of him an old bull, worn with age, lying on the prairie. Two wolves were seated on their haunches before him, their tongues lolling from their mouths, whilst the buffalo was impotently rolling his ponderous head from side to side, his blood-shot eyes glaring fiercely at his tormentors, and flakes of foam, mixed with blood, dropping from his mouth over his long shaggy beard. La Bonté was transfixed; he dared scarcely to breathe lest the animal should be alarmed and escape. Weak as it was, he could hardly have followed it, and, knowing that his own and companion's life

[4] Carrion. Ruxton's note.

hung upon the success of his shot, he scarcely had strength to raise his rifle. By dint of extraordinary exertions and precautions, which were totally unnecessary, for the poor old bull had not a move in him, the hunter approached within shot. Lying upon the ground, he took a long steady aim, and fired. The buffalo raised its matted head, tossed it wildly for an instant, and, stretching out its limbs convulsively, turned over on its side and was dead.

Killbuck heard the shot, and crawling from under the little shanty which covered his bed, saw, to his astonishment, La Bonté in the act of butchering a buffalo within two hundred yards of camp. "Hurraw for you!" he faintly exclaimed; and exhausted by the exertion he had used, and perhaps by the excitement of an anticipated feast, fell back and fainted.

However, the killing was the easiest matter, for when the huge carcass lay dead upon the ground, our hunter had hardly strength to drive the blade of his knife through the tough hide of the old patriarch. Then having cut off as much of the meat as he could carry, eating the while sundry portions of the liver, which he dipped in the gall-bladder by way of relish, La Bonté cast a wistful look upon the half-starved wolves, who now loped round and round, licking their chops, only waiting until his back was turned to fall to with appetite equal to his own, and capabilities of swallowing and digesting far superior. La Bonté looked at the buffalo, and then at the wolves, levelled his rifle and shot one dead, at which the survivor scampered off without delay.

Arrived at camp, packing in a tolerable load of the best part of the animal—for hunger lent him strength—he found poor Killbuck lying on his back, deaf to time, and to all appearances gone under. Having no salvolatile or vinaigrette at hand, La Bonté flapped a lump of raw fleece into his patient's face, and this instantly revived him. Then taking the sick man's shoulder, he raised him tenderly into a sitting posture, and invited, in kindly accents, "the old hos to feed," thrusting at the same time a tolerable slice of liver into his hand, which the patient looked at wistfully and vaguely for a few short moments, and then greedily devoured. It was nightfall by the time that La Bonté, assisted by many intervals of hard eating, packed in the last of the meat, which formed a goodly pile around the fire.

"Poor bull" it was in all conscience: the labour of chewing a mouthful of the "tender loin" was equal to a hard day's hunt; but to them, poor starved fellows, it appeared the richest of meat. They still preserved a small tin pot, and in this, by stress of eternal boiling, La Bonté contrived to make some strong soup, which soon restored his sick companion to marching order. For himself, as soon as a good meal had filled him, he was strong as ever, and employed himself in drying the remainder of the meat for future use. Even the wolf, bony as he was, was converted into meat, and rationed them several days. Winter, however, had set in with such severity, and Killbuck was still so weak, that La Bonté determined to remain in his present position until spring, as he now found that buffalo frequently visited the valley, as it was more bare of snow than the lowlands, and afforded them better pasture; and one morning he had the satisfaction of seeing a band of seventeen bulls within long rifle-shot of the camp, out of which four of the fattest were soon laid low by his rifle.

They still had hard times before them, for towards spring the buffalo again disappeared; the greater part of their meat had been spoiled, owing to there not being sufficient sun to dry it thoroughly; and when they resumed their journey they had nothing to carry with them, and had a desert before them without game of any kind. We pass over what they suffered. Hunger, thirst, and Indians assaulted them at times, and many miraculous and hair-breadth escapes they had from such enemies.

CHAPTER VI

THE TRAIL TO OREGON, followed by traders and emigrants, crosses the Rocky Mountains at a point known as the South Pass, where a break in the chain occurs of such moderate and gradual elevation as to permit the passage of waggons with tolerable facility. The Sweet Water Valley runs nearly to the point where the dividing ridge of the Pacific and Atlantic waters throws off its streams to their respective oceans. At one end of this valley, and situated on the right bank of the Sweet Water, a huge isolated mass of granitic rock rises to the height of three hundred feet, abruptly from the plain. On the smooth and scarped surface presented by one of its sides, are rudely carved the names and initials of traders, trappers, travellers and emigrants, who have here recorded the memorial of their sojourn in the remote wilderness of the Far West. The face of the rock is covered with names familiar to the mountaineers as those of the most renowned of their hardy brotherhood; while others again occur, better known to the science and literature of the Old World than to the unlearned trappers of the Rocky Mountains. The huge mass is a well-known landmark to the Indians and mountaineers; and travellers and emigrants hail it as the half-way beacon between the frontiers of the United States and the still distant goal of their long and perilous journey.[1]

It was a hot sultry day in July. Not a breath of air relieved the intense and oppressive heat of the atmosphere, unusual here

[1] Independence Rock, the "Register of the Desert." It is on the left bank of the Sweetwater, instead of on the right bank, as Ruxton says.

where pleasant summer breezes, and sometimes stronger gales, blow over the elevated plains with the regularity of trade-winds. The sun, at its meridian height, struck the dry sandy plain and parched the drooping buffalo-grass on its surface, and its rays, refracted and reverberating from the heated ground, distorted every object seen through its lurid medium. Straggling antelope, leisurely crossing the adjoining prairie, appeared to be gracefully moving in mid-air; whilst a scattered band of buffalo bulls loomed huge and indistinct in the vapoury distance. In the timbered valley of the river deer and elk were standing motionless in the water, under the shade of the overhanging cottonwoods, seeking a respite from the persevering attacks of swarms of horseflies and mosquitos; and now and then the heavy splash was heard, as they tossed their antlered heads into the stream, to free them from the venomous insects that buzzed incessantly about them. But in the sandy prairie, beetles of an enormous size were rolling in every direction huge balls of earth, pushing them with their hind legs with comical perseverance; cameleons darted about, assimilating the hue of their grotesque bodies with the colour of the sand: groups of prairie-dog houses were seen, each with its inmate barking lustily on the roof; whilst under cover of nearly every bush of sage or cactus a rattlesnake lay glittering in lazy coil. Tantalising the parched sight, the neighbouring peaks of the lofty Wind River Mountains glittered in a mantle of sparkling snow, whilst Sweet Water Mountain, capped in cloud, looked gray and cool, in striking contrast to the burned up plains which lay basking at its foot.

Resting their backs against the rock (on which, we have said, are *now* carved the names of many travellers), and defended from the powerful rays of the sun by its precipitous sides, two white men quietly slept. They were gaunt and lantern-jawed, and clothed in tattered buckskin. Each held a rifle across his knees, but—strange sight in this country—one had its pan thrown open, which was rust-eaten and contained no priming; the other's hammer was without a flint. Their faces were as if covered with mahogany-coloured parchment; their eyes were sunken; and as their jaws fell listlessly on their breasts, their cheeks were hollow, with the bones nearly protruding from the skin. One was in the prime of manhood, with handsome features; the other, considerably past the middle age, was stark and stern. Months of dire privation had brought them to this pass. The elder of the two was Killbuck, of mountain fame; the other hight La Bonté.

The former opened his eyes, and saw the buffalo feeding on the plain. "Ho, boy," he said, touching his companion, "thar's meat a-runnin."

La Bonté looked in the direction the other pointed, stood up, and hitching round his pouch and powder-horn, drew the stopper from the latter with his teeth, and placing the mouth in the palm of his left hand, turned the horn up and shook it.

"Not a grain," he said—"not a grain, old hos."

"Wagh!" exclaimed the other, "we'll have to eat afore long," and rising, walked into the prairie. He had hardly stepped two paces, when, passing close to a sage bush, a rattlesnake whizzed a note of warning with its tail. Killbuck grinned, and taking the wiping-stick from his rifle-barrel, tapped the snake on the head, and, taking it by the tail, threw it to La Bonté, saying, "hyar's meat, any how." The old fellow followed up his success by slaying half-a-dozen more, and brought them in skewered through the head on his wiping-stick. A fire was soon kindled, and the snakes as soon roasting before it; when La Bonté, who sat looking at the buffalo which fed close to the rock, suddenly saw them raise their heads, snuff the air, and scamper towards him. A few minutes afterwards a huge shapeless body loomed in the refracted air, approaching the spot where the buffalo had been grazing. The hunters looked at it and then at each other, and ejaculated "Wagh!" Presently a long white mass showed more distinctly, followed by another, and before each was a string of animals.

"Waggons, by hos and beaver! Hurrah for Conestoga!" exclaimed the trappers in a breath, as they now observed two white-tilted waggons, drawn by several pairs of mules, approaching the very spot where they sat. Several mounted men were riding about the waggons, and two on horseback, in advance of all, were approaching the rock, when they observed the smoke curling from the hunters' fire. They halted at sight of this, and one of the two, drawing a long instrument from a case, which Killbuck voted a rifle, directed it towards them for a moment, and then, lowering it, again moved forward.

As they drew near, the two poor trappers, although half-dead with joy, still retained their seats with Indian gravity and immobility of feature, turning now and then the crackling snakes which lay on the embers of the fire. The two strangers approached. One, a man of some fifty years of age, of middle height and stoutly built, was clad in a white shooting-jacket, of cut unknown in mountain tailoring, and a pair of trousers of the well-known material called "shepherd's plaid"; a broad-brimmed Panama shaded his face, which was ruddy with health and exercise; a belt round the waist supported a handsome bowie-knife, and a double-barelled fowling-piece was *slung* across his shoulder.[2]

His companion was likewise dressed in a light shooting-jacket, of many pockets and dandy cut, rode on an English saddle and in *boots*, and was armed with a superb double rifle, glossy from the case, and bearing few marks of use or service. He was a tall, fine-looking fellow of thirty, with light hair and complexion; a scrupulous beard and mustache; a wide-awake hat, with a short pipe stuck in the band, but not very black with smoke; an elaborate powder-horn over his shoulder, with a Cairngorm in the butt as large as a plate; a blue handkerchief tied round his throat in a sailor's knot, and the collar of his shirt turned carefully over it. He had, moreover, a tolerable idea of his very correct appearance, and wore Woodstock gloves.

The trappers looked at them from head to foot, and the more they looked the less could they make them out.

[2] William Drummond Stewart, on one of his famous hunting expeditions, presumably that of 1843.

"H——!" exclaimed La Bonté emphatically.

"This beats grainin' bull-hide slick," broke in Killbuck as the strangers reined up at the fire, the younger dismounting, and staring with wonder at the weather-beaten trappers.

"Well, my men, how are you?" he rattled out. "Any game here? By jove!" he suddenly exclaimed, seizing his rifle, as at that moment a large buzzard, the most unclean of birds, flew into the topmost branch of a cottonwood, and sat, a tempting shot. "By Jove, there's a chance!" cried the mighty hunter; and, bending low, started off to approach the unwary bird in the most approved fashion of northern deer-stalkers. The buzzard sat quietly, and now and then stretched its neck to gaze upon the advancing sportsman, who on such occasions threw himself flat on the ground, and remained motionless, in dread of alarming the bird. It was worth while to look at the countenance of old Killbuck as he watched the antics of the "bourgeois" hunter. He thought at first that the dandy rifleman had really discovered game in the bottom, and was nothing loth that there was a chance of his seeing meat; but when he understood the object of such manœuvres, and saw the quarry the hunter was so carefully approaching, his mouth grinned from ear to ear, and, turning to La Bonté, he said, "Wagh! *he's* some —*he* is!"

Nothing doubting, however, the stranger approached the tree on which the bird was sitting, and, getting well under it, raised his rifle and fired. Down tumbled the bird; and the successful hunter, with a loud shout, rushed frantically towards it, and bore it in triumph to the camp, earning the most sovereign contempt from the two trappers by the achievement.

The other stranger was a quieter character. He, too, smiled as he witnessed the exultation of his younger companion (whose horse, by the way, was scampering about the plain), and spoke kindly to the mountaineers, whose appearance was clear evidence of the sufferings they had endured. The snakes by this time were cooked, and the trappers gave their new acquaintances the never-failing invitation to "sit and eat." When the

latter, however, understood what the viands were, their looks
expressed the horror and disgust they felt.

"Good God!" exclaimed the elder, "you surely cannot eat
such disgusting food?"

"This niggur doesn't savy what disgustin is," gruffly answered
Killbuck; "but them as carries empty paunch three days an'
more, is glad to get 'snake-meat' I'm thinkin."

"What! you've no ammunition, then?"

"*Well*, we haven't."

"Wait till the waggons come up, and throw away that abom-
inable stuff, and you shall have something better, I promise,"
said the elder of the strangers.

"Yes," continued the younger, "some hot preserved soup,
hotch-potch, and a glass of porter, will do you good."

The trappers looked at the speaker, who was talking Greek
(to them). They thought the bourgeois were making fun, and
did not half like it, so answered simply, "Wagh! h——'s full of
hosh-posh and porter."

Two large waggons presently came up, escorted by some
eight or ten stout Missourians. Sublette[3] was amongst the number, well known as a mountain trader, and under whose guidance the present party, which formed a pleasure expedition
at the expense of a Scotch sportsman, was leisurely making its
way across the mountains to the Columbia. As several mountaineers were in company, Killbuck and La Bonté recognised
more than one friend, and the former and Sublette were old
compañeros. As soon as the animals were unhitched, and camp
formed on the banks of the creek, a black cook set about preparing a meal. Our two trapping friends looked on with astonishment as the sable functionary drew from the waggon the
different articles he required to furnish forth a feed. Hams,
tongues, tins of preserved meats, bottles of pickles, of porter,
brandy, coffee, sugar, flour, were tumbled promiscuously on
the prairie; whilst pots and pans, knives, forks, spoons, plates,
&c. &c. displayed their unfamiliar faces to the mountaineers.

3 William L. Sublette was a leader of this expedition of 1843.

"Hosh-posh and porter" did not now appear such Utopian articles as they had first imagined; but no one can understand the relish, but those who have fared for years on simple meat and water, with which they accepted the invitation of the Capen (as they called the Scotchman) to "take a horn of liquor." Killbuck and La Bonté sat in the same position as when we first surprised them asleep under the shadow of Independence Rock, regarding the profuse display of comestibles with scarce-believing eyes, and childishly helpless by the novelty of the scene. Each took the proffered half-pint cup, filled to the brim with excellent brandy—(no tee-totallers they!)—looked once at the amber-coloured surface, and with the usual mountain pledge of "here's luck!" tossed off the grateful liquor at a breath. This prepared them in some measure for what was yet in store for them. The Scotchman bestirred the cook in his work, and soon sundry steaming pots were lifted from the fire, and the skillets emptied of their bread—the contents of the former poured in large flat pans, while panikins were filled with smoking coffee. The two trappers needed no second invitation, but, seizing each a panful of steaming stew, drew the butcher knives from their belts, and fell to lustily—the hospitable Scotchman plying them with more and more, and administering corrective noggins of brandy the while; until at last they were fain to cry enough, wiped their knives on the grass, and placed them in their sheaths—a sign that human nature could no more. How can pen describe the luxury of the smoke that followed, to lips which had not kissed pipe for many months, and how the fragrant honey-dew from Old Virginia was relishingly puffed!

But the Scotchman's bounty did not stop here. He soon elicited from the lips of the hunters the narrative of their losses and privations, and learned that they now, without ammunition and scarcely clothed, were on their way to Platte Fort,[4] to

---

[4] Ruxton may be referring to Fort Laramie, or to its neighbor, Fort Platte. The latter, at the junction of the Laramie and North Platte rivers, was a trading post established by Lancaster P. Lupton, who had resigned his lieutenancy in the First Dragoons in 1836 and entered the fur trade of the West. In 1837

hire themselves to the Indian traders in order to earn another outfit, wherewith once more to betake themselves to their perilous employment of trapping. What was their astonishment to see their entertainer presently lay out upon the ground two piles of goods, each consisting of a four-point Mackinaw, two tin canisters of powder, with corresponding lead and flints, a pair of mocassins, a shirt, and sufficient buckskin to make a pair of pantaloons; and how much the more was the wonder increased when two excellent Indian horses were presently lassoed from the cavallada, and with mountain saddle, bridle, and lariats complete, together with the two piles of goods described, presented to them "on the prairie" or "gift-free," by the kind-hearted stranger, who would not even listen to thanks for the most timely and invaluable present.[5]

Once more equipped, our two hunters, filled with good brandy and fat buffalo meat, again wended on their way; their late entertainers continuing their pleasure trip across the gap of the South Pass, intending to visit the Great Salt Lake, or Timponogos, of the West.[6] The former were bound for the North Fork of the Platte, with the intention of joining one of the numerous trapping parties which rendezvous at the American Fur Company's post on that branch of the river. On a fork of Sweet Water, however, not two days after the meeting with the Scotchman's waggons, they encountered a band of a dozen

he established Fort Lupton on the South Platte, near the town of Fort Lupton, Colorado. His Fort Platte, a competitor with Fort Laramie (earlier known as Fort William and then as Fort John) was short-lived. Sybille and Adams owned it in 1843, according to *The Journals of Theodore Talbot* (edited by Charles H. Carey [Portland, 1931]).

[5] We have found no contemporary record that the W. D. Stewart party of 1843 actually found two starving trappers at Independence Rock, as narrated here. Matt Field's sketches in the *New Orleans Picayune* mention no such incident and the Missouri Historical Society reports, in a letter of August 8, 1950, that neither Field's diary nor that of William L. Sublette mentions any such incident at Independence Rock.

[6] The Stewart party did not continue to the Great Salt Lake, but upon reaching the Green River Valley turned northward, and after a season of hunting and recreation returned to St. Louis. See an account of the trip by William Clark Kennerly, one of the young members, in *Persimmon Hill* (Norman, 1948), 143–67. Sketches about the trip, written by Matt Field, were run in the *New Orleans Picayune* of 1843–44.

mountaineers, mounted on fine horses, and well armed and equipped, travelling along without the usual accompaniment of a mulada of pack-animals, two or three mules alone being packed with meat and spare ammunition. The band was proceeding at a smart rate, the horses moving with the gait peculiar to American animals, known as *"pacing"* or *"racking,"* in Indian file—each of the mountaineers with a long heavy rifle resting across the horn of his saddle. Amongst them our two friends recognised Markhead, who had been one of the party dispersed months before by the Blackfeet on one of the head streams of the Yellow Stone, which event had been the origin of the dire sufferings of Killbuck and La Bonté. Markhead, after running the gauntlet of numerous Indians, through the midst of whose country he passed with his usual temerity and utter disregard to danger, suffering hunger, thirst, and cold—those every-day experiences of mountain life—riddled with balls, but with three scalps hanging from his belt, made his way to a rendezvous on Bear River, whence he struck out for the Platte in early spring, in time to join the band he now accompanied, who were on a horse-stealing expedition to the Missions of Upper California.[7] Little persuasion did either Killbuck or La Bonté require to join the sturdy free-booters. In five minutes they had gone "files-about," and at sundown were camping on the well-tim-

[7] The plentiful bands of California horses had made a strong appeal to Anglo-Americans from the time the first company of trappers crossed the mountains and deserts to enter the lush pastures of California valleys. Jedediah Smith drove a band before him when he made his exit from the territory, and Joe Walker's famous exploring and trapping expedition of 1833 turned out to be, according to one of its members (William Craig), more of a horse-stealing expedition than anything else.

The dusky traders who in 1829 inaugurated commercial traffic between the far-flung Mexican provinces of New Mexico and California brought their serapes and woolens over the tortuous Old Spanish Trail by pack horse to barter for the prized horses and mules of California. The more irresponsible traders soon found it easier to procure the animals by raid than by trade. Horse-stealing became a regular feature of the traffic. American trappers joined or led marauding parties and soon such names as Peg-leg Smith, Charlefou, and Bill Williams were known and feared in California.

Ruxton is about to relate a rather typical trapper excursion beyond the Sierras to exact tribute from missions and ranches.

bered bottom of "Little Sandy," feasting once more on delicate hump-rib and tender loin.

For California, ho!

Fourteen good rifles in the hands of fourteen mountain men, stout and true, on fourteen strong horses, of true Indian blood and training—fourteen cool heads, with fourteen pairs of keen eyes in them, each head crafty as an Indian's, directing a right arm strong as steel, and a heart as brave as grizzly bear's.[8] Before them a thousand miles of dreary desert or wilderness, overrun by hostile savages, thirsting for the white man's blood; famine and drought, the arrows of wily hordes of Indians—and, these dangers past, the invasion of the civilised settlements of whites, the least numerous of which contained ten times their number of armed and bitter enemies—the sudden swoop upon their countless herds of mules and horses, the fierce attack and bloody slaughter—such were the consequences of the expedi-

---

[8] The dating and chronology of this California horse-stealing expedition is confusing. The number in the party would suggest that this may be the expedition of 1840–41. The leader, as indicated below, was the famous Captain Joseph R. Walker. The prefect of Los Angeles reported to the secretary of state of California on February 10, 1841, that Walker with two companions and in charge of twelve Americans had come in to procure horses.

The William D. Stewart expedition of 1843 would appear to be the one that rescued Killbuck and La Bonté just before the setting out of the raiding party for California. But Walker's known travels of 1843–44 do not conform to the Ruxton account here. In 1843 Walker went to California as guide to the Chiles emigrant party. The next spring he catches up with the Frémont expedition returning east along the Old Spanish Trail.

Some known facts in Walker's career point to 1845–46 as the date of the horse-stealing raid that Ruxton describes. In July of 1845, Captain P. St. George Cooke, with the Kearny Dragoons, met Walker a little west of Independence Rock and wrote: "This afternoon [July 8] Mr. Walker, whom we met at Independence Rock and who is now on his way to California, visited our camp: he has picked up a small party at Fort Laramie; and wild-looking creatures they are—white and red."—Cooke, *Scenes and Adventures in the Army* (Philadelphia, 1859), 389. Later that year Walker guided the main branch of Frémont's party by Walker's Pass, over the Sierras, and was in San Jose in February of 1846. Soon thereafter he and his party rounded up a band of horses and drove them east. Edwin Bryant met him at Fort Bridger on July 17, 1846.—*What I Saw in California* (New York, 1848), 143. Walker's party had 400 to 500 horses along. They took them to the Bent's Fort vicinity, where they disposed of part of them to United States troops enroute to New Mexico. J. W. Abert's Journal of 1846, in "Notes of a Military Reconnoissance," 30 Cong., 1 sess., *House Ex. Doc. 41*, 420, 432.

tion these bold mountaineers were now engaged in. Fourteen lives of any fourteen enemies who would be rash enough to stay them, were, any day you will, carried in the rifle barrels of these stout fellows; who, in all the proud consciousness of their physical qualities, neither thought, nor cared to think, of future perils; and rode merrily on their way, rejoicing in the dangers they must necessarily meet. Never a more daring band crossed the mountains; a more than ordinary want of caution characterised their march, and dangers were recklessly and needlessly invited, which even the older and more cold-blooded mountaineers seemed not to care to avoid. They had, each and all, many a debt to pay the marauding Indians. Grudges for many privations, for wounds and loss of comrades, rankled in their breasts; and not one but had suffered more or less in property and person at the hands of the savages, within a few short months. Threats of vengeance on every Redskin they met were loud and deep; and the wild war-songs round their nightly camp-fires, and grotesque scalp-dances, borrowed from the Indians, proved to the initiated that they were, one and all, "half-froze for hair." Soon after Killbuck and La Bonté joined them, they one day suddenly surprised a band of twenty Sioux, scattered on a small prairie and butchering some buffalo they had just killed. Before they could escape, the whites were upon them with loud shouts, and in three minutes the scalps of eleven were dangling from their saddle-horns.

Struggling up mountains, slipping down precipices, dashing over prairies which resounded with their Indian songs, charging the Indians wherever they met them, and without regard to their numbers; frightening with their lusty war-whoops the miserable Diggers, who were not unfrequently surprised while gathering roots in the mountain plains, and who, scrambling up the rocks and concealing themselves, like sage rabbits, in holes and corners, peered, chattering with fear, as the wild and noisy troop rode by. Scarce drawing rein, they passed rapidly the heads of Green and Grand Rivers, through a country abounding in game and in excellent pasture; encountering in the upland valleys, through which meandered the well-timbered creeks on which they made their daily camps, many a band of Yutas, through whom they dashed at random, caring not whether they were friends or foes. Passing many other heads of streams, they struck at last the edge of the desert, lying along the southeastern base of the Great Salt Lake, and which extends in almost unbroken sterility to the foot of the range of the Sierra Nevada—a mountain chain, capped with perpetual snow, that bounds the northern[9] extremity of a singular tract of country, walled by mountains and utterly desert, whose salt lagoons and lakes, although fed by many streams, find no outlet to the ocean, but are absorbed in the spongy soil or thirsty sand, which characterise the different portions of this deserted tract. In the "Grand Basin,"[10] it is reported, neither human nor animal life can be supported. No oases cheer the wanderer in the unbroken solitude of the vast wilderness. More than once the lone trapper has penetrated, with hardy enterprise, into the salt plains of the basin; but no signs of beaver or fur-bearing animal rewarded the attempt.[11] The ground is scantily covered with coarse unwholesome grass that mules and horses refuse to eat; and the water of the springs, impregnated with the impurities of the soil through which it percolates, affords but nauseating draughts to the thirsty traveller.

In passing from the more fertile uplands to the lower plains, as they descended the streams, the timber on their banks became scarcer, and the groves more scattered. The rich buffalo or *grama* grass was exchanged for a coarser species, on which the hard-worked animals soon grew poor and weak. The thickets of plum and cherry, of box-alder and quaking ash, which had

---

[9] The Sierra Nevada chain bounds the western extremity of the Great Basin. Other geographical features of the region are not accurately described by Ruxton.

[10] J. C. Frémont, on his second far western expedition (1843-44), encircled and named the Great Basin.

[11] The desert region of Nevada and western Utah is hardly so barren as here described. There are small streams and oases. When Peter Skene Ogden in 1828 led his band of British trappers west of Salt Lake and discovered the river that for a time bore his name but later was unfortunately christened the Humboldt, he found beaver plentiful and made an excellent catch.

hitherto fringed the creeks, and where the deer and bear loved
to resort—the former to browse on the leaves and tender shoots,
the latter to devour the fruit—now entirely disappeared, and
the only shrub seen was the eternal sage-bush, which flourishes
everywhere in the western regions in uncongenial soils where
other vegetation refuses to grow. The visible change in the
scenery had also a sensible effect on the spirits of the mountaineers. They travelled on in silence through the deserted
plains; the hi-hi-hiya of their Indian chants was no longer heard
enlivening the line of march. More than once a Digger of the
Pi-yutah tribe took himself and hair, in safety, from their path,
and almost unnoticed; but as they advanced they became more
cautious in their movements, and testified, by the vigilant watch
they kept, that they anticipated hostile attacks even in these
arid wastes. They had passed without molestation through the
country infested by the bolder Indians. The mountain Yutes,
not relishing the appearance of the hunters, had left them unmolested; but they were now entering a country inhabited by
the most degraded and abject of the western tribes; who, nevertheless, ever suffering from the extremities of hunger, have their
brutish wits sharpened by the necessity of procuring food, and
rarely fail to levy a contribution of rations, of horse or mule
flesh, on the passenger in their inhospitable country. The brutish cunning and animal instinct of these wretches is such, that
although arrant cowards, their attacks are more feared than
those of bolder Indians. These people—called the Yamparicas
or Root-Diggers—are, nevertheless, the degenerate descendants
of those tribes which once overran that portion of the continent of North America now comprehended within the boundaries of Mexico, and who have left such startling evidences in
their track of a comparatively superior state of civilisation.
They now form an outcast tribe of the great nation of the
Apache, which extends under various names from the Great
Salt Lake along the table-lands on each side the Sierra Madre
to the tropic of Cancer, where they merge into what are called
the Mexican Indians. The whole of this nation is characterised

by most abject cowardice; and they even refuse to meet the helpless Mexicans in open fight—unlike the Yutah or Comanche, who carry bold and open warfare into the territories of their civilised enemy, and never shrink from hand to hand encounter. The Apaches and the degenerate Diggers pursue a cowardly warfare, hiding in ambush, and shooting the passer-by with arrows; or, dashing upon him at night when steeped in sleep, they bury their arrow to the feather in his heaving breast. As the Mexicans say, "*Sin ventaja, no salen*"; they never attack without odds. But they are not the less dangerous enemies on this account; and by the small bands of trappers who visit their country, they are the more dreaded by reason of this coward and wolfish system of warfare.

To provide against surprise, therefore, as the hunters rode along, flankers were extended *en guerilla* on each side, mounting the high points to reconnoitre the country, and keeping a sharp look-out for the Indian sign. At night the animals were securely hobbled, and a horse-guard posted round them—a service of great danger, as the stealthy cat-like Diggers are often known to steal up silently, under cover of the darkness, towards the sentinel, shoot him with their arrows, and, approaching the animals, cut the hobbles and drive them away unseen.

One night they encamped on a creek where was but little of the coarsest pasture, and that little scattered here and there; so that they were compelled to allow their animals to roam farther than usual from camp in search of food. Four of the hunters, however, accompanied them to guard against surprise; whilst but half of those in camp laid down to sleep, the others, with rifles in their hands, remaining prepared for any emergencies. This day they had killed one of their two pack-mules for food, game not having been met with for several days; but the animal was so poor, that it scarcely afforded more than one tolerable meal to the whole party.

A short time before the dawn of day an alarm was given; the animals were heard to snort violently; a loud shout was heard, followed by the sharp crack of a rifle, and the tramp of galloping horses plainly showed that a stampede had been effected. The whites instantly sprang to their arms, and rushed in the direction of the sounds. The body of the cavallada, however, had luckily turned, and, being headed by the mountaineers, were surrounded and secured, with the loss of only three, which had probably been mounted by the Indians.

Day breaking soon after, one of their band was discovered to be missing; and it was then found that a man who had been standing horse-guard at the time of the attack, had not come into camp with his companions. At that moment a thin spiral column of smoke was seen to rise from the banks of the creek, telling but too surely the fate of the missing mountaineer. It was the signal of the Indians to their people that a "*coup*" had been struck, and that an enemy's scalp remained in their triumphant hands.

"H——!" exclaimed the trappers in a breath; and soon imprecations and threats of revenge, loud and deep, were showered upon the heads of the treacherous Indians. Some of the party rushed to the spot where the guard had stood, and there lay the body of their comrade, pierced with lance and arrow, the scalp gone, and the body otherwise mutilated in a barbarous manner. Five were quickly in the saddle, mounted upon the strongest horses, and flying along the track of the Indians, who had made off towards the mountains with their prize and booty. We will not follow them in their work of bloody vengeance, save by saying that they followed the savages to their village, into which they charged headlong, recovered their stolen horses, and returned to camp at sundown with thirteen scalps dangling from their rifles, in payment for the loss of their unfortunate companion.[12]

[12] In Frémont's expedition to California, on a somewhat similar occasion, two mountaineers, one the celebrated Kit Carson, the other a St. Louis Frenchman named Godey, and both old trappers, performed a feat surpassing the one described above, inasmuch as they were but two, who charged into an Indian village to rescue some stolen horses, and avenge the slaughter of two New Mexicans who had been butchered by the Indians; both which objects

In their further advance, hunger and thirst were their daily companions; they were compelled to kill several of their animals for food, but were fortunate enough to replace them by a stroke of good luck in meeting a party of Indians returning from an excursion against one of the Californian settlements with a tolerably large band of horses. Our hunters met this band one fine morning, and dashed into the midst at once; half a dozen Indians bit the dust, and twenty horses were turned over from red to white masters in as many seconds, which remounted those whose animals had been eaten, and enabled the others to exchange their worn-out steeds for fresh ones. This fortunate event was considered a *coup*, and the event was celebrated by the slaughter of a fat young horse, which furnished an excellent supper that night—a memorable event in these starveling regions.

They were now devouring their horses and mules at the rate of one every alternate day; for, so poor were the animals, that one scarcely furnished an ample meal for the thirteen hungry hunters. They were once more reduced to the animals they rode on; and after a fast of twenty-four hours' duration, were debating on the propriety of drawing lots as to whose Rosinante should fill the kettle, when some Indians suddenly appeared making signs of peace upon the bluff, and indicating a disposition to enter the camp for the purpose of trading. Being invited to approach, they offered to trade a few dressed elk-skins; but being asked for meat, they said that their village was a long way off, and they had nothing with them but a small portion of some game they had lately killed. When requested to produce this, they hesitated, but the trappers looking hungry and angry at the same moment, an old Indian drew from under his blanket several flaps of portable dried meat which he declared was bear's. It was but a small ration amongst so many; but being divided, was quickly laid upon the fire to broil. The meat was stringy, and of whitish colour, altogether unlike any flesh

they effected, returning to camp with the lost animals and a couple of propitiatory scalps. Ruxton's note.

the trappers had before eaten. Killbuck was the first to discover this. He had been quietly masticating the last mouthful of his portion, the stringiness of which required more than usual dental exertion, when the novelty of the flavour struck him as something singular. Suddenly his jaws ceased their work, he thought a moment, took the morsel from his mouth, looked at it intently, and dashed it into the fire.

"Man-meat, by G——!" he cried out; and at the words every jaw stopped work: the trappers looked at the meat and each other.

"I'm dog-gone if it ain't!" cried old Walker, looking at his piece, "and white meat at that, wagh!" (and report said it was not the first time he had tasted such viands);[13] and the conviction seizing each mind, every mouthful was quickly spat into the fire, and the ire of the deceived whites was instantly turned upon the luckless providers of the feast. They saw the storm that was brewing, and without more ado turned tail from the camp, and scuttled up the bluffs, where, turning round, they fired a volley of arrows at the tricked mountaineers, and instantly disappeared.

However, the desert and its nomad pilferers were at length passed; the sandy plains became grass-covered prairies; the monstrous cottonwood on the creeks was replaced by oak and ash; the surface of the country grew more undulating, and less broken up into cañons and ravines; elk and deer leaped in the bottoms, and bands of antelope dotted the plains, with occasional troops of wild horses, too wary to allow the approach of man. On the banks of a picturesque stream called the San Joaquim,[14] the party halted a few days to recruit themselves and animals, feasting the while on the fattest of venison and other

13 Although this is not unlikely, in view of Walker's many crossings of the deserts, we have found no authenticated recorded instance of Walker's eating man meat.

14 The San Joaquin flows north through the central valley of California and debouches into San Francisco Bay.

Ruxton apparently has his mountaineers cross Nevada by the Humboldt River route, the one Walker explored in 1833, although the geographic description is vague and makes no mention of a crossing of the Sierra Nevadas.

game. They then struck to the southeast for two days, until they reached a branch of the "Las Animas," a clear stream running through a pretty valley, well timbered and abounding in game. Here, as they wound along the river-banks, a horseman suddenly appeared upon the bluff above them, galloping at a furious rate along the edge. His dress approached in some degree to civilised attire. A broad-brimmed sombrero surmounted his swarthy face; a coloured blanket, through a slit in which his head was thrust, floated in the air from his shoulders; leathern leggings encased his lower limbs; and huge spurs jingled on his heels. He rode in a high-peaked Mexican saddle, his feet thrust in ponderous stirrups, and in his hand swung a coil of ready lasso, his only offensive arm. One of the trappers knew a little Spanish, and instantly hailed him.

"*Compadre*," he shouted, "*por onde va?*" The Californian reined in suddenly, throwing the horse he rode on its very haunches, and darting down the bluff, galloped unhesitatingly into the midst of the hunters.

"*Americanos!*" he exclaimed glancing at them; and continued, smiling—"*Y caballos quieren, por eso vienen tan lejitos. Jesus, que mala gente!*" "It's horses you want, and for this you come all this way. Ah, what rogues you are!"

He was an Indian, employed at the Mission of San Fernando, distant three days' journey from their present position, and was now searching for a band of horses and mules which had strayed. San Fernando, it appeared, had once before been visited by a party of mountain free-traders, and the Indian therefore divined the object of the present one. He was, he told them, "*un Indio, pero mansito*": an Indian, but a tame one;[15] "*de mas, Christiano*"; a Christian moreover (exhibiting a small cross which hung round his neck). There were many people about

---

The only alternate route to California that our veteran travelers would have taken was the one from Salt Lake to Southern California by way of Las Vegas. This course would not have taken them to the San Joaquin and the subsequent route southeast that Ruxton indicates.

[15] The Mexicans call the Indians living near the Missions and engaged in agriculture, *mansos*, or *mansitos*, tame. Ruxton's note.

the mission, he said, who knew how to fight, and had plenty of arms; and there were enough to "eat up" the "*Americanos, sin frijoles,*" without beans, as he facetiously observed. For his part, however, he was friendly to the *Americanos;* he had once met a man of that nation who was a good sort of fellow, and had made him a present of tobacco, of which he was particularly fond. Finding this hint did not take, he said that the horses and mules belonging to the mission were innumerable— "like that," he added, sweeping his hand to all points of the compass over the plain, to intimate that they would cover that extent; and he could point out a large herd grazing nearer at hand than the mission, and guarded but by three *vaqueros.* Regaled with venison, and with a smoke of his coveted tobacco, he rode off, and made his way to the mission without delay; conveying the startling intelligence that a thousand Americans were upon them.

The next morning the thirteen doughty mountaineers quietly resumed their journey, moving leisurely along towards the object of their expedition.

It will not be out of place here to digress a little, in order to describe the singular features of the establishments formed in those remote regions by the Catholic church, as nuclei round which to concentrate the wandering tribes that inhabit the country, with a view to give them the benefit of civilised example, and to wean them from their restless nomadic habits.

The establishment of missions in Upper California is coeval with the first settlement of Southern Mexico.[16] No sooner had Spanish rule taken a firm foothold in the Aztec empire, than the avowed primary object of the military expedition began to be carried into effect. "To save the souls" of the savage and barbarous subjects of their most Catholic majesties was ever inculcated upon the governors of the conquered country as the

[16] This is hardly true, for though California was visited by Cabrillo as early as 1542, the actual settlement of the province did not begin until late in the eighteenth century. The first of the Spanish missions of California was founded at San Diego in 1769.

grand object to be sought after, as soon as tranquillity was par-
tially restored by the submission of the Mexicans; and the cross,
the sacred emblem of the Catholic faith, was to be upraised in
the remotest corners of the country, and the natives instructed
and compelled to worship it, in lieu of the grotesque images of
their own idolatrous religion.

To carry into effect these orthodox instructions, troops of
pious priests, of friars and monks of every order, and even of
saintly nuns, followed in the wake of the victorious armies of
Cortez; and girding up their loins with zealous fervour and en-
thusiasm, and with an enterprise and hardihood worthy of buc-
caneers, they pushed their adventurous way far into the bowels
of the land, preaching devoutly and with commendable perseverance to savages who did not understand a syllable of what
they so eloquently discoursed; and returning, after the lapse
of many months passed in this first attempt, with glowing accounts of the *"muy buen indole,"* the very ductile disposition
of the savages, and of the thousands they had converted to *"la
santa fé catolica."*

Ferdinand and Isabel, of glorious memory, at once beat up
for volunteers. Crowds of Franciscan monks, greasy Capu-
chinos, and nuns of orthodox odour, joined the band; and saints
even of the feminine gender, long since canonised and up aloft
amongst the goodly muster of saints and martyrs, put foot once
more on *terra firma*, and, rosary in hand, crossed the seas to
participate in the good work. As proof of this latter fact, one
Venabides, a Franciscan, whose veracity is beyond impeach-
ment, declared that, while preaching in the regions now known
as New Mexico, one million Indians from the *"rumbo"* known
as Cibolo, a mighty nation, approached his temporary pulpit
on the Río Grande, and requested in a body the favour of being
baptised. Struck with the singularity of this request from Indians with whom he had as yet held no communication, and
with conscientious scruple as to whether he would be justified
in performing such ceremony without their having received
previous instructions, he hesitated a few moments before mak-

ing an answer. At this juncture, the Indians espied a medallion which hung around his neck, bearing the effigy of a certain saint of extraordinary virtue. At sight of this they fell on their knees before it; and it was some time before they found words (in what language does not appear) to explain to the holy father that the original of that effigy, which hung pendant from his neck, had been long amongst them instructing them in the elements of the Christian religion, and had only lately disappeared; informing them that certain reverend men would shortly appear in the land, who would finish the good work she had devoutly commenced, and clench the business by baptising the one million miserable sinners who now knelt before El Padre Venabides.

"*Valgame Dios!*" reverently exclaimed that worthy man, "*qui milagro es este*" [what a miracle is this I hear]; and casting up his eyes, and speaking slowly, as if he weighed every word, and taxing his memory of the historical calendar of saints, continued—

"*Se murió—equella—santissima—muger—en el ano 175—es decir—ya hacen—mil—quatro—cientos—anos.*" [That most holy woman died in the year 175, that is to say, one thousand four hundred years ago.][17]

"Oh, what a strange thing is this!" the padre continues devoutly. "After so many ages spent in heaven in company of the angels, of most holy men, and of virgins the most pure; and, perhaps, also in the company of my worthy and esteemed friend and patron Don Vincente Carvajal y Calvo, who died a few years ago in San Lucar of Xeres (bequeathing me certain arrobas of dry wine, of a class I greatly esteem—for which act he deserved to be canonised, and, I have no doubt, is), the said Don Vincente Carvajal y Calvo being, moreover, a man of the purest and holiest thoughts (*Dios mio!* what a *puchero* that man always had on his table!), this holy woman comes here—to these wild and remote regions; this holy woman (who died fifteen hundred years ago), abandoning the company of angels, of holy

[17] The brackets here and in the preceding paragraph are Ruxton's.

men, and sanctified women and virgins, and also of Don Vincente Carvajal y Calvo (that worthy man!)—comes here, I say,
where there are neither *pucheros*, nor *garbanzos*, nor dry wine,
nor sweet wine, neither of Xeres, nor of Val de Peñas, nor of
Peralta; where" (sobbed the padre, and bellowed the last word)
"there is—nothing either to eat or to drink. *Valgame Puríssima
María!* And what is the name of this holy woman? the world
will ask," continues Venabides. "Santa Clara of Carmona is her
name, one well known in my native country, who leaves heaven
and all its joys, wends her way to the distant wilds of New
Spain, and spends years in inducting the savage people to the
holy faith. Truly a pious work, and pleasing to God!"[18]

Thus spoke Venabides the Franciscan, and no doubt he believed what he said; and many others in Old Spain were fools
enough to believe it too, for the shaven heads flocked over in
greater numbers, and the cry was ever "still they come."

Along the whole extent of the tablelands, not an Indian tribe
but was speedily visited by the preaching friars and monks; and,
in less than a century after the conquest of Mexico by the Spaniards, these hardy and enthusiastic frayles had pushed their way
into the inhospitable regions of New Mexico, nearly two thousand miles distant from the valley of Anáhuac.[19] How they succeeded in surmounting the natural obstacles presented by the
wild and barren deserts they traversed; how they escaped the
infinite peril they encountered at every step, at the hands of the
savage inhabitants of the country, with whose language they
were totally unacquainted, is sufficient puzzle to those who, in
the present day, have attempted a journey in the same regions.

---

[18] From a manuscript obtained in Santa Fé of New Mexico, describing the
labours of the missionaries Fray Augustin Ruiz, Venabides, and Macos, in the
year 1585. Ruxton's note. In his previous work, *Adventures in Mexico and
the Rocky Mountains*, Ruxton refers to the same missionaries as Ruiz, Venabides, and Marcos. Father Ruiz, usually known as Rodríguez, was killed by
the Indians. See *The Gallegos Relation of the Rodríguez Expedition to New
Mexico* (edited by G. P. Hammond and A. Rey [Santa Fé, 1927]). The "V"
and "B" are often interchanged in Spanish, and "Venabides" is often found
"Benavides."

[19] Anáhuac was the valley of Mexico City.

However, it is impossible not to admire the hardihood of these holy pioneers of civilisation, who, totally unfitted by their former mode of life for undergoing such hardships as they must have anticipated, threw themselves into the wilderness with fearless and stubborn zeal.

For the most part, however, they found the Indians exceedingly hospitable and well disposed; and it was not until some time after—when, receiving from the missionary monks glowing, and not always very truthful accounts of the riches of the country in which they had located themselves, the governors of Mexico dispatched armed expeditions under adventurous desperadoes to take and retain possession of the said country, with orders to compel the submission of the native tribes, and enforce their obedience to the authority of the whites— that the simple and confiding Indians began to see the folly they had committed in permitting the residence amongst them of these superior beings, whom they had first looked upon as more than mortal, but who, when strong enough to do so, were not long in throwing off the mask, and proving to the simple savages that they were much "more human than divine."

Thus, in the province of New Mexico, Fray Augustin Ruiz, with his co-preachers Marcos and Venabides, were kindly received by the native inhabitants, and we have seen how one million (?) Indians came from the *"rumbo"* of the Cibolo, ready and willing to receive the baptismal sacrament. This Cibolo,[20] or Sivulo, as it is written in some old MSS., is, by the way, mysteriously alluded to by the monkish historians who have written on this region, as being a kingdom inhabited by a very superior class of Indians to any met with between Anáhuac and the Vale of Taos—in the enjoyment of a high state of civilisation, inhabiting a well-built city, the houses of which were three stories high, and having attained considerable per-

[20] Cibola was one of the fabled lands sought by Coronado in his famed expedition of 1540. See Herbert E. Bolton, *Coronado, Knight of Pueblos and Plains* (New York and Albuquerque, 1949). The Seven Cities of Cibola were usually interpreted as being the Zuñi towns on the boundary between modern New Mexico and Arizona. *Cibola* was Spanish for "buffalo."

fection in the domestic arts. This, notwithstanding the authority of Don Francisco Vásquez Coronado, who visited Cibolo, and of Solis and Venegas, who have guaranteed the assertion, must be received *cum grano salis;* but, at all events, the civilisation of the mysterious Cibolo may be compared to that of the Aztec empire, under Montezuma, at the time of the Spanish Conquest, both being egregiously exaggerated by the historians of the day. Cibolo was situated on a river called Tegue. At this day, neither name is known to the inhabitants of New Mexico. If pate-shaven Venabides had held his tongue, New Mexico might now be in the peaceful possession of the Catholic Missions, and the property of the Church of Mexico pretty considerably enhanced by the valuable *placeres*, or gold washings, which abound in that province.[21] Full, however, of the wonderful miracle of Santa Clara of Carmona, which had been brought to light through the agency of the medallion at the end of his *rosario*, Fray Venabides must needs return to Spain, and humbug poor old Fernando, and even the more sensible Isabel, with wonderful accounts of the riches of the country he had been instrumental in exploring, and of the excellent disposition of the natives to receive the word of God. Don Juan Oñate[22] was, therefore, quickly dispatched to take possession; and in his train followed twelve Castilian families of *sangre azul*, to colonise the newly-acquired territory. The names of these still remain, disgraced by the degenerate wretches who now bear them, but in whom scarce a drop of blood remains which ever filtered from the veins of the paladins of Old Castile.

Then commenced the troublous times. The missions were upheld by dint of steel alone; and, on every occasion, the Indians rose, and often massacred their white persecutors. The colonists were more than once driven bodily from New Mexico,

[21] Ruxton, in his previously cited book, tells of the principal New Mexican gold placer, which was discovered in 1828 and was located about twenty miles south of Santa Fé.

[22] The career of Oñate, the founder of New Mexico and the first white colonizer of southwestern United States, is given in G. P. Hammond, *Don Juan de Oñate and the Founding of New Mexico* (Santa Fé, 1927).

and were only reinstated by the aid of large bodies of armed men.[23]

In California, however, they managed these things better. The wily monks took care to keep all interlopers from the country, established themselves in snug quarters, instructed the Indians in agriculture, and soon gained such an ascendency over them, that no difficulty was experienced in keeping them under proper and wholesome restraint. Strong and commodious missions were built and fortified, well stored with arms and ammunition, and containing sufficient defenders to defy attack. Luxuriant gardens and thriving vineyards soon surrounded these isolated stations: the plains waved with golden corn; whilst domestic cattle, thriving on the rich pasture, and roaming far and near, multiplied and increased a hundred-fold.[24]

Nothing can be more beautiful than the appearance of one of these missions, to the traveller who has lately passed the arid and barren wilderness of the Northwest. The *adobe* walls of the convent-looking building, surmounted by cross and belfry,

[23] There was but one general and successful uprising in New Mexico's Spanish history. The Pueblos, under the medicine man, Popé, rose in 1680, murdered over 400 Spanish settlers—about one-sixth the white population—and drove the remainder down the river to El Paso. Don Diego de Vargas effected the reconquest of the province, beginning in 1692.

[24] The California missions had generally prospered, having extensive tilled acres and large flocks and herds. The mission was the most successful of Spain's frontier institutions—the others being the *presidio* (fort) and the *pueblo* (town). Supported jointly by church and state, the mission held the wild Indian tribes in check and gradually taught husbandry to the neophytes. The purpose was to convert the natives into Christian, law-abiding subjects. The government looked upon the mission as a temporary institution that would quickly achieve its objective in a given area and then move on to new frontiers. But experience proved that the desired result could not be attained in the ten-year period originally allotted, and so the missions were continued decade after decade.

After Mexico won independence from Spain, in 1821, the movement for secularization of the missions gained ground, being pressed jointly by those wishing to free the Indians, and those interested in opportunities for grabbing the wealth of the missions. The decree ordering secularization of the California missions was issued in 1833, but it was carried into effect by gradual stages. The Administrators, appointed to manage the mission property, often were inefficient or were culpable in their duties. By devious ways the mission lands came into possession of private individuals, frequently friends of California governors.

are generally hidden in a mass of luxuriant vegetation. Fig-trees, bananas, cherry, and apple, leaf-spreading platanos, and groves of olives, form umbrageous vistas, under which the sleek monks delight to wander; gardens, cultivated by their own hands, testify to the horticultural skill of the worthy padres; whilst vineyards yield their grateful produce to gladden the hearts of the holy exiles in these western solitudes. Vast herds of cattle roam half-wild on the plains, and bands of mules and horses, whose fame has even reached the distant table-lands of the Rocky Mountains, and excited the covetousness of the hunters —and thousands of which, from the day they are foaled to that of their death, never feel a saddle on their backs—cover the country. Indians (*Mansitos*) idle round the skirts of these vast herds (whose very numbers keep them together), living, at their own choice, upon the flesh of mule, or ox, or horse.

CHAPTER VII

THE MISSION OF SAN FERNANDO[1] is situated on a small river called Las Animas, a branch of the Los Martires. The convent is built at the neck of a large plain, at the point of influx of the stream from the broken spurs of the sierra. The savana is covered with luxuriant grass, kept down, however, by the countless herds of cattle which pasture on it. The banks of the creek are covered with a lofty growth of oak and poplar, which near the Mission have been considerably thinned for the purpose of affording fuel and building material for the increasing settlement. The convent stands in the midst of a grove of fruit-trees, its rude tower and cross peeping above them, and contrasting picturesquely with the wildness of the surrounding scenery. Gardens and orchards lie immediately in front of the building, and a vineyard stretches away to the upland ridge of the valley. The huts of the Indians are scattered here and there, built of stone and adobe, sometimes thatched with flags and boughs, but comfortable enough. The convent itself is a substantial building, of the style of architec-

---

[1] The Mission San Fernando, Rey de Espana, located near the town of San Fernando at the northern outskirts of Los Angeles, was founded September 8, 1797. The population, that had reached 1000 by 1820, declined thereafter, but the livestock was generally undiminished. The inventory of June, 1840, showed 4,130 cattle, 2,637 horses, 2,500 sheep, 60 mules, 33 asses, and 30 hogs. Hubert Howe Bancroft, *History of California* (7 vols., San Francisco, 1890), III, 647.

Whether or not this is really the mission Ruxton means to describe is questionable. He was never in California and much of the detail given is doubtless manufactured from his knowledge of Spain, Mexico, and New Mexico. His later references to the distance of the mission from Los Angeles, and from the Spanish Trail, suggest that he is referring to a mission farther north than San Fernando—probably nearer the vicinity of San Luis Obispo.

ture characterising monastic edifices in most parts of the world. Loopholes peer from its plastered walls, and on a flat portion of the roof a comically mounted gingall or wall-piece, carrying a two-pound ball, threatens the assailant in time of war. At one end of the oblong building, a rough irregular arch of sun-burned bricks is surmounted by a rude cross, under which hangs a small but deep-toned bell—the wonder of the Indian *peones,* and highly venerated by the frayles themselves, who received it as a present from a certain venerable archbishop of Old Spain, and who, whilst guarding it with reverential awe, tell wondrous tales of its adventures on the road to its present abiding place.

Of late years the number of the canonical inmates of the convent has been much reduced—there being but four priests now to do the duties of the eleven who formerly inhabited it: Fray Augustin, a Capuchin of due capacity of paunch, being at the head of the holy quartette. Augustin is the conventual name of the reverend father, who fails not to impress upon such casual visitants to that *ultima Thule* as he deems likely to appreciate the information, that, but for his humility, he might add the sonorous appellations of Ignacio Sabanal-Morales-y Fuentes—his family being of the best blood of Old Castile, and known there since the days of Ruy Gómez—el Campéador—possessing, moreover, half the *"vega"* of the Ebro, &c., where, had fate been propitious, he would now have been the sleek superior of a rich Capuchin convent, instead of vegetating, a leather-clad frayle, in the wilds of California Alta.

Nevertheless, his lot is no bad one. With plenty of the best and fattest meat to eat, whether of beef or venison, of bear or mountain mutton; with good wine and brandy of home make, and plenty of it; fruit of all climes in great abundance; wheaten or corn bread to suit his palate; a tractable flock of natives to guide, and assisted in the task by three brother shepherds; far from the strife of politics or party—secure from hostile attack (not quite, by-the-by), and eating, drinking, and sleeping away his time, one would think that Fray Augustin Ignacio Sabanal-

Morales-y Fuentes had little to trouble him, and had no cause to regret even the *vega* of Castilian Ebro, held by his family since the days of el Campéador.

One evening Fray Augustin sat upon an adobe bench, under the fig-tree shadowing the porch of the Mission. He was dressed in a goat-skin jerkin, softly and beautifully dressed, and descending to his hips, under which his only covering—tell it not in Gath!—was a long linen shirt, reaching to his knees, and lately procured from Puebla de los Angeles, as a sacerdotal garment. Boots, stockings, or unmentionables, he had none. A cigarito, of tobacco rolled in corn shuck, was occasionally placed between his lips; whereupon huge clouds of smoke rushed in columns from his mouth and nostrils. His face was of a golden yellow colour, relieved by arched and very black eyebrows; his shaven chin was of most respectable duplicity—his corporation of orthodox dimensions. Several Indians and half-breed Mexican women were pounding Indian corn on metates near at hand; whilst sundry beef-fed urchins of whitey-brown complexion sported before the door, exhibiting, as they passed Fray Augustin, a curious resemblance to the strongly marked features of that worthy padre. They were probably his nieces and nephews—a class of relations often possessed in numbers by priests and monks.

The three remaining brothers were absent from the Mission; Fray Bernardo, hunting elk in the sierra; Fray José, gallivanting at Puebla de los Angeles, ten days' journey distant;[2] Fray Cristoval, lassoing colts upon the plain. Augustin, thus left to his own resources, had just eaten his vespertine *frijolitos* and *chile colorado,* and was enjoying a post-cœnal smoke of fragrant *pouche* under the shadow of his own fig-tree.

Whilst thus employed, an Indian dressed in Mexican attire approached him hat in hand, and, making a reverential bow, asked his directions concerning domestic business of the Mission.

[2] If the mission were ten days distant from Los Angeles, it would not be San Fernando.

"*Hola!* friend José," cried Fray Augustin in a thick guttural voice, "*pensabo yo*—I was thinking that it was very nearly this time three years ago when those '*malditos Americanos*' came by here and ran off with so many of our cavallada."

"True, reverend father," answered the administrador, "just three years ago, all but fifteen days: I remember it well. *Malditos sean*—curse them!"

"How many did we kill, José?"

"*Quizas moochos*—a great many, I dare say. But they did not fight fairly—charged right upon us, and gave us no time to do anything. They don't know how to fight, these *Mericanos;* come right at you, before you can swing a lasso, hallooing like *Indios Bravos*."

"But, José, how many did they leave dead on the field?"

"Not one."

"And we?"

"*Valgame Dios!* thirteen dead, and many more wounded."

"That's it! Now if these savages come again (and the Chemeguaba, who came in yesterday, says he saw a large trail), we must fight *adentro*—within—outside is no go; for as you very properly say, José, these Americans don't know how to fight, and kill us before—before we can kill them. *Vaya!*"

At this moment there issued from the door of the Mission Don Antonio Velez Trueba, a Gachupin—that is, a native of Old Spain—a wizened old hidalgo refugee, who had left the mother country on account of his political opinions, which were stanchly Carlist, and had found his way—how, he himself scarcely knew—from Mexico to San Francisco in Upper California, where, having a most perfect contempt for every thing Mexican, and hearing that in the Mission of San Fernando, far away, were a couple of Spanish padres of "*sangre regular*," he had started into the wilderness to ferret them out; and having escaped all dangers on the route (which, however, were hardly dangers to the Don, who could not realise the idea of scalptaking savages), had arrived with a whole skin at the Mission. There he was received with open arms by his countryman Fray

Augustin, who made him welcome to all the place afforded, and there he harmlessly smoked away his time; his heart far away on the banks of the Genil and in the grape-bearing *vegas* of his beloved Andalusia, his withered *cuerpo* in the sierras of Upper California. Don Antonio was the walking essence of a Spaniard of the *ancien régime*. His family dated from the Flood, and with the exception of sundry refreshing jets of Moorish blood, injected into the Truebas during the Moorish epoch, no strange shoot was ever engrafted on their genealogical tree. The marriages of the family were ever confined to the family itself—never looking to fresh blood in a station immediately below it, which was not *hidalgueño;* nor above, since any thing higher in rank than the Trueba y Trueba family, *no habia,* there was not.

Thus, in the male and female scions of the house, were plainly visible the ill effects of breeding "in and in." The male Truebas were sadly degenerate Dons, in body as in mind—compared to their ancestors of Boabdil's day; and the *señoritas* of the name were all eyes, and eyes alone, and hardly of such stamp as would have tempted that amorous monarch to bestow a kingdom for a kiss, as ancient ballads tell.

> "*Dueña de la negra toca,*
> *Por un beso de tu boca,*
> *Diera un reyno, Boabdil;*
> *Y yo por ello, Cristiana,*
> *Te diera de buena gana*
> *Mil cielos, si fueran mil.*"

Come of such poor stock, and reared on tobacco smoke and "*gazpacho,*" Don Antonio would not have shone, even amongst pigmy Mexicans, for physical beauty. Five feet high, a frame-work of bones covered with a skin of Andalusian tint, the Trueba stood erect and stiff in all the consciousness of his "*sangre regular.*" His features were handsome, but entirely devoid of flesh, his upper lip was covered with a jet-black mustache mixed with gray, his chin was bearded "like the pard." Everyone around him clad in deer and goat skin, our Don walked conspicuous in shining suit of black—much the worse for wear, it must be confessed—with beaver hat sadly battered, and round his body and over his shoulder an unexceptionable "*capa*" of the amplest dimensions. Asking, as he stepped over him, the pardon of an Indian urchin who blocked the door, and bowing with punctilious politeness to the sturdy *mozas* who were grinding corn, Don Antonio approached our friend Augustin, who was discussing warlike matters with his administrador.

"*Hola!* Don Antonio, how do you find yourself, sir?"

"Perfectly well, and your very humble servant, reverend father; and your worship also, I trust you are in good health?"

"*Sin novedad*—without novelty"; which, since it was one hour and a half since our friends had separated to take their siestas, was not impossible.

"Myself and the worthy José," continued Fray Augustin, "were speaking of the vile invasion of a band of North American robbers, who three years since fiercely assaulted this peaceful Mission, killing many of its inoffensive inhabitants, wounding many more, and carrying off several of our finest colts and most promising mules to their dens and caves in the Rocky Mountains. Not with impunity, however, did they effect this atrocity. José informs me that many of the assailants were killed by my brave Indians. How many said you, José?"

"*Quizas-mo-o-ochos*," answered the Indian.

"Yes, probably a great multitude," continued the padre; "but, unwarned by such well-merited castigation, it has been reported to me by a Chemeguaba *mansito*, that a band of these audacious marauders are now on their road to repeat the offence, numbering many thousands, well mounted and armed; and to oppose these white barbarians it behoves us to make every preparation of defence."[3]

[3] From the report to the Governor of California by the Head of the Mission, in reference to the attacks by the American mountaineers. Ruxton's note.

"There is no cause for alarm," answered the Andaluz. "I (tapping his breast) have served in three wars: in that glorious one '*de la Independencia*,' when our glorious patriots drove the French like sheep across the Pyrenees; in that equally glorious one of 1821; and in the late magnanimous struggle for the legitimate rights of his majesty Charles V, king of Spain (doffing his hat), whom God preserve. With that right arm," cried the spirited Don, extending his shrivelled member, "I have supported the throne of my kings—have fought for my country, mowing down its enemies before me; and with it," vehemently exclaimed the Gachupin, working himself into a perfect frenzy, "I will slay these *Norte Americanos*, should they dare to show their faces in my front. Adios, Don Augustin Ignacio Sabanal-Morales-y Fuentes," he cried, doffing his hat with an earth-sweeping bow: "I go to grind my sword. Till then adieu."

"A countryman of mine!" said the frayle, admiringly, to the administrador. "With him by our side we need not to fear: neither *Norte Americanos*, nor the devil himself, can harm us when he is by."

Whilst the Trueba sharpens his Tizona, and the priest puffs volumes of smoke from his nose and mouth, let us introduce to the reader one of the *muchachitas*, who knelt grinding corn on the metate, to make *tortillas* for the evening meal. Juanita was a stout wench from Sonora, of Mexican blood, hardly as dark as the other women who surrounded her, and with a drop or two of the Old Spanish blood struggling with the darker Indian tint to colour her plump cheeks. An *enagua* (a short petticoat) of red serge was confined round her waist by a gay band ornamented with beads, and a chemisette covered the upper part of the body, permitting, however, a prodigal display of her charms. Whilst pounding sturdily at the corn, she laughed and joked with her fellow-labourers upon the anticipated American attack, which appeared to have but few terrors for her. "*Que vengan*," she exclaimed—"let them come; they are only men, and will not molest us women. Besides, I have seen these white men before—in my own country, and they are fine fellows, very tall, and as white as the snow on the sierras. Let them come, say I!"

"Only hear the girl!" cried another: "if these savages come, then will they kill Pedrillo, and what will Juanita say to lose her sweetheart?"

"Pedrillo!" sneered the latter; "what care I for Pedrillo? *Soy Mejicana, yo*—a Mexican girl am I, I'd have you know, and don't demean me to look at a wild Indian. Not I, indeed, by my salvation! What I say is, let the *Norte Americanos* come."

At this juncture Fray Augustin called for a glass of *aguardiente*, which Juanita was dispatched to bring, and, on presenting it, the church-man facetiously inquired why she wished for the Americans, adding, "Don't think they'll come here—no, no: here we are brave men, and have Don Antonio with us, a noble fellow, well used to arms." As the words were on his lips, the clattering of a horse's hoofs was heard rattling across the loose stones and pebbles in the bed of the river, and presently an Indian herder galloped up to the door of the Mission, his horse covered with foam, and its sides bleeding from spur-wounds.

"Oh, *padre mio!*" he cried, as soon as he caught sight of his reverence, "*vienen los Americanos*—the Americans, the Americans are upon us. *Ave Maria puríssima*—more than ten thousand are at my heels!"

Up started the priest and shouted for the Don.

That hidalgo presently appeared, armed with the sword that had graced his thigh in so many glorious encounters, the sword with which he had mowed down the enemies of his country, and by whose aid he now proposed to annihilate the American savages should they dare to appear before him.

The alarm was instantly given; *peones, vaqueros* hurried from the plains; and *milpas*, warned by the deep-toned bell, which soon rung out its sonorous alarum. A score of mounted Indians, armed with gun and lasso, dashed off to bring intelligence of the enemy. The old gingall on the roof was crammed with powder and bullets to the very muzzle, by the frayle's own hand. Arms were brought and piled in the *sala*, ready for use.

The padre exhorted, the women screamed, the men grew pale and nervous, and thronged within the walls. Don Antonio, the fiery Andaluz, alone remained outside, flourishing his whetted sabre, and roaring to the padre, who stood on the roof with lighted match, by the side of his formidable cannon, not to be affrighted. "That he, the Trueba, was there, with his Tizona, ready to defeat the devil himself should he come on."

He was deaf to the entreaties of the priest to enter.

"*Siempre en el frente*—Ever in the van," he said, was the war-cry of the Truebas.

But now a cloud of dust was seen approaching from the plain, and presently a score of horsemen dashed headlong towards the Mission. "*El enemigo*," shouted Fray Augustin; and, without waiting to aim, he clapped his match to the touch-hole of the gun, harmlessly pointed to the sky, and crying out "*in el nombre de Dios*"—in God's name—as he did so, was instantly knocked over and over by the recoil of the piece, then was as instantly seized by some of the Indian garrison, and forced through the trap-door into the building; whilst the horsemen (who were his own scouts) galloped up with the intelligence that the enemy was at hand, and in overwhelming force.

Thereupon the men were all mounted, and formed in a body before the building, to the amount of more than fifty, well armed with guns or bows and arrows. Here the gallant Don harangued them, and infusing into their hearts a little of his own courage, they eagerly demanded to be led against the enemy. Fray Augustin re-appeared on the roof, gave them his blessing, advised them to give no quarter, and, with slight misgivings, saw them ride off to the conflict.

About a mile from the Mission, the plain gradually ascended to a ridge of moderate elevation, on which was a growth of dwarf oak and ilex. To this point the eyes of the remaining inmates of the convent were earnestly directed, as at this point the enemy was first expected to make his appearance. Presently a few figures were seen to crown the ridge, clearly defined against the clear evening sky. Not more than a dozen mounted men composed this party, which all imagined must be doubtless the vanguard of the thousand invaders. On the summit of the ridge they halted a few minutes, as if to reconnoitre; and by this time the Californian horsemen were halted in the plain, midway between the Mission and the ridge, and distant from the former less than half-a-mile, so that all the operations were clearly visible to the lookers-on.

The enemy wound slowly, in Indian file, down the broken ground of the descent; but when the plain was reached, they formed into something like a line, and trotted fearlessly towards the Californians. These began to sit uneasily in their saddles; nevertheless they made a forward movement, and even broke into a gallop, but soon halted, and again huddled together. Then the mountaineers quickened their pace, and their loud shout was heard as they dashed into the middle of the faltering troop. The sharp cracks of the rifles were heard, and the duller reports of the smooth-bored pieces of the Californians; a cloud of smoke and dust arose from the plain, and immediately half-a-dozen horses, with empty saddles, broke from it, followed quickly by the Californians, flying like mad across the level. The little steady line of the mountaineers advanced, and puffs of smoke arose, as they loaded and discharged their rifles at the flying horsemen. As the Americans came on, however, one was seen to totter in his saddle, the rifle fell from his grasp, and he tumbled head-long to the ground. For an instant his companions surrounded the fallen man, but again forming, dashed towards the Mission, shouting fierce war-whoops, and brandishing aloft their long and heavy rifles. Of the defeated Californians some jumped off their horses at the door of the Mission, and sought shelter within; others galloped off towards the sierra in panic-stricken plight. Before the gate, however, still paced valiantly the proud hidalgo, encumbered with his cloak, and waving with difficulty his sword above his head. To the priest and women, who implored him to enter, he replied with cries of defiance, of "*Viva Carlos Quinto,*" and "Death or glory." He shouted in vain to the flying crowd to halt; but, seeing their panic was beyond hope, he clutched his weapon more firmly as the Americans dashed at him, closed his teeth and his eyes, thought once of the *vega* of his beloved Genil, and of Granada la Florida, and gave himself up for lost. Those inside the Mission, when they observed the flight of their cavalry, gave up the defence as hopeless; and already the charging mountaineers were almost under the walls when they observed the curious figure of the little Don making demonstrations of hostility.

"Wagh!" exclaimed the leading hunter (no other than our friend La Bonté), "here's a little crittur as means to do all the fighting"; and seizing his rifle by the barrel, he poked at the Don with the butt-end, who parried the blow, and with such a sturdy stroke, as nearly severed the stock in two. Another mountaineer rode up, and, swinging his lasso overhead, threw the noose dexterously over the Spaniard's head, and as it fell over his shoulders, drew it taut, thus securing the arms of the pugnacious Don as in a vice.

"*Quartel!*" cried the latter; "*por Dios, quartel!*"

"Quarter be d——!" exclaimed one of the whites, who understood Spanish; "who's agoin' to hurt you, you little crittur?"

By this time Fray Augustin was waving a white flag from the roof, in token of surrender; and soon after he appeared trembling at the door, beseeching the victors to be merciful and to spare the lives of the vanquished, when all and every thing in the Mission would be freely placed at their disposal.

"What does the niggur say?" asked old Walker,[4] the leader of the mountaineers, of the interpreter.

"Well, he talks so queer, this hos can't rightly make it out."

"Tell the old coon then to quit that, and make them darned greasers clear out of the lodge, and pock some corn and shucks here for the animals, for they're nigh give out."

[4] Joseph Reddeford Walker, famous mountaineer. The first of his many trips to California was made in 1833, as leader of a contingent of Bonneville's trappers. They opened the Humboldt River route that became the principal road of the forty-niners. Walker was one of the most noteworthy of the Mountain Men and his name is encountered frequently in the literature of the fur trade period.

This being conveyed to him in mountain Spanish, which fear alone made him understand, the padre gave orders to the men to leave the Mission, advising them, moreover, not to recommence hostilities, as himself was kept as hostage, and if a finger was lifted against the mountaineers, he would be killed at once, and the Mission burned to the ground. Once inside, the hunters had no fear of attack, they could have kept the building against all California; so, leaving a guard of two outside the gate, and first seeing their worn-out animals supplied with piles of corn and shucks, they made themselves at home, and soon were paying attention to the hot *tortillas*, meat, and chile colorado which were quickly placed before them, washing down the hot-spiced viands with deep draughts of wine and brandy. It would have been amusing to have seen the faces of these rough fellows as they gravely pledged each other in the grateful liquor, and looked askance at the piles of fruit served by the attendant Hebes. These came in for no little share of attention, it may be imagined; but the utmost respect was paid to them, for your mountaineer, rough and bear-like though he be, never, by word or deed, offends the modesty of a woman, although sometimes obliged to use a compulsory wooing, when time is not allowed for regular courtship, and not unfrequently known to jerk a New Mexican or Californian beauty behind his saddle, should the obdurate parents refuse consent to their immediate union. It tickled the Americans not a little to have all their wants supplied, and to be thus waited upon, by what they considered the houris of paradise; and after their long journey, and the many hardships and privations they had suffered, their present luxurious situation seemed scarcely real.

The Hidalgo, released from the durance vile of the lasso, assisted at the entertainment; his sense of what was due to the "*sangre regular*" which ran in his veins being appeased by the fact, that he sat *above* the wild uncouth mountaineers, these preferring to squat crosslegged on the floor in their own fashion, to the uncomfortable and novel luxury of a chair. Killbuck, indeed, seemed to have quite forgotten the use of such pieces of furniture. On Fray Augustin offering him one, and begging him, with many protestations, to be seated, that old mountain worthy looked at it, and then at the padre, turned it round, and at length comprehending the intention, essayed to sit. This he effected at last, and sat grimly for some moments, when, seizing the chair by the back, he hurled it out the open door, exclaiming—"Wagh! this coon aint hamshot anyhow, and don't want such fixins, he don't"; and gathering his legs under his body, reclined in the manner customary to him. There was a prodigious quantity of liquor consumed that night, the hunters making up for their many banyans; but as it was the pure juice of the grape, it had little or no effect upon their hard heads. They had not much to fear from attacks on the part of the Californians; but, to provide against all emergencies, the padre and Gachupin were "hobbled," and confined in an inner room, to which there was no ingress nor egress save through the door which opened into the apartment where the mountaineers lay sleeping, two of the number keeping watch. A fandango with the Indian girls had been proposed by some of them, but Walker placed a decided veto on this. He said "they had need of sleep now, for there was no knowing what to-morrow might bring forth; that they had a long journey before them, and winter was coming on; they would have to 'streak' it night and day, and sleep when their journey was over, which would not be until Pike's Peak was left behind them. It was now October, and the way they'd have to hump it back to the mountains would take the gristle off a painter's tail."

Young Ned Wooton was not to the fore when the roll was called. He was courting the Sonora wench Juanita, and to some purpose, for we may at once observe, that the maiden accompanied the mountaineer to his distant home, and at the present moment is sharing his lodge on Hardscrabble creek of the upper Arkansa, having been duly and legally married by Fray Augustin before their departure.[5]

[5] Later he calls him "Dick." This experience in California is not mentioned in Conard's account of Wootton, *"Uncle Dick" Wootton, the Pioneer Fron-*

But now the snow on the ridge of the Sierra Madre, and the nightly frosts; the angular flights of geese and ducks constantly passing overhead; the sober tints of the foliage, and the dead leaves that strew the ground; the withering grass on the plain, and the cold gusts, sometimes laden with snow and sleet, that sweep from the distant snow-clad mountains—all these signs warn us to linger no longer in the tempting valley of San Fernando, but at once to pack our mules to cross the dreary and desert plains and inhospitable sierras; and to seek with our booty one of the sheltered bayous of the Rocky Mountains.

On the third day after their arrival, behold our mountaineers again upon the march, driving before them—with the assistance of a half-a-dozen Indians, impressed for the first few days of the journey until the cavallada get accustomed to travel without confusion—a band of four hundred head of mules and horses, themselves mounted on the strongest and fleetest they could select from at least a thousand.

Fray Augustin and the Hidalgo, from the house-top, watched them depart: the former glad to get rid of such unscrupulous guests at any cost, the latter rather loath to part with his boon companions, with whom he had quaffed many a *quartillo* of Californian wine. Great was the grief, and violent the sobbing, when all the girls in the Mission surrounded Juanita to bid her adieu; as she, seated *en cavalier* on an easy pacing mule, bequeathed her late companions to the keeping of every saint in the calendar, and particularly to the great St. Ferdinand himself, under whose especial tutelage all those in the Mission were supposed to live. Pedrillo, poor forsaken Pedrillo, a sullen sulky half-breed, was overcome, not with grief, but with anger at the slight put upon him, and vowed revenge. He of the *"sangre*

tiersman of the Rocky Mountain Region. However, it is probably true, as Ruxton undoubtedly met Wootton at Pueblo early in 1847, and Wootton lived on the upper Arkansas in the early eighteen fifties. Wootton was born in Virginia in 1816 and first came west over the Santa Fé Trail to Bent's Fort in 1836. He lived the trapper's life in the eighteen forties, drove sheep to California in the early fifties, and in his last years operated a toll road over Raton Pass and kept a stage station and inn at the northern entrance to the road (a little south of Trinidad, Colorado).

regular," having not a particle of enmity in his heart, waved his arm—that arm with which he had mowed down the enemies of Carlos Quinto—and requested the mountaineers, if ever fate should carry them to Spain, not to fail to visit his *quinta* in the *vega* of Genil, which, with all in it, he placed at their worships' disposal—*con muchissima franqueza.*

Fat Fray Augustin likewise waved his arm, but groaned in spirit as he beheld the noble band of mules and horses, throwing back clouds of dust on the plain where they had been bred. One noble roan stallion seemed averse to leave his accustomed pasture, and again and again broke away from the band. Luckily old Walker had taken the precaution to secure the *"bell mare"* of the herd, and mounted on her rode ahead, the animals all following their well-known leader. As the roan galloped back, the padre was in ecstasy. It was a favourite steed, and one he would have gladly ransomed at any price.

"*Ya viene, ya viene!*" he cried out, "now, now it's coming! hurrah for the roan!" but, under the rifle of a mountaineer, one of the Californians dashed at it, a lasso whirling round his head, and turning and twisting like a doubling hare, as the horse tried to avoid him, at last threw the open coil over the animal's head, and led him back in triumph to the band.

"*Maldito sea aquel Indio*—curse that Indian!" quoth the padre, and turned away.

And now our sturdy band—less two who had gone under—were fairly on their way. They passed the body of their comrade who had been killed in the fight before the Mission; the wolves, or Indian dogs, had picked it to the bones; but a mound near-by, surrounded by a rude cross, showed where the Californians (seven of whom were killed) had been interred—the pile of stones at the foot of the cross testifying that many an *ave maria* had already been said by the poor Indians, to save the souls of their slaughtered companions from the pangs of purgatory.

For the first few days progress was slow and tedious. The confusion attendant upon driving so large a number of animals over a country without trail or track of any description, was sufficient to prevent speedy travelling; and the mountaineers, desirous of improving the pace, resolved to pursue a course more easterly, and to endeavour to strike the great SPANISH TRAIL, which is the route followed by the New Mexicans in their journeys to and from the towns of Puebla de los Angeles and Santa Fé.[6] This road, however, crosses a long stretch of desert country, destitute alike of grass and water, save at a few points, the regular halting-places of the caravans; and as but little pasture is to be found at these places at any time, there was great reason to doubt, if the Santa Fé traders had passed this season, that there would not be sufficient grass to support the numerous cavallada, after the herbage had been laid under contribution by the traders' animals. However, a great saving of time would be effected by taking this trail, although it wound a considerable distance out of the way to avoid the impassable chain of the Sierra Nevada—the gap in those mountains through which the Americans had come being far to the southward,[7] and at this late season probably obstructed by the snow.

Urged by threats and bribes, one of the Indians agreed to guide the cavalcade to the trail, which he declared was not more than five days' distant. As they advanced, the country became wilder and more sterile—the valleys, through which several small streams coursed, being alone capable of supporting so large a number of animals. No time was lost in hunting for game; the poorest of the mules and horses were killed for provisions, and the diet was improved by a little venison when a deer casually presented itself near the camping ground. Of Indians they had seen not one; but they now approached the country of the Diggers, who infest the district through which the Spanish trail passes, laying contributions on the caravans of traders, and who have been, not inaptly, termed the "Arabs

[6] The Old Spanish Trail. For a general account, see LeRoy R. Hafen, "The Old Spanish Trail, Santa Fé to Los Angeles," in the *Huntington Library Quarterly*, Vol. XI, No. 2 (February, 1948), 149-60.

[7] He probably means northward.

of the American desert." The Californian guide now earnestly entreated permission to return, saying, that he should lose his life if he attempted to pass the Digger country alone on his return. He pointed to a snow-covered peak, at the foot of which the trail passed; and leave being accorded, he turned his horse's head towards the Mission of San Fernando.

Although the cavallada travelled, by this time, with much less confusion than at first, still, from the want of a track to follow, great trouble and exertion were required to keep the proper direction. The bell-mare led the van, carrying Walker, who was better acquainted with the country than the others; another hunter, of considerable distinction in the band, on a large mule, rode by his side. Then followed the cavallada, jumping and frisking with each other, stopping whenever a blade of grass showed, and constantly endeavouring to break away to green patches which sometimes presented themselves in the plains. Behind the troop, urging them on by dint of loud cries and objurgations, rode six mountaineers, keeping as much as possible in a line. Two others were on each flank to repress all attempts to wander, and keep the herd in a compact body. In this order the caravan had been crossing a broken country, up and down ridges, all day, the animals giving infinite trouble to their drivers, when a loud shout from the advanced guard put them all upon the *qui-vive*. Old Walker was seen to brandish the rifle over his head and point before him, and presently the cry of "The trail! the trail!"[8] gladdened all hearts with the anticipation of a respite from the harassing labour of mule-driving. Descending a broken ridge, they at once struck into a distinct and tolerably well-worn track, into which the cavallada turned as easily and instinctively as if they had all their lives been accustomed to travel on beaten roads. Along this they travelled

[8] This is doubtless suggested by Frémont's account of his trip over a similar route in 1844. Frémont wrote: ". . . after a difficult march of eighteen miles a general shout announced that we had struck the great object of our search— THE SPANISH TRAIL." Ruxton was familiar with Frémont's report, as he cites the famous incident of Carson and Godey recovering horses along the Old Spanish Trail from a robber band of Indians.

merrily—their delight being, however, alloyed by frequent in-dications that hunger and thirst had done their work on the mules and horses of the caravans which had preceded them on the trail. They happened to strike it in the centre of a long stretch of desert, extending sixty miles without either water or pasture; and many animals had perished here, leaving their bones to bleach upon the plain. The soil was sandy, but rocks and stones covered the surface, disabling the feet of many of the young horses and mules; several of which, at this early stage of the journey, were already abandoned. Traces of the wretched Diggers became very frequent; these abject creatures resorting to the sandy plains for the purpose of feeding upon the lizards which there abound. As yet they did not show; only at night they prowled around the camp, waiting a favourable oppor-tunity to run the animals. In the present instance, however, many of the horses having been left on the road, the Diggers found so plentiful a supply of meat as to render unnecessary any attack upon the formidable mountaineers.

One evening the Americans had encamped, earlier than usual, on a creek well-timbered with willow and quaking-ash, and affording tolerable pasture; and although it was still rather early, they determined to stop here, and give the animals an oppor-tunity to fill themselves. Several deer had jumped out of the bottom as they entered it; and La Bonté and Killbuck had sallied from the camp with their rifles, to hunt and endeavour to pro-cure some venison for supper. Along the river banks, herds of deer were feeding in every direction, within shot of the belt of timber; and the two hunters had no difficulty in approaching and knocking over two fine bucks within a few paces of the thicket. They were engaged in butchering the animals, when La Bonté, looking up from his work, saw half-a-dozen Indians dodging among the trees, within a few yards of himself and Killbuck. At the same instant two arrows *thudded* into the car-cass of the deer over which he knelt, passing but a few inches from his head. Hollowing to his companion, La Bonté immedi-ately seized the deer, and, lifting it with main strength, held it as a shield before him, but not before an arrow had struck him in the shoulder. Rising from the ground he retreated, behind cover, yelling loudly to alarm the camp, which was not five hundred yards' distant on the other side of the stream. Kill-buck, when apprised of the danger, ran bodily into the plain, and, keeping out of shot of the timber, joined La Bonté, who now, out of arrow-shot, threw down his shield of venison and fired his rifle at the assailants. The Indians appeared at first afraid to leave the cover; but three or four more joining them, one a chief, they advanced into the plain, with drawn bows, scattering wide apart, and running swiftly towards the whites, in a zigzag course, in order not to present a steady mark to their unerring rifles. The latter were too cautious to discharge their pieces, but kept a steady front, with rifle at shoulder. The In-dians evidently disliked to approach nearer; but the chief, an old grizzled man, incited them by word and gesture—running in advance and calling upon the others to follow him.

"Ho, boy!" exclaimed Killbuck to his companion, "that old coon must go under, or we'll get rubbed out by these darned critturs."

La Bonté understood him. Squatting on the ground, he plant-ed his wiping-stick firmly at the extent of his left arm, and resting the long barrel of his rifle on his left hand, which was supported by the stick, he took a steady aim and fired. The Indian, throwing out his arms, staggered and let fall his bow—tried hard to recover himself, and then fell forward on his face. The others, seeing the death of their chief, turned and made again for the cover. "You darned critturs," roared Killbuck, "take that!" and fired his rifle at the last one, tumbling him over as dead as a stone. The camp had also been alarmed. Five of them waded across the creek and took the Indians in rear; their rifles cracked within the timber, several more Indians fell, and the rest quickly beat a retreat. The venison, however, was not forgotten; the two deer were packed into camp, and did the duty of mule-meat that night.

This lesson had a seasonable effect upon the Diggers, who

made no attempt on the cavallada that night or the next; for the camp remained two days to recruit the animals.

We will not follow the party through all the difficulties and perils of the desert route, nor detail the various devilries of the Diggers, who constantly sought opportunities to stampede the animals, or, approaching them in the night as they grazed, fired their arrows indiscriminately at the herd, trusting that dead or disabled ones would be left behind, and afford them a good supply of meat. In the month of December, the mountaineers crossed the great dividing ridge of the Rocky Mountains, making their way through the snowy barrier with the utmost difficulty, and losing many mules and horses in the attempt. On passing the ridge, they at once struck the head-springs of the Arkansa river, and turned into the Bayou Salade.[9] Here they found a village of Arapahos, and were in no little fear of leaving their cavallada with these dexterous horse-thieves. Fortunately the chief in command was friendly to the whites, and restrained his young men; and a present of three horses insured his good offices. Still, the near neighbourhood of these Indians being hardly desirable, after a few days' halt, the Americans were again on their way, and halted finally at the juncture of the Fontaine-qui-bout with the Arkansa, where they determined to construct a winter camp. They now considered themselves at home, and at once set about building a log-shanty capable of containing them all, and a large corral for securing the animals at night, or in case of Indian alarms. This they effected by felling several large cottonwoods, and throwing them in the form of a horse-shoe: the entrance, however, being narrower than in that figure, and secured by upright logs, between which poles were fixed to be withdrawn at pleasure. The house, or "fort"—as any thing in the shape of a house is called in these parts, where, indeed, every man must make his house a castle—was loop-holed on all sides, and boasted a turf chimney of rather primitive construction; but which answered the

[9] If they took such a trail, and in December, it was a very unusual procedure.

purpose of drawing the smoke from the interior.[10] Game was plentiful all around; bands of buffalo were constantly passing the Arkansa; and there were always deer and antelope within sight of the fort. The pasture, too, was good and abundant—being the rich grama or buffalo grass, which, although rather dry at this season, still retains its fattening qualities; and the animals soon began to improve wonderfully in condition and strength.

Of the four hundred head of mules and horses with which they had started from California, but one-half reached the Arkansa. Many had been killed for food (indeed they had furnished the only provisions during the journey), many had been stolen by the Indians, or shot by them at night; and many had strayed off and not been recovered. We have omitted to mention that the Sonora girl, Juanita, and her spouse, Ned Wooton, remained behind at Roubideau's fort and rendezvous on the Uintah, which our band had passed on the other side of the mountains, whence they proceeded with a party to Taos in New Mexico, and resided there for some years, blessed with a fine family, &c. &c. &c., as the novels end.[11]

As soon as the animals were fat and strong, they were taken down the Arkansa to Bent's Indian trading fort, about sixty miles below the mouth of Fontaine-qui-bout. Here a ready sale was found for them,[12] mules being at that time in great demand on the frontier of the United States, and every season the Bents carried across the plains to Independence a considerable number collected in the Indian country, and in the upper settlements of New Mexico. As the mountaineers descended the Arkansa, a little incident occurred, and some of the party very unexpectedly encountered an old friend. Killbuck and La

[10] Fort Pueblo, on the Arkansas, at the mouth of Fountain Creek, was in existence in 1842.

[11] This varies a bit from his previous story that Wootton and Juanita were living in 1847 on the Hardscrabble branch of the Arkansas.

[12] In the summer of 1846 Joe Walker had California horses and mules at Pueblo and brought down some to Bent's Fort, where he sold them to the soldiers and others who had come with Colonel Price's troops. See Abert's report of 1846, "Notes of a Military Reconnoissance," 420, 432.

Bonté, who were generally compañeros, were riding some distance ahead of the cavallada, passing at the time the mouth of the Huerfano or Orphan Creek, when, at a long distance before them, they saw the figure of a horseman, followed by two loose animals, descending the bluff into the timbered bottom of the river. Judging the stranger to be Indian, they spurred their horses and galloped in pursuit, but the figure ahead suddenly disappeared. However, they quickly followed the track, which was plain enough in the sandy bottom, that of a horse and two mules. Killbuck scrutinised the "sign," and puzzled over it a considerable time; and at last exclaimed—"Wagh! this sign's as plain as mon beaver to me; look at that hos-track, boy; did ye ever see that afore?"

"*Well*, I have!" answered La Bonté, peering down at it: "that ar shuffle-toe seems handy to me now, I *tell* you."

"The man as used to ride that hos is long gone under, but the hos, darn the old crittur, is old Bill Williams's, I'll swar by hook."

"Well, it ain't nothin else," continued La Bonté, satisfying himself by a long look; "it's the old boy's hos as shure as shootin: and them Rapahos has rubbed him out at last, and raised his animals. Ho, boy! let's lift their hair."

"Agreed," answered Killbuck; and away they started in pursuit, determined to avenge the death of their old comrade.

They followed the track through the bottom and into the stream, which it crossed, and, passing a few yards up the bank, entered the water again, when they could see nothing more of it. Puzzled at this, they sought on each side the river, but in vain; and, not wishing to lose more time in the search, they proceeded through the timber on the banks to find a good camping-place for the night, which had been their object in riding in advance of the cavallada. On the left bank, a short distance before them, was a heavy growth of timber, and the river ran in one place close to a high bluff, between which and the water was an almost impervious thicket of plum and cherry trees. The grove of timber ended before it reached this point, and

but few scattered trees grew in the little glade which inter-
vened, and which was covered with tolerable grass. This being
fixed upon as an excellent camp, the two mountaineers rode
into the glade, and dismounted close to the plum and cherry
thicket, which formed almost a wall before them, and an excellent shelter from the wind. Jumping off their horses, they were
in the act of removing the saddles from their backs, when a
shrill neigh burst from the thicket not two yards behind them;
a rustling in the bushes followed, and presently a man dressed
in buck-skin, and rifle in hand, burst out of the tangled brush,
exclaiming in an angry voice—

"Do 'ee hy'ar now? I was nigh upon gut-shootin some of e'e—
I was now; thought e'e was darned Rapahos, I did, and câched
right off."

"Ho, Bill! what, old hos! not gone under yet?" cried both
the hunters. "Give us your paw."

"Do'ee now, if hy'ar ar'nt them boys as was rubbed out on
Lodge Pole (creek) a time ago. Do'ee hy're? if this aint 'some'
now, I wouldn't say so."

Leaving old Bill Williams and our two friends to exchange
their rough but hearty greetings, we will glance at that old
worthy's history since the time when we left him câching in
the fire and smoke on the Indian battle-ground in the Rocky
Mountains. He had escaped fire and smoke, or he would not
have been here on Arkansa with his old grizzled Nez-percé
steed. On that occasion, the veteran mountaineer had lost his
two pack-animals and all his beaver. He was not the man, however, to want a horse or mule as long as an Indian village was
near at hand. Skulking, therefore, by day in cañons and deep
gorges of the mountains, and travelling by night, he followed
closely on the trail of the victorious savages, bided his time,
struck his "coup," and recovered a pair of pack-horses, which
was all he required. Ever since, he had been trapping alone in
all parts of the mountains; had visited the rendezvous but twice
for short periods, and then with full packs of beaver; and was
now on his way to Bent's Fort, to dispose of his present loads

of peltry, enjoy one good carouse on Taos whisky, and then return to some hole or corner in the mountains which he knew of, to follow in the spring his solitary avocation. He too had had his share of troubles, and had many Indian scrapes but passed safely through all, and scarcely cared to talk of what he had done, so matter-of-fact to him were the most extraordinary of his perilous adventures.

Arrived at Bent's Fort, the party disposed of their cavallada, and then—respect for the pardonable weaknesses of our mountain friends prompts us to draw a veil over the furious orgies that ensued. A number of hunters and trappers were "in" from their hunting-grounds, and a village of Shians and some lodges of Kioways were camped round the fort. As long as the liquor lasted, and there was good store of alcohol as well as of Taos whisky, the Arkansa resounded with furious mirth—not unmixed with graver scenes; for your mountaineer, ever quarrelsome in his cups, is quick to give and take offence, when rifles alone can settle the difference, and much blood is spilt upon the prairie in his wild and frequent quarrels.

Bent's Fort is situated on the left or northern bank of the river Arkansa, about one hundred miles from the foot of the Rocky Mountains—on a low and level bluff of the prairie which here slopes gradually to the water's-edge. The walls are built entirely of adobes—or sun-burned bricks—in the form of a hollow square, at two corners of which are circular flanking towers of the same material. The entrance is by a large gateway into the square, round which are the rooms occupied by the traders and employés of the host. These are small in size, with walls coloured by a white-wash made of clay found in the prairie. Their flat roofs are defended along the exterior by parapets of adobe, to serve as a cover to marksmen firing from the top; and along the coping grow plants of cactus of all the varieties common in the plains. In the centre of the square is the press for packing the furs; and there are three large rooms, one used as a store and magazine, another as a council-room, where the Indians assemble for their "talks," whilst the third is the common dining-hall, where the traders, trappers, and hunters, and all employés, feast upon the best provender the game-covered country affords. Over the culinary department presided of late years a fair lady of colour, Charlotte by name, who was, as she loved to say, "de onlee lady in de dam Injun country," and who moreover was celebrated from Long's Peak to the Cumbres Espanolás[13] for slap-jacks and pumpkin pies.

Here congregate at certain seasons the merchants of the plains and mountains, with their stocks of peltry. Chiefs of the Shian, the Kioway, and Arapaho, sit in solemn conclave with the head traders, and smoke the "calumet" over their real and imaginary grievances. Now O-cun-no-whurst, the Yellow Wolf, grand chief of the Shian,[14] complains of certain grave offences against the dignity of his nation! A trader from the "big lodge" (the fort) has been in his village, and before the trade was opened, in laying the customary chief's gift "on the prairie"[15] has not "opened his hand," but "squeezed out his present between his fingers" grudgingly and with too sparing measure. This was hard to bear, but the Yellow Wolf would say no more!

Tah-kai-buhl or, "he who jumps," is deputed from the Kioway to warn the white traders not to proceed to the Canadian to trade with the Comanche. That nation is mad—a "heap mad" with the whites, and has "dug up the hatchet" to "rub out" all who enter its country. The Kioway loves the paleface, and gives him warning (and "he who jumps" looks as if he deserves something "on the prairie" for his information).

Shawh-noh-qua-mish, "the peeled lodge-pole," is there to excuse his Arapaho braves, who lately made free with a band of horses belonging to the fort. He promises the like shall never happen again, and he, Shawh-noh-qua-mish, speaks with a "single tongue." Over clouds of tobacco and kinnik-kinnik, these grave affairs are settled and terms arranged.

[13] The Spanish Peaks, or the Huajatolla (Breasts of the World), just west of the city of Walsenburg, Colorado.

[14] J. W. Abert, who visited with Yellow Wolf at Bent's Fort in 1845 and 1846, made a portrait of him.

[15] Indian expression for free gift. Ruxton's note.

In the corral, groups of leather-clad mountaineers, with "decks" of "euker" and "seven up," gamble away their hard-earned peltries. The employés—mostly St. Louis Frenchmen and Canadian voyageurs—are pressing packs of buffalo skins, beating robes, or engaged in other duties of a trading fort. Indian squaws, the wives of mountaineers, strut about in all the pride of beads and fanfaron, jingling with bells and bugles, and happy as paint can make them. Hunters drop in with animals packed with deer or buffalo meat to supply the fort; Indian dogs look anxiously in at the gateway, fearing to enter and encounter the enmity of their natural enemies, the whites: and outside the fort, at any hour of the day or night, one may safely wager to see a dozen coyotes or prairie wolves loping round, or seated on their haunches, and looking gravely on, waiting patiently for some chance offal to be cast outside. Against the walls, groups of Indians, too proud to enter without an invitation, lean, wrapped in their buffalo robes, sulky and evidently ill at ease to be so near the whites without a chance of fingering their scalp-locks; their white lodges shining in the sun, at a little distance from the river-banks; their horses feeding in the plain beyond.

The appearance of the fort is very striking, standing as it does hundreds of miles from any settlement, on the vast and lifeless prairie, surrounded by hordes of hostile Indians, and far out of reach of intercourse with civilised man; its mud-built walls inclosing a little garrison of a dozen hardy men, sufficient to hold in check the numerous tribes of savages ever thirsting for their blood. Yet the solitary stranger passing this lone fort, feels proudly secure when he comes within sight of the "stars and stripes" which float above the walls.[16]

[16] This excellent description of Bent's Fort is from Ruxton's own observations on his visit there in the spring of 1847.

CHAPTER VIII

GAIN WE MUST TAKE A JUMP with La Bonté over a space of several months; when we find him, in company of half a dozen trappers, amongst them his inseparable compañero Killbuck, camped on the Greenhorn creek, *en route* to the settlements of New Mexico. They have a few mules packed with beaver for the Taos market; but this expedition has been planned more for pleasure than profit—a journey to Taos valley being the only civilised relaxation coveted by the mountaineers. Not a few of the present band are bound thither with matrimonial intentions; the belles of Nuevo Mejico being to them the *ne plus ultra* of female perfection, uniting most conspicuous personal charms (although coated with cosmetic *alegría*—an herb, with the juice of which the women of Mexico hideously bedaub their faces) with all the hard-working industry of Indian squaws. The ladies, on their part, do not hesitate to leave the paternal abodes, and eternal tortilla-making, to share the perils and privations of the American mountaineers in the distant wilderness. Utterly despising their own countrymen, whom they are used to contrast with the dashing white hunters who swagger in all the pride of fringe and leather through their towns—they, as is but natural, gladly accept husbands from the latter class; preferring the stranger, who possesses the heart and strong right arm to defend them, to the miserable cowardly *"pelados,"* who hold what little they have on sufferance of savage Indians, but one degree superior to themselves.

Certainly no band of hunters that ever appeared in the vale of Taos, numbered in its ranks a properer lot of lads than those now camped on Greenhorn, intent on matrimonial foray into the settlements of New Mexico. There was young Dick Wooton, who was "some" for his inches, being six feet six, and as straight and strong as the barrel of his long rifle. Shoulder to shoulder with this "boy," stood Rube Herring, and not a hair's-breadth difference in height or size between them. Killbuck, though mountain winters had sprinkled a few snow-flakes on his head, *looked up* to neither; and La Bonté held his own with any mountaineer who ever set a trap in sight of Long's Peak or the Snowy Range. Marcelline—who, though a Mexican, de-spised his people and abjured his blood, having been all his life in the mountains with the white hunters—looked down easily upon six feet and odd inches. In form a Hercules, he had the symmetry of an Apollo; with strikingly handsome features, and masses of long black hair hanging from his slouching beaver over the shoulders of his buckskin hunting shirt. He, as he was wont to say, was "no dam Spaniard, but 'mountainee man,' wagh!" Chabonard[1] a half-breed, was not lost in the crowd;—and, the last in height, but the first in every quality which con-stitutes excellence in a mountaineer, whether of indomitable courage, or perfect indifference to death or danger; with an iron frame capable of withstanding hunger, thirst, heat, cold, fatigue and hardships of every kind; of wonderful presence of mind, and endless resource in time of great peril; with the instinct of an animal, and the moral courage of a *man*—who was "taller" for his inches than KIT CARSON, paragon of mountaineers?[2] Small in stature, and slenderly limbed, but with muscles of wire, with a fair complexion and quiet intelligent features, to look at Kit none would suppose that the mild-looking being before him was an incarnate devil in Indian fight, and had raised more hair from head of Redskins than any two men in the western

[1] Doubtless Baptiste Charbonneau, son of Bird Woman.

[2] Since the time of which we speak, Kit Carson has distinguished himself in guiding the several U. S. exploring expeditions, under Frémont, across the Rocky Mountains, and to all parts of Oregon and California; and for his services, the President of the United States presented the gallant mountaineer with the commission of lieutenant in a newly raised regiment of mounted riflemen, of which his old leader Frémont is appointed colonel. Ruxton's note.

country; and yet, thirty winters had scarcely planted a line or furrow on his clean-shaven face. No name, however, was better known in the mountains—from Yellow Stone to Spanish Peaks, from Missouri to Columbia River—than that of Kit Carson, "raised" in Boonlick, county of Missouri State, and a credit to the diggings that gave him birth.[3]

On Huerfano or Orphan Creek, so called from an isolated *butte* which stands on a prairie near the stream, our party fell in with a village of Yutah Indians, at that time hostile to the whites. Both parties were preparing for battle, when Killbuck, who spoke the language, went forward with signs of peace, and after a talk with several chiefs, entered into an armistice, each party agreeing not to molest the other. After trading for a few deer-skins which the Yutahs are celebrated for dressing delicately fine, the trappers moved hastily on out of such dangerous company, and camped under the mountain on Oak Creek, where they forted in a strong position, and constructed a corral in which to secure their animals at night. At this point is a tolerable pass through the mountains, where a break occurs in the range, whence they gradually decrease in magnitude until they meet the sierras of Mexico, which connect the two mighty chains of the Andes and the Rocky Mountains. From the summit of the dividing ridge, to the eastward, a view is had of the vast sea of prairie which stretches away from the base of the mountains, in dreary barrenness, for nearly a thousand miles, until it meets the fertile valley of the great Missouri. Over this boundless expanse, nothing breaks the uninterrupted solitude of the view. Not a tree or atom of foliage relieves the eye; for the lines of scattered timber which belt the streams running from the mountains, are lost in the shadow of their stupendous height, and beyond this nothing is seen but the bare surface of the rolling prairie. In no other part of the chain are the grand characteristics of the Far West more strikingly displayed than

[3] In May of 1847, Ruxton descended the Arkansas with a part of the company that had recently come from California with Carson. Kit had hurried ahead with his dispatches for Washington. See E. L. Sabin, *Kit Carson Days, 1809–1868* (New York, 1935), 550–79.

from this pass.[4] The mountains here rise, on the eastern side, abruptly from the plain, and the view over the great prairies is not therefore obstructed by intervening ridges. To the westward the eye sweeps over the broken spurs which stretch from the main range in every direction; whilst distant peaks, for the most part snow-covered, are seen at intervals rising isolated above the range. On all sides the scene is wild and dismal.

Crossing by this pass, the trappers followed the Yutah trail over a plain, skirting a pine-covered ridge, in which countless herds of antelope, tame as sheep, were pasturing. Numerous creeks intersect it, well timbered with oak, pine, and cedar, and well stocked with game of all kinds. On the eleventh day from leaving the Huerfano, they struck the Taos valley settlement on Arroyo Hondo,[5] and pushed on at once to the village of Fernandez—sometimes, but improperly, called Taos.[6] As the dashing band clattered through the village, the dark eyes of the *reboso*-wrapped *muchachas* peered from the doors of the adobe houses, each mouth armed with cigarito, which was at intervals removed to allow utterance to the salutation to each hunter as he trotted past of *Adios, Americanos*—"Welcome to Fernandez!" and then they hurried off to prepare for the fandango, which invariably followed the advent of the mountaineers. The men, however, seemed scarcely so well pleased; but leaned sulkingly against the walls, their serapes turned over the left shoulder, and concealing the lower part of the face, the hand appearing from its upper folds only to remove the eternal cigarro from their lips. They, from under their broad-brimmed sombreros, scowled with little affection upon the stalwart hunters, who clattered past them, scarcely deigning to glance

[4] Sangre de Cristo (Blood of Christ) Pass, over the Sangre de Cristo Range. Ruxton's geographical description here is accurate, as he traversed the region in the winter of 1846–47.

[5] Deep Wash, or Creek, location of Turley's Mill and scene of the attack during the Taos Uprising of January, 1847, described by Ruxton in his first book. See *Ruxton of the Rockies*, 221–24. The trappers have skirted broad, level San Luis Valley, taking in reverse the route Ruxton had traveled from New Mexico to the upper Arkansas River.

[6] Present Taos, New Mexico.

at the sullen *Peládos,* but paying incomprehensible compliments to the buxom wenches who smiled at them from the doors. Thus exchanging salutations, they rode up to the house of an old mountaineer, who had long been settled here with a New Mexican wife, and who was the recognised entertainer of the hunters when they visited Taos valley, receiving in exchange such peltry as they brought with them.

No sooner was it known that *Los Americanos* had arrived, than nearly all the householders of Fernandez presented them-selves to offer the use of their *"salas"* for the fandango which invariably celebrated their arrival. This was always a profitable event; for as the mountaineers were generally pretty well "flush" of cash when on their "spree," and as open-handed as an Indian could wish, the sale of whisky, with which they re-galed all comers, produced a handsome return to the fortunate individual whose room was selected for the fandango. On this occasion the *sala* of the Alcalde Don Cornelio Vegil[7] was se-lected and put in order; a general invitation was distributed; and all the dusky beauties of Fernandez were soon engaged in arraying themselves for the fête. Off came the coats of dirt and *"alegría"* which had bedaubed their faces since the last *"fun-cion,"* leaving their cheeks clear and clean. Water was pro-fusely used, and their *cuerpos* were doubtless astonished by the unusual lavation. Their long black hair was washed and combed, plastered behind their ears, and plaited into a long queue, which hung down their backs. *Enaguas* of gaudy colour (red most affected) were donned, fastened round the waist with ornamented belts, and above this a snow-white *camisita* of fine linen was the only covering, allowing a prodigal dis-play of their charms. Gold and silver ornaments, of antiquated pattern, decorate their ears and necks; and massive crosses of the precious metals, wrought from the gold or silver of their

[7] Cornelio Vigil, partner with Ceran St. Vrain in ownership of one of the large land grants in Colorado and Kit Carson's cousin by marriage, was a friend of the Americans. When General Kearny set up a government after taking over control of New Mexico in 1846, Vigil was prefect of Taos. He was killed, along with Americans, in the uprising of January 19, 1847.

own *placeres*, hang pendant on their breasts. The *enagua* or petticoat, reaching about halfway between the knee and ancle, displays their well-turned limbs, destitute of stockings, and their tiny feet, thrust into quaint little shoes (*zapatitos*) of Cinderellan dimensions. Thus equipped, with the *reboso* drawn over their heads and faces, out of the folds of which their brilliant eyes flash like lightning, and each pretty mouth armed with its cigarito, they coquettishly enter the fandango.[8] Here, at one end of a long room, are seated the musicians, their instruments being generally a species of guitar, called *heaca, bandolin*, and an Indian drum, called *tombé*—one of each. Round the room groups of New Mexicans lounge, wrapped in the eternal serape, and smoking of course, scowling with jealous eyes at the more favoured mountaineers. These, divested of their hunting-coats of buckskins, appear in their bran-new shirts of gaudy calico, and close fitting buckskin pantaloons, with long fringes down the outside seam from the hip to the ancle; with mocassins, ornamented with bright beads and porcupine quills. Each, round his waist, wears his mountain-belt and scalp-knife, ominous of the company he is in, and some have pistols sticking in their belt.

The dances—save the mark!—are without form or figure, at least those in which the white hunters sport the "fantastic toe." Seizing his partner round the waist with the gripe of a grisly bear, each mountaineer whirls and twirls, jumps and stamps; introduces Indian steps used in the "scalp" or "buffalo" dances, whooping occasionally with unearthly cry, and then subsiding into the jerking step, raising each foot alternately from the ground, so much in vogue in Indian ballets. The hunters have the floor all to themselves. The Mexicans have no chance in such physical force dancing; and if a dancing *Peládo*[9] steps into the ring, a lead-like thump from a galloping mountaineer quick-

[8] The word *fandango*, in New Mexico, is not applied to the peculiar dance known in Spain by that name, but designates a ball or dancing meeting. Ruxton's note.

[9] Nickname for the idle fellows hanging about a Mexican town, translated into "Greasers" by the Americans. Ruxton's note.

ly sends him sprawling, with the considerate remark—"Quit, you darned Spaniard! you can't 'shine' in this crowd."

During a lull, *guagés*[10] filled with whisky go the rounds— offered to and seldom refused by the ladies—sturdily quaffed by the mountaineers, and freely swallowed by the *Peládos*, who drown their jealousy and envious hate of their entertainers in potent *aguardiente*. Now, as the *guagés* are oft refilled and as often drained, and as night advances, so do the spirits of the mountaineers become more boisterous, while their attentions to their partners become warmer—the jealousy of the natives waxes hotter thereat—and they begin to show symptoms of re- senting the endearments which the mountaineers bestow upon their wives and sweethearts. And now, when the room is filled to crowding—with two hundred people, swearing, drinking, dancing, and shouting—the half-dozen Americans monopolising the fair, to the evident disadvantage of at least threescore scowl- ing *Peládos*, it happens that one of these, maddened by whisky and the green-eyed monster, suddenly seizes a fair one from the waist-encircling arm of a mountaineer, and pulls her from her partner. Wagh!—La Bonté—it is he—stands erect as a pillar for a moment, then raises his hand to his mouth, and gives a ringing war-whoop—jumps upon the rash *Peládo*, seizes him by the body as if he were a child, lifts him over his head, and dashes him with the force of a giant against the wall.

The war, long threatened, has commenced; twenty Mexicans draw their knives and rush upon La Bonté, who stands his ground, and sweeps them down with his ponderous fist, one after another, as they throng around him. "Howgh-owgh- owgh-owgh-h!" the well-known war-whoop, bursts from the throats of his companions, and on they rush to the rescue. The women scream, and block the door in their eagerness to escape; and thus the Mexicans are compelled to stand their ground and fight. Knives glitter in the light, and quick thrusts are given and parried. In the centre of the room the whites stand shoulder to shoulder—covering the floor with Mexicans by their stalwart

10 Cask-shaped gourds. Ruxton's note.

blows; but the odds are fearful against them, and other assailants crowd up to supply the place of those who fall.

Alarm being given by the shrieking women, reinforcements of *Peládos* rushed to the scene of action, but could not enter the room, which was already full. The odds began to tell against the mountaineers, when Kit Carson's quick eye caught sight of a high stool or stone, supported by three long heavy legs. In a moment he had cleared his way to this, and in another the three legs were broken off and in the hands of himself, Dick Wooton, and La Bonté. Sweeping them round their heads, down came the heavy weapons amongst the Mexicans with wonderful effect—each blow, dealt by the nervous arms of Wooton and La Bonté, mowing down a good half-dozen of the assailants. At this the mountaineers gave a hearty whoop, and charged the wavering enemy with such resistless vigor, that they gave way and bolted through the door, leaving the floor strewed with wounded, many most dangerously; for, as may be imagined, a thrust from the keen scalp-knife by the nervous arm of a mountaineer was no baby blow, and seldom failed to strike home— up to the "Green River"[11] on the blade.

The field being won,[12] the whites, too, beat a quick retreat to the house where they were domiciled, and where they had left their rifles. Without their trusty weapons they felt, indeed, unarmed; and not knowing how the affair just over would be followed up, lost no time in making preparations for defence. However, after great blustering on the part of the *prefecto*, who, accompanied by a *posse comitatus* of "Greasers," pro-

[11] The knives used by the hunters and trappers are manufactured at the "Green River" works, and have that name stamped upon the blade. Hence the mountain term for doing any thing effectually is "up to Green River." Ruxton's note. For an excellent article on Green River knives, see Arthur Woodward, "Up to Green River," in *The Westerners Brand Book, Los Angeles Corral, 1948* (Los Angeles, 1949), 141–46.

[12] Some readers of the serial publication of this story having expressed doubt as to the plausibility of certain incidents, including this fight at the fandango, Ruxton wrote (as quoted below in Appendix A) to his editors: "The Mexican fandango *is true to the letter....* I myself, with three trappers, cleared a fandango at Taos, armed only with bowie-knives—some score Mexicans, at least, being in the room."

ceeded to the house, and demanded the surrender of all concerned in the affair—which proposition was received with a
yell of derision—the business was compounded by the mountaineers promising to give sundry dollars to the friends of two
of the Mexicans, who died during the night of their wounds,
and to pay for a certain amount of masses to be sung for the
repose of their souls in purgatory. Thus the affair blew over;
but for several days the mountaineers never showed themselves
in the streets of Fernandez without their rifles on their shoulders, and refrained from attending fandangos for the present,
and until the excitement had cooled down.

A bitter feeling, however, existed on the part of the men;
and one or two offers of a matrimonial nature were rejected by
the papas of certain ladies who had been wooed by some of the
white hunters, and their hands formally demanded from the
respective padres.

La Bonté had been rather smitten with the charms of one
Dolores Salazar—a buxom lass, more than three parts Indian in
her blood, but confessedly the "beauty" of the Vale of Taos.
She, by dint of eye, and of nameless acts of elaborate coquetry,
with which the sex so universally bait their traps, whether in
the salons of Belgravia, or the *rancherias* of New Mexico, contrived to make considerable havoc in the heart of our mountaineer; and when once Dolores saw she had made an impression, she followed up her advantage with all the arts the most
civilised of her sex could use when fishing for a husband.

La Bonté, however, was too old a hunter to be easily caught;
and, before comitting himself, he sought the advice of his tried
companion Killbuck. Taking him to a retired spot without the
village, he drew out his pipe and charged it—seated himself
cross-legged on the ground, and, with Indian gravity, composed himself for a "talk."

"Ho, Killbuck!" he began, touching the ground with the
bowl of his pipe, and then turning the stem upwards for *"medicine"*—"Hyar's a child feels squamptious like, and nigh upon
'gone beaver,' *he* is—wagh!"

"Wagh!" exclaimed Killbuck, all attention.

"Old hos," continued the other; "thar's no use câching any-how what a niggur feels—so hyar's to 'put out.' You're good for beaver *I* know; at deer or buffler, or darned red Injun either, you're 'some.' Now that's a fact. 'Off-hand,' or 'with a rest,' you make 'em 'come.' You knows the 'sign' of Injuns slick— Blackfoot or Sioux, Pawnee or Burntwood, Zeton, Rapaho, Shian, or Shoshonée, Yutah, Piyutah, or Yamhareek—their trail's as plain as writin', old hos, to you."

"Wagh!" grunted Killbuck, blushing bronze at all these compliments.

"Your sight ain't bad. Elks is elk; black-tail deer ain't white-tails; and b'ar is b'ar to you, and nothin' else, a long mile off and more."

"Wa-agh!"

"Thar ain't a track as leaves its mark upon the plains or mountains but you can read off-hand; that I've see'd myself. But tell me, old hos, can you make understand the 'sign' as shows itself in a woman's breast?"

Killbuck removed the pipe from his mouth, raised his head, and puffed a rolling cloud of smoke into the air—knocked the ashes from the bowl, likewise made his "medicine"—and answered thus:

"From Red River, away up north amongst the Britishers, to Heely (Gila) in the Spanish country—from old Missoura to the sea of Californy, I've trapped and hunted. I knows the Injuns and thar 'sign,' and they knows *me*, I'm thinkin. Thirty winters has snowed on me in these hyar mountains, and a niggur or a Spaniard[13] would larn 'some' in that time. This old tool" (tapping his rifle) "shoots 'center,' *she* does; and if thar's game afoot, this child knows 'bull' from 'cow,' and ought to could. That deer is deer, and goats is goats, is plain as paint to any but a greenhorn. Beaver's a cunning crittur, but I've trapped a 'heap'; and at killing meat when meat's a-running, I'll 'shine'

[13] Always alluding to Mexicans, who are invariably called Spaniards by the Western Americans. Ruxton's note.

in the biggest kind of crowd. For twenty year I packed a squaw along. Not one, but a many. First I had a Blackfoot—the darndest slut as ever cried for fofarraw. I lodge-poled her on Colter's Creek, and made her quit. My buffler hos, and as good as four packs of beaver, I gave for old Bull-tail's daughter. He was head chief of the Ricaree, and 'came' nicely 'round' me. Thar was'nt enough scarlet cloth, nor beads, nor vermilion in Sublette's packs for her. Traps wouldn't buy her all the fofarraw she wanted; and in two years I'd sold her to Cross-Eagle for one of Jake Hawkin's guns—this very one I hold in my hands. Then I tried the Sioux, the Shian, and a Digger from the other side, who made the best mocassins as ever *I* wore. She was the best of all, and was rubbed out by the Yutahs in the Bayou Salade. Bad was the best; and after she was gone under I tried no more.

"Afore I left the settlements I know'd a white gal, and she was some punkins. I have never seed nothing as 'ould beat her. Red blood won't 'shine' any ways you fix it; and though I'm hell for 'sign,' a woman's breast is the hardest kind of rock to me, and leaves no trail that I can see of. I've hearn you talk of a gal in Memphis county; Mary Brand you called her oncest. The gal I said *I* know'd, her name I disremember, but she stands afore me as plain as Chimley Rock on Platte, and thirty year and more har'nt changed a feature in her face, to me.

"If you ask this child, he'll tell you to leave the Spanish slut to her Greasers, and hold on till you take the trail to old Missoura, whar white and Christian gals are to be had for axing. Wagh!"

La Bonté rose to his feet. The mention of Mary Brand's name decided him; and he said—

"Darn the Spaniard! she cant shine with me; come, old hos! let's move."

And, shouldering their rifles, the two compañeros returned to the Ranch. More than one of the mountaineers had fulfilled the object of their journey, and had taken to themselves a partner from amongst the belles of Taos, and now they were preparing for their return to the mountains. Dick Wooton was the only unfortunate one. He had wooed a damsel whose parents peremptorily forbade their daughter to wed the hunter, and he therefore made ready for his departure with considerable regret.

The day came, however. The band of mountaineers were already mounted, and those with wives in charge were some hours on the road, leaving the remainder quaffing many a stirrup-cup before they left. Dick Wooton was as melancholy as a buffalo bull in spring; and as he rode down the village, and approached the house of his lady-love, who stood wrapped in *reboso*, and cigarito in mouth, on the sill of the door, he turned away his head as if dreading to say adios. La Bonté rode beside him, and a thought struck him.

"Ho, Dick!" he said, "thar's the gal, and thar's the mountains: shoot sharp's the word."

Dick instantly understood him, and was "himself again." He rode up to the girl as if to bid her adieu, and she came to meet him. Whispering one word, she put her foot upon his, was instantly seized round the waist, and placed upon the horn of his saddle. He struck spurs into his horse, and in a minute was out of sight, his three companions covering his retreat, and menacing with their rifles the crowd which was soon drawn to the spot by the cries of the girl's parents, who had been astonished spectators of the daring rape.

The trapper and his bride, however, escaped scatheless, and the whole party effected a safe passage of the mountains, and reached the Arkansa, where the band was broken up—some proceeding to Bent's Fort, and others to the Platte, amongst whom were Killbuck and La Bonté, still in company.

These two once more betook themselves to trapping, the Yellow Stone being their chief hunting-ground. But we must again leap over months and years, rather than conduct the reader through all their perilous wanderings, and at last bring him back to the camp on Bijou, where we first introduced him to our mountaineers; and as we have already followed them on the Arapaho trail, which they pursued to recover their stolen animals from a band of that nation, we will once again seat ourselves at the camp on Boiling Spring, where they had met a strange hunter[14] on a solitary expedition to the Bayou Salade, and whose double-barreled rifle had excited their wonder and curiosity.

From him they learned also that a large band of Mormons were wintering on the Arkansa, *en route* to the Great Salt Lake and Upper California; and as our hunters had before fallen in with the advanced guard of these fanatic emigrants, and felt no little wonder that such helpless people should undertake so long a journey through the wilderness, the stranger narrated to them the history of the sect, which we will also shortly transcribe for the benefit of the reader.

[14] Ruxton himself.

CHAPTER IX

THE MORMONS WERE ORIGINALLY of the sect known as "Latter-day Saints,"[1] which sect flourishes wherever Anglo-Saxon gulls are found in sufficient numbers to swallow the egregious nonsense of fanatic humbugs who fatten upon their credulity. In the United States they especially abounded; but, the creed becoming "slow," one Joe Smith,[2] a *smart* man, arose from its ranks, and instilled a little life into the decaying sect.

Joe, better known as the "Prophet Joe," was taking his siesta one fine day, upon a hill in one of the New England States, when an angel suddenly appeared to him, and made known the locality of a new Bible or Testament, which contained the history of the lost tribes of Israel; that these tribes were no other than the Indian nations which possessed the continent of America at the time of its discovery, and the remains of which still existed in their savage state; that, through the agency of Joe, these were to be reclaimed, collected into the bosom of a church to be there established, according to principles which would be found in the wonderful book—and which church was gradually to receive into its bosom all other churches, sects, and persuasions, with "unanimity of belief and perfect brotherhood."

After a certain probation, Joe was led in body and spirit to the mountain by the angel who first appeared to him, was pointed out the position of the wonderful book, which was covered by a flat stone, on which would be found two round pebbles, called Urim and Thummim, and through the agency

[1] The full name of the sect is Church of Jesus Christ of Latter-day Saints; commonly called Mormons. The headquarters of the church is now in Salt Lake City, Utah, which was colonized by the Mormons in July of 1847.

[2] Joseph Smith was the founder of the sect, organized on April 6, 1830.

of which the mystic characters inscribed on the pages of the book were to be deciphered and translated. Joe found the spot indicated without any difficulty, cleared away the earth, and discovered a hollow place formed by four flat stones; on removing the topmost one of which sundry plates of brass presented themselves, covered with quaint and antique carving; on the top lay Urim and Thummim (commonly known to the Mormons as Mummum and Thummum, the pebbles of wonderful virtue), through which the miracle of reading the plates of brass was to be performed.

Joe Smith, on whom the mantle of Moses had so suddenly fallen, carefully removed the plates and hid them, burying himself in woods and mountains whilst engaged in the work of translation. However, he made no secret of the important task imposed upon him, nor of the great work to which he had been called. Numbers at once believed him, but not a few were deaf to belief, and openly derided him. Being persecuted (as the sect declares, at the instigation of the authorities), and many attempts being made to steal his precious treasure, Joe, one fine night, packed his plates in a sack of beans, bundled them into a Jersey waggon, and made tracks for the West. Here he completed the great work of translation, and not long after gave to the world the "Book of Mormon," a work as bulky as the Bible, and called "of Mormon," for so was the prophet named by whose hand the history of the lost tribes had been handed down in the plates of brass thus miraculously preserved for thousands of years, and brought to light through the agency of Joseph Smith.

The fame of the Book of Mormon spread over all America, and even to Great Britain and Ireland. Hundreds of proselytes flocked to Joe, to hear from his lips the doctrine of Mormonism; and in a very brief period the Mormons became a numerous and recognised sect, and Joe was at once, and by universal acclamation, installed as the head of the Mormon church, and was ever known by the name of the "Prophet Joseph."

However, from certain peculiarities in their social system,

the Mormons became rather unpopular in the settled States, and at length moved bodily into Missouri, where they purchased several tracts of land in the neighbourhood of Independence. Here they erected a large building, which they called the Lord's Store, where goods were collected on the common account, and retailed to members of the church at moderate prices. All this time their numbers increased in a wonderful manner, and immigrants from all parts of the States, as well as Europe, continually joined them. As they became stronger, they grew bolder and more arrogant in their projects. They had hitherto been considered as bad neighbours, on account of their pilfering propensities, and their utter disregard of the conventional decencies of society—exhibiting the greatest immorality, and endeavouring to establish amongst their society a universal concubinage. This was sufficient to produce an ill feeling against them on the part of their neighbours, the honest Missourians; but they still tolerated their presence amongst them, until the Saints openly proclaimed their intention of seizing upon the country, and expelling by force the present occupants—giving, as their reason, that it had been revealed to their prophets that the "Land of Zion" was to be possessed by themselves alone.

The sturdy Missourians began to think this was a little too strong, and that, if they permitted such aggressions any longer, they would be in a fair way of being despoiled of their lands by the Mormon interlopers. At length matters came to a crisis, and the Saints, emboldened by the impunity with which they had hitherto carried out their plans, issued a proclamation to the effect that all in that part of the country, who did not belong to the Mormon persuasion, must "clear out," and give up possession of their lands and houses.[3] The Missourians collected in a body, burned the printing-press from which the proclamation had emanated, seized several of the Mormon leaders, and, after inflicting a summary chastisement, "tarred and feathered" them, and let them go.

To revenge this insult, the Mormons marshalled an army of

[3] Ruxton's account is distorted by a strong anti-Mormon bias.

Saints, and marched upon Independence, threatening vengeance against the town and people. Here they met, however, a band of sturdy backwoods-men, armed with rifles, determined to defend the town against the fanatic mob, who, not relishing their appearance, refused the encounter, and surrendered their leaders at the first demand. The prisoners were afterwards released, on condition that the Mormons left that part of the country without delay.

Accordingly, they once more "took up their beds and walked," crossing the Missouri to Clay County, where they established themselves, and would finally have formed a thriving settlement but for their own acts of wilful dishonesty. At this time their blasphemous mummery knew no bounds. Joe Smith, and other prophets who had lately arisen, were declared to be chosen of God; and it was the general creed that, on the day of judgment, the former would take his stand on the right hand of the judgment-seat, and that none would pass into the kingdom of heaven without his seal and touch. One of their tenets was the faith in "spiritual matrimony." No woman, it appeared, would be admitted into heaven unless "passed" by a saint. To qualify them for this, it was necessary that the woman should first be received by the guaranteeing Mormon as an "earthly wife," in order that he did not pass in any of whom he had no knowledge. The consequences of this state of things may be imagined. The most debasing immorality was a precept of the order, and an almost universal concubinage existed amongst the sect, which at this time numbered at least forty thousand. Their disregard to the laws of decency and morality was such as could not be tolerated in any class of civilised society.

Again did the honest Missourians set their faces against this pernicious example, and when the county to which the Mormons had removed became more thickly settled, they rose to a man against the modern Gomorrah. The Mormons, by this time, having on their part gained considerable accession to their strength, thought to set the laws at defiance, organised and armed large bodies of men, in order to maintain the ascendency over the legitimate settlers, and bid fair to constitute an *"imperium in imperio"* in the State, and become the sole possessors of the public lands. This, of course, could not be tolerated. Governor Boggs at once ordered out a large force of State militia to put down this formidable demonstration, marched against the Mormons, and suppressed the insurrectionary movement without bloodshed.

From Clay County, they moved still farther into the wilds, and settled at last in Caldwell County, where they built the town of "Far West," and here they remained for the space of three years.

During this time they were continually receiving converts to the faith, and many of the more ignorant country people were disposed to join them, being only deterred by the fear of incurring ridicule from the stronger-minded. The body of the Mormons seeing this, called upon their prophet, Joe Smith, to perform a miracle in public before all comers, which was to prove to those of their own people who still doubted the doctrine, the truth of what it advanced—(the power of performing miracles was steadfastly declared to be in their hands by the prophets)—and to enlist those who wavered in the Mormon cause.

The prophet instantly agreed, and declared that, upon a certain day, he would walk across the broad waters of the Missouri without wetting the the soles of his feet. On the appointed day, the river banks were thronged by an expectant crowd. The Mormons sang hymns of praise in honour of their prophet, and were proud of the forthcoming miracle, which was to set finally at rest all doubt as to his power and sanctity.

This power of performing miracles, and effecting miraculous cures of the sick, was so generally believed by the Mormons, that physic was never used amongst them. The prophets visited the beds of the sick, and laid hands upon them, and if, as of course was most invariably the case, the patient died, it was attributed to his or her want of faith; but if, on the contrary, the patient recovered, there was universal glorification on the miraculous cure.

Joe Smith was a tall, fine-looking man, of most plausible address, and possessed the gift of the gab in great perfection. At the time appointed for the performance of the walking-water miracle, he duly attended on the river banks, and descended barefoot to the edge of the water.

"My brethren!" he exclaimed in a loud voice, "this day is a happy one to me, to us all, who venerate the great and only faith. The truth of our great and blessed doctrine will now be proved before the thousands I see around me. You have asked me to prove by a miracle that the power of the prophets of old has been given to me. I say unto you, not only to me, but to all who have faith. I have faith, and can perform miracles—that faith empowers me to walk across the broad surface of that mighty river without wetting the soles of my unworthy feet; but if ye are to *see* this miracle performed, it is necessary that ye have faith also, not only in yourselves, but in me. Have ye this faith in yourselves?"

"We have, we have!" roared the crowd.

"Have ye the faith in me, that ye believe I can perform this miracle?"

"We have, we have!" roared the crowd.

"Then," said Joe Smith, coolly walking away, "with such faith do ye know well that I *could*, but it boots not that I *should*, do it; therefore, my brethren, doubt no more"—and Joe put on his boots and disappeared.

Being again compelled to emigrate, the Mormons proceeded into the state of Illinois, where, in a beautiful situation, they founded the new Jerusalem, which, it had been declared by the prophet Mormon, should rise out of the wilderness of the west, and where the chosen people should be collected under one church, and governed by the elders after a "spiritual fashion."

The city of Nauvoo soon became a large and imposing settlement. An enormous building, called the Temple of Zion, was erected, half church, half hotel, in which Joe Smith and the other prophets resided—and large storehouses were connected with it, in which the goods and chattels belonging to the community were kept for the common good.

However, here, as every where else, they were continually quarreling with their neighbours; and as their numbers increased, so did their audacity. A regular Mormon militia was again organised and armed, under the command of experienced officers, who had joined the sect; and now the authority of the state government was openly defied. In consequence, the executive took measures to put down the nuisance, and a regular war commenced, and was carried on for some time, with no little bloodshed on both sides; and this armed movement is known in the United States as the Mormon war. The Mormons, however, who, it seemed, were much better skilled in the use of the tongue than the rifle, succumbed: the city of Nauvoo was taken, Joe Smith and other ringleading prophets captured; and the former, in an attempt to escape from his place of confinement was seized and shot. The Mormons declare he had long foretold his own fate, and that when the rifles of the firing party who were his executioners were levelled at the prophet's breast, a flash of lightning struck the weapons from their hands, and blinded for a time the eyes of the sacrilegious soldiers.

With the death of Joe Smith the prestige of the Mormon cause declined; but still thousands of proselytes joined them annually, and at last the state took measures to remove them altogether, as a body, from the country.

Once again they fled, as they themselves term it, before the persecutions of the ungodly! But this time their migration was far beyond the reach of their enemies, and their intention was to place between them the impassable barrier of the Rocky Mountains, and to seek a home and resting-place in the remote regions of the Far West.

This, the most extraordinary migration of modern times, commenced in the year 1845: but it was not till the following year that the great body of the Mormons turned their backs

upon the settlements of the United States, and launched boldly
out into the vast and barren prairies, without any fixed destination as a goal to their endless journey. For many months, long
strings of Pittsburg and Conestoga waggons, with herds of
horses and domestic cattle, wound their way towards the Indian frontier, with the intention of rendezvousing at Council
Bluffs on the Upper Missouri. Here thousands of waggons were
congregated, with their tens of thousands of men, women, and
children, anxiously waiting the route from the elders of the
church, who on their parts scarcely knew whither to direct the
steps of the vast crowd they had set in motion. At length the
indefinite destination of Oregon and California was proclaimed,
and the long train of emigrants took up the line of march. It
was believed the Indian tribes would immediately fraternise
with the Mormons, on their approaching their country; but
the Pawnees quickly undeceived them by running off with
their stock on every opportunity. Besides these losses, at every
camp, horses, sheep, and oxen strayed away and were not recovered, and numbers died from fatigue and want of provender; so that, before they had been many weeks on their journey,
nearly all their cattle, which they had brought to stock their
new country, were dead or missing, and those that were left
were in most miserable condition.

They had started so late in the season, that the greater part
were compelled to winter on the Platte,[4] on Grand Island,
and in the vicinity, where they endured the greatest privations
and sufferings from cold and hunger. Many who had lost their
stock lived upon roots and pig-nuts; and scurvy, in a most
malignant form, and other disorders, carried off numbers of
the wretched fanatics.

Amongst them were many substantial farmers from all parts
of the United States, who had given up their valuable farms,
sold off all their property, and were dragging their irresponsible and unfortunate families into the wilderness—carried away

[4] Most of the Mormons wintered on the west bank of the Missouri, at
Winter Quarters, now Florence, a few miles north of Omaha, Nebraska.

by their blind and fanatic zeal in this absurd and incredible faith. There were also many poor wretches from different parts of England, mostly of the farm-labouring class, with wives and families, crawling along with helpless and almost idiotic despair, but urged forward by the fanatic leaders of the movement, who promised them a land flowing with milk and honey to reward them for all their hardships and privations.

Their numbers were soon reduced by want and disease. When too late, they often wished themselves back in the old country, and sighed many a time for the beer and bacon of former days, now preferable to the dry buffalo meat (but seldom obtainable) of the Far West.

Evil fortune pursued the Mormons, and dogged their steps. The year following, some struggled on towards the promised land, and of these a few reached Oregon and California. Many were killed by hostile Indians; many perished of hunger, cold, and thirst, in passing the great wilderness; and many returned to the States, penniless and crestfallen, and heartily cursing the moment in which they had listened to the counsels of the Mormon prophet. The numbers who reached their destination of Oregon, California, and the Great Salt Lake, are computed at 20,000, of whom the United States had an unregretted riddance.[5]

One party had followed the troops of the American government intended for the conquest of New Mexico and the Californias. Of these a battalion was formed, and part of it proceeded to Upper California; but the way being impracticable for waggons, some seventy families proceeded up the Arkansa, and wintered near the mountains,[6] intending to cross to the

[5] Brigham Young, principal leader of the sect after the death of Smith, led his coreligionists to the valley beside the Great Salt Lake.

[6] The sick members of the Mormon Battalion and the families that accompanied them wintered near the mouth of Fountain Creek and the site of Pueblo, Colorado. They went there because a band of Mormon converts from Monroe County, Mississippi, had already taken up temporary quarters there in the summer of 1846. For an account of this temporary colony, see LeRoy R. Hafen and F. M. Young, "The Mormon Settlement at Pueblo during the Mexican War," in the *Colorado Magazine*, Vol. IX, No. 4 (July, 1932), 121–36.

Platte the ensuing spring, and join the main body of emigrants on their way by the south pass of the Rocky Mountains.

In the wide and well-timbered bottom of the Arkansa, the Mormons had erected a street of log shanties, in which to pass the inclement winter. These were built of rough logs of cottonwood, laid one above the other, the interstices filled with mud, and rendered impervious to wind or wet. At one end of the row of shanties was built the "church" or temple—a long building of huge logs, in which the prayer-meetings and holdings-forth took place. The band wintering on the Arkansa were a far better class than the generality of Mormons, and comprised many wealthy and respectable farmers from the western states, most of whom were accustomed to the life of woodmen, and were good hunters. Thus they were enabled to support their families upon the produce of their rifles, frequently sallying out to the nearest point of the mountains with a waggon, which they would bring back loaded with buffalo, deer, and elk meat, thereby saving the necessity of killing any of their stock of cattle, of which but few remained.

The mountain hunters found this camp a profitable market for their meat and deer-skins, with which the Mormons were now compelled to clothe themselves, and resorted there for that purpose—to say nothing of the attraction of the many really beautiful Missourian girls who sported their tall graceful figures at the frequent fandangos. Dancing and preaching go hand in hand in Mormon doctrine, and the "temple" was generally cleared for a hop two or three times during the week, a couple of fiddles doing the duty of orchestra. A party of mountaineers came in one day, bringing some buffalo meat and dressed deer-skins, and were invited to be present at one of these festivals.

Arrived at the temple, they were rather taken aback by finding themselves in for a sermon, which one of the elders delivered preparatory to the "physical exercises." The preacher was one Brown—called, by reason of his commanding a company of Mormon volunteers, "Cap'en Brown"[7]—a hard-featured, black-coated man of five-and-forty, correctly got up in black continuations and white handkerchief round his neck, a costume seldom seen at the foot of the Rocky Mountains. The Cap'en, rising, cleared his voice, and thus commenced, first turning to an elder (with whom there was a little rivalry in the way of preaching), "Brother Dowdle!" (brother Dowdle blushed and nodded—he was a long tallow-faced man, with black hair combed over his face), "I feel like holding forth a little this afternoon, before we glorify the Lord,—a—a—in the—a—holy dance. As there are a many strange gentlemen now—a—present, it's about right to tell 'em—a—what our doctrine just is, and so I tells 'em right off what the Mormons is. They are the chosen of the Lord; they are the children of glory, persecuted by the hand of man: they flies here to the wilderness, and, amongst the *Injine* and the buffler, they lifts up their heads, and cries with a loud voice, Susannah, and hurray for the promised land! Do you believe it? I *know* it.

"They wants to know whar we're going. Whar the church goes—thar we goes. Yes, to hell, and pull the devil off his throne —that's what we'll do. Do you believe it? I *know* it.

"Thar's milk and honey in that land as we're goin' to, and the lost tribes of Israel is thar, and will jine us. They say as we'll starve on the road, bekase thar's no game and no water; but thar's manna up in heaven, and it'll rain on us, and thar's prophets among us as can make the water 'come.' Can't they, brother Dowdle?"

"*Well*, they can."

"And now, what have the Gen*tiles* and the Philis*tines* to say against us Mormons? They says we're thieves, and steal hogs; yes, d—— 'em! they say we has as many wives as we like. So we have. I've twenty—forty, myself, and mean to have as many more as I can get. But it's to pass unfortunate females into heaven that I has 'em—yes, to prevent 'em going to roaring flames and damnation that I does it.

"Brother Dowdle," he continued, in a hoarse, low voice, "I've

[7] James Brown, Captain of Company C.

'give out,' and think we'd better begin the exercises grettful to the Lord."

Brother Dowdle rose, and, after saying that "he didn't feel like saying much, begged to remind all hands, that dancing was solemn music like, to be sung with proper devotion, and not with laughing and talking, of which he hoped to hear little or none; that joy was to be in their hearts, and not on their lips; that they danced for the glory of the Lord, and not their own amusement, as did the Gen*tiles*." After saying thus, he called upon brother Ezra to "strike up": sundry couples stood forth, and the ball commenced.

Ezra of the violin was a tall, shambling Missourian, with a pair of "homespun" pantaloons thrust into the legs of his heavy boots. Nodding his head in time with the music, he occasionally gave instructions to such of the dancers as were at fault, singing them to the tune he was playing, in a dismal nasal tone—

> "Down the centre—hands across,"
> "You, Jake Herring—thump it,"
> "Now, you all go right a-head—
> Every one of you hump it.
> Every one of you—*hump it*."

The last words being the signal that all should clap the steam on, which they did *con amore*, and with comical seriousness.

A mountaineer, Rube Herring, whom we have more than once met in the course of this narrative, became a convert to the Mormon creed, and held forth its wonderful doctrines to such of the incredulous trappers as he could induce to listen to him. Old Rube stood nearly six feet six in height, and was spare and bony in make. He had picked up a most extraordinary cloth coat amongst the Mormons, which had belonged to some one his equal in stature. This coat, which was of a snuff-brown colour, had its waist about a hand's span from the nape of Rube's neck, or about a yard above its proper position, and the skirts reached to his ancles. A slouching felt-hat covered his head, from which long black hair escaped, hanging in flakes

over his lantern-jaws. His pantaloons of buckskin were shrunk
with wet, and reached midway between his knees and ancles,
and his huge feet were encased in mocassins of buffalo-cow skin.

Rube was never without the book of Mormon in his hand,
and his sonorous voice might be heard, at all hours of the day
and night, reading passages from its wonderful pages. He stood
the badgering of the hunters with most perfect good humor,
and said there never was such a book as that ever before printed;
that the Mormons were the "biggest kind" of prophets, and
theirs the best faith ever man believed in.

Rube had let out one day that he was to be hired as guide by
this party of Mormons to the Great Salt Lake; but their destination being changed, and his services not required, a wonderful
change came over his mind. He was, as usual, book of Mormon
in hand, when brother Brown announced the change in their
plans; at which the book was cast into the Arkansa, and Rube
exclaimed—"Cuss your darned Mummum and Thummum!
thar's not one among you knows 'fat cow' from 'poor bull,'
and you may go h—— for me." And turning away, old Rube
spat out a quid of tobacco and his Mormonism together.[8]

Amongst the Mormons was an old man, named Brand, from
Memphis county, state of Tennessee, with a family of a daughter and two sons, the latter with their wives and children.[9] Brand

[8] Rube Herring was in the Mormon colony at San Bernardino, California,
in the eighteen fifties. There he opposed the church and was a bitter enemy
of the Mormons. He was later a justice of the peace in San Bernardino. See
data on Herring in George W. Beattie and Helen P. Beattie, *Heritage of the
Valley, San Bernardino's First Century* (Pasadena, 1939).

[9] Ruxton first used the name "Chase," but upon his expressing regret that
he had used what he said was the real name, *Blackwood's Magazine* changed
it to "Brand."

There were three Chases in the Mormon Battalion—Abner, John D., and
Hiram B. Abner Chase, of Company D, died of chills and fever while with
a sick detachment going from Santa Fé to the Mormon Pueblo on the Arkan-
sas.—"Journal History," Mormon Church archives, Salt Lake City. John D.
Chase, son of Abner Chase and Amy Scott, was a corporal in Company B.
At Pueblo he married Almira, a daughter of Captain Higgins. See Daniel
Tyler, *A Concise History of the Mormon Battalion in the Mexican War*
(Salt Lake City, 1881), 120, 125; and Andrew Jenson, *Latter-day Saints Biographical Encyclopedia* (Salt Lake City, 1901), 738. Hiram B. Chase was a
member of Company A.—Tyler, *A Concise History*, 119.

was a wiry old fellow, nearly seventy years of age, but still
stout and strong, and wielded axe or rifle better than many a
younger man. If truth be told, he was not a very red-hot Mormon, and had joined them as much for the sake of company to
California, whither he had long resolved to emigrate, as from
any implicit credence in the faith. His sons were strapping
fellows, of the sterling stuff that the Western pioneers are made
of; his daughter Mary, a fine woman of thirty, for whose state
of single blessedness there must doubtless have been sufficient
reason; for she was not only remarkably handsome, but was
well known in Memphis to be the best-tempered and most in-
dustrious young woman in those diggings. She was known to
have received several advantageous offers, all of which she had
refused; and report said, that it was from having been disappointed in very early life in an *affaire du cœur*, at an age when
such wounds sometimes strike strong and deep, leaving a scar
difficult to heal. Neither his daughter, nor any of his family,
had been converted to the Mormon doctrine, but had ever kept
themselves aloof, and refused to join or associate with them;
and, for this reason, the family had been very unpopular with
the Mormon families on the Arkansa; and hence, probably, one
great reason why they now started alone on their journey.

Spring had arrived, and it was time the Mormons should start
on their long journey; but whether already tired of the sample
they had had of life in the wilderness, or fearful of encountering
the perils of the Indian country, not one amongst them, with
the exception of old Brand, seemed inclined to pursue the journey farther. That old backwoodsman, however, was not to be
deterred, but declared his intention of setting out alone, with
his family, and risking all the dangers to be anticipated.[10]

Abner and John D. Chase came from Vermont and there are no Chase
women folk listed among the Mormons at Pueblo. These facts indicate that
the family Ruxton refers to as being joined by La Bonté was not named Chase.

[10] The one family that fits most of Ruxton's descriptions and is the one
that set out from Pueblo ahead of the main party of Mormons was the Crow
family. It left the Mormon Pueblo in April; the rest of the Mormon families
and the soldiers did not leave until May 24. The Crow party reached Fort

One fine sunny evening in April of 1847, when the cotton-woods on the banks of the Arkansa began to put forth their buds, and robins and blue-birds—harbingers of spring—were hopping, with gaudy plumage, through the thickets, three white tilted Conestoga waggons emerged from the timbered bottom of the river, and rumbled slowly over the prairie, in the direction of the Platte's waters. Each waggon was drawn by eight oxen, and contained a portion of the farming imple-ments and household utensils of the Brand family. The teams were driven by the young boys, the men following in rear with shouldered rifles—Old Brand himself, mounted on an Indian horse, leading the advance. The women were safely housed under the shelter of the waggon tilts, and out of the first the

Laramie in about three weeks, and was encamped there two weeks before Brigham Young and his Pioneer Band arrived on June 1.—*William Clayton's Journal* (Salt Lake City, 1921), 215; Howard Egan, *Pioneering the West, 1846 to 1878* (Richmond, Utah, 1917), 64–65; and the "Pioneer Journal of Heber C. Kimball," in the *Utah Genealogical and Historical Magazine*, Vol. XXXI, No. 1 (January, 1940), 20.

According to records in the Genealogical Library of the Mormon Church in Salt Lake City, Robert Crow was born in Green County, Tennessee, about 1794. After a short sojourn in Utah, he continued on to California, where he died, at Sacramento. His wife, Elizabeth Brown Crow, was born in South Carolina, April 1, 1795, and was baptized into the Mormon Church in 1838. Their twenty-year-old son, Walter H. Crow, was baptized at Pueblo on October 12, 1846. It is uncertain whether other members of the Crow family were members of the Mormon faith in 1847.

Mr. and Mrs. Robert Crow and their nine children (ages 11 to 27), two grandchildren, son-in-law (George W. Therlkel), and three other men made up the party of seventeen. President Heber C. Kimball in his "Journal" gives the names: Robert Crow, Elizabeth Crow, Benjamin B. Crow, Harriet Crow, Elizabeth Jane Crow, William Parker Crow, Isa Vinda Exene Crow, Ira Minda Almarene Crow, John McHenry Crow, Walter H. Crow, George W. Therlkill, Matilda Jane Therlkill, Milton Howard Therlkill, James William Therlkill, Archibald Little, James Chesney, and Lewis B. Myers. Kimball reports this party as having 5 wagons, 1 cart, 11 horses, 24 oxen, 22 cows, 3 bulls, and 7 calves.

Although the Crow party traveled west from Fort Laramie to the Salt Lake Valley with Brigham Young's Pioneer Band, they held themselves as a separate unit. In fact Clayton complains (in his *Journal*, 223) that Crow's hunter (Myers) kills a deer, "but they are unwilling to conform to the rules of the camp in dividing and reserve it all to themselves."

The Crows' eldest daughter, Harriet (probably the Mary Brand of Rux-ton's love story) was born in 1822 and so was age 25 in 1847.—Mormon Church genealogical records, Salt Lake City.

mild face of Mary Brand smiled adieu to many of her old companions who had accompanied them thus far, and now wished them "God-speed" on their long journey. Some mountaineers, too, galloped up, dressed in buckskin, and gave them rough greeting—warning the men to keep their "eyes skinned," and look out for the Arapahos, who were out on the waters of the Platte. Presently all retired, and then the huge waggons and the little company were rolling on their solitary way through the deserted prairies—passing the first of the many thousand miles which lay between them and the "setting sun," as the Indians style the distant regions of the Far West. And on, without casting a look behind him, doggedly and boldly marched old Brand, followed by his sturdy family.

They made but a few miles that evening, for the first day the *start* is all that is effected; and nearly the whole morning is taken up in getting fairly underweigh. The loose stock had been sent off earlier, for they had been collected and corralled the previous night; and, after a twelve hours' fast, it was necessary they should reach the end of the day's journey betimes. They found the herd grazing in the bottom of the Arkansa, at a point previously fixed upon for their first camp. Here the oxen were unyoked, and the waggons drawn up to form the three sides of a small square. The women then descended from their seats, and prepared the evening meal. A huge fire was kindled before the waggons, and round this the whole party collected; whilst large kettles of coffee boiled on it, and hoe-cakes baked upon the embers.

The women were sadly down-hearted, as well they might be, with the dreary prospect before them; and poor Mary, when she saw the Mormon encampment shut out from her sight by the rolling bluffs, and nothing before her but the bleak, barren prairie, could not divest herself of the idea that she had looked for the last time on civilised fellow-creatures, and fairly burst into tears.

In the morning the heavy waggons rolled on again, across the upland prairies, to strike the trail used by the traders in passing from the south fork of the Platte to the Arkansa. They had for guide a Canadian voyageur, who had been in the service of the Indian traders, and knew the route well, and who had agreed to pilot them to Fort Lancaster,[11] on the north fork of the Platte. Their course led for about thirty miles up the Boiling Spring River, whence they pursued a northeasterly course to the dividing ridge which separates the waters of the Platte and Arkansa.[12] Their progress was slow, for the ground was saturated with wet, and exceedingly heavy for the cattle, and they scarcely advanced more than ten miles a-day.

At the camp-fire at night, Antoine, the Canadian guide, amused them with tales of the wild life and perilous adventures of the hunters and trappers who make the mountains their home; often extorting a scream from the women by the description of some scene of Indian fight and slaughter, or beguiling them of a commiserating tear by the narrative of the sufferings and privations endured by those hardy hunters in their arduous life.

Mary listened with the greater interest, since she remembered that such was the life which had been led by one very dear to her—by one, long supposed to be dead, of whom she had never but once, since his departure, nearly fifteen years before, heard a syllable. Her imagination pictured him as the bravest and most daring of these adventurous hunters, and conjured up his figure charging through the midst of whooping savages, or stretched on the ground perishing from wounds, or cold, or famine.

Amongst the characters who figured in Antoine's stories, a hunter named La Bonté was made conspicuous for deeds of hardiness and daring. The first mention of the name caused the blood to rush to Mary's face: not that she for a moment imagined it was her La Bonté, for she knew the name was a common one; but, associated with feelings which she had never got the

11 More commonly called Fort Lupton. It was the trading post of Lancaster P. Lupton, and was located about a mile north of the present town of Fort Lupton, Colorado.

12 The route was up the Jimmy's Camp branch of Fountain Creek.

better of, it recalled a sad epoch in her former life, to which she could not look back without mingled pain and pleasure.

Once only, and about two years after his departure, had she ever received tidings of her former lover. A mountaineer had returned from the Far West to settle in his native State, and had found his way to the neighbourhood of old Brand's farm. Meeting him by accident, Mary, hearing him speak of the mountain hunters, had inquired, tremblingly, after La Bonté. Her informant knew him well—had trapped in company with him —and had heard at the trading fort, whence he had taken his departure for the settlements, that La Bonté had been killed on the Yellow Stone by Blackfeet; which report was confirmed by some Indians of that nation. This was all she had ever learned of the lover of her youth.

Now, upon hearing the name of La Bonté so often mentioned by Antoine, a vague hope was raised in her breast that he was still alive, and she took an opportunity of questioning the Canadian closely on the subject.

"Who was this La Bonté, Antoine, whom you say was so brave a mountaineer?" she asked one day.

"J'ne sais pas, he vas un beau garçon, and strong comme le diable—enfant de garce, mais he pas not care a dam for les sauvages, pe gar. He shoot de centare avec his carabine; and ride de cheval comme one Comanche. He trap heap castor (what you call beevare), and get plenty dollare—mais he open hand vare wide—and got none too. Den, he hont vid de Blackfoot and avec de Cheyenne, and all round de montaignes he hont dam sight."

"But, Antoine, what became of him at last? and why did he not come home, when he made so many dollars?" asked poor Mary.

"Enfant de garce, mais pourquoi he com home? Pe gar, de montaigne-man, he love de montaigne and de prairie more better dan he love de grandes villes—même de Saint Louis ou de Montreal. Wagh! La Bonté, well he one montaigne-man, wagh! He love de buffaloe, an de chevreaux plus que de bœuf and de mouton, may be. Mais on-dit dat he have autre raison—dat de gal he lofe in Missouri not lofe him, and for dis he not go back. Mais now he go ondare, m' on dit. He vas go to de Californe, may be to steal de hos and de mule—pe gar, and de Espagnols rub him out, and take his hair, so he mort."

"But are you sure of this?" she asked, trembling with grief.

"Ah, now, j'ne suis pas sûr, mais I tink you know dis La Bonté. Enfant de garce, maybe you de gal in Missouri he lofe, and not lofe him. Pe gar! 'fant de garce! fort beau garçon dis La Bonté, pourquoi you ne l'aimez pas? Maybe he not gone ondare. Maybe he turn op, autre-fois. De trappares, dey go ondare tree, four, ten times, mais dey turn op twenty time. De sauvage not able for kill La Bonté, ni de dam Espagnols. Ah, non! ne craignez pas; pe gar, he not gone ondare encore."

Spite of the good-natured attempts of the Canadian, poor Mary burst into a flood of tears: not that the information took her unawares, for she long had believed him dead; but because the very mention of his name awoke the strongest feelings within her breast, and taught her how deep was the affection she had felt for him whose loss and violent fate she now bewailed.

As the waggons of the lone caravan roll on towards the Platte, we return to the camp where La Bonté, Killbuck, and the stranger, were sitting before the fire when last we saw them:—Killbuck loquitur.

"The doins of them Mormon fools can't be beat by Spaniards, stranger. Their mummums and thummums you speak of won't 'shine' whar Injuns are about; nor pint out a trail, whar nothin crossed but rattler-snakes since fust it snow'd on old Pike's Peak. If they pack along them *profits*, as you tell of, who can make it rain hump-ribs and marrow-guts when the crowd gets out of the buffler range, they are 'some,' now, that's a fact. But this child don't believe it. I'd laugh to get a sight on these darned Mormonites, I would. They're 'no account,' I guess; and it's the 'meanest' kind of action to haul their women critters and their young 'uns to sech a starving country as the Californys."

"They are not all Mormons in the crowd," said the strange hunter; "and there's one family amongst them with some smart-ish boys and girls, I tell you. Their name's Brand."

La Bonté looked up from the lock of his rifle, which he was cleaning—but either didn't hear, or, hearing, didn't heed, for he continued his work.

"And they are going to part company," continued the stranger, "and put out alone for Platte and the South Pass."

"They'll lose their hair, I'm thinking," said Killbuck, "if the Rapahos are out thar."

"I hope not," continued the other, "for there's a girl amongst them worth more than that."

"Poor beaver!" said La Bonté, looking up from his work, "I'd hate to see any white gal in the hands of Injuns, and of Rapahos worse than all. Where does she come from, stranger?"

"Down below St. Louis, from Tennessee, I've heard them say."

"Tennessee," cried La Bonté—"hurrah for the old State! What's her name, stran—" At this moment Killbuck's old mule pricked her ears and snuffed the air, which action catching La Bonté's eye, he rose abruptly, without waiting a reply to his question, and exclaimed, "The old mule smells Injuns, or I'm a Spaniard!"

The hunter did the old mule justice, and she well maintained her reputation as the best "guard" in the mountains; for in two minutes an Indian stalked into the camp, dressed in a cloth capote, and in odds and ends of civilised attire.

"Rapaho," cried Killbuck, as soon as he saw him; and the Indian catching the word, struck his hand upon his breast, and exclaimed, in broken Spanish and English mixed, "*Si, si*, me Arapaho, white man *amigo*. Come to camp—eat heap *carne*— me *amigo* white man. Come from Pueblo—hunt cibola—me gun break—*no puedo matar nada: mucha hambre* (very hungry) —heap eat."

Killbuck offered his pipe to the Indian, and spoke to him in his own language, which both he and La Bonté well understood. They learned that he was married to a Mexican woman, and lived with some hunters at the Pueblo fort on the Arkansa. He volunteered the information that a war party of his people were out on the Platte trail to intercept the Indian traders on their return from the North Fork; and as some "Mormones" had just started with three waggons in that direction, he said his people would make a "*roise*." Being *muy amigo* himself to the whites, he cautioned his present companions from crossing to the "divide," as the "braves," he said, were a "heap" mad, and their hearts were "big," and nothing in the shape of white skin would live before them.

"Wagh!" exclaimed Killbuck, "the Rapahos know me, I'm thinking; and small gain they've made against this child. I've knowed the time when my gun cover couldn't hold more of their scalps."

The Indian was provided with some powder, of which he stood in need; and, after gorging as much meat as his capacious stomach would hold, he left the camp, and started into the mountain.

The next day our hunters started on their journey down the river, travelling leisurely, and stopping wherever good grass presented itself. One morning they suddenly struck a wheel trail, which left the creek banks and pursued a course at right angles to it, in the direction of the "divide." Killbuck pronounced it but a few hours old, and that of three waggons drawn by oxen.

"Wagh!" he exclaimed, "if them poor devils of Mormonites ain't going head first into the Rapaho trap. They'll be 'gone beaver' afore long."

"Ay," said the strange hunter, "these are the waggons belonging to old Brand, and he has started alone for Laramie. I hope nothing will happen to them."

"Brand!" muttered La Bonté. "I knowed that name mighty well once, years agone; and should hate the worst kind that mischief happened to any one who bore it. This trail's as fresh as paint; and it goes against me to let these simple critters help

the Rapahos to their own hair. This child feels like helping
'em out of the scrape. What do you say, old hos?"

"I thinks with you, boy," answered Killbuck, "and go in for
following this waggon trail, and telling the poor critters that
there's danger ahead of them. What's your talk, stranger?"

"I go with you," shortly answered the latter; and both followed quickly after La Bonté, who was already trotting smart-
ly on the trail.

Meanwhile the three waggons, containing the household
goods of the Brand family, rumbled slowly over the rolling
prairie, and towards the upland ridge of the "divide," which,
studded with dwarf pine and cedar thickets, rose gradually
before them. They travelled with considerable caution, for already the quick eye of Antoine had discovered recent Indian
sign upon the trail, and, with mountain quickness, had at once
made it out to be that of a war party; for there were no horses
with them, and, after one or two of the moccasin tracks, the
mark of a rope which trailed upon the ground was sufficient
to show him that the Indians were provided with the usual
lasso of skin, with which to secure the horses stolen in the expedition. The men of the party were consequently all mounted
and thoroughly armed, the waggons moved in a line abreast,
and a sharp look-out was kept on all sides. The women and
children were all consigned to the interior of the waggons;
and the latter had also guns in readiness, to take their part in
the defence should an attack be made.

However, they had seen no Indians, and no fresh sign, for
two days after they left the Boiling Spring River, and they
began to think they were well out of their neighbourhood.
One evening they camped on a creek called Black Horse, and,
as usual, had corralled the waggons, and forted as well as circumstances would permit, when three or four Indians suddenly appeared on a bluff at a little distance, and, making sig-
nals of peaceable intentions, approached the camp. Most of
the men were absent at the time, attending to the cattle or
collecting fuel, and only old Brand and one of his young grand-

children, about fourteen years old, remained in camp. The Indians were hospitably received, and regaled with a smoke, after which they began to evince their curiosity by examining every article lying about, and signifying their wishes that it should be given to them. Finding their hints were not taken, they laid hold of several things which took their fancies, and, amongst others, of the pot which was boiling on the fire, and with which one of them was about very coolly to walk off, when old Brand, who up to this moment had retained possession of his temper, seized it out of the Indian's hand, and knocked him down. One of the others instantly began to draw the buckskin cover from his gun, and would no doubt have taken summary vengeance for the insult offered to his companion, when Mary Brand courageously stepped up to him, and, placing her left hand upon the gun which he was in the act of uncovering, with the other pointed a pistol at his breast.

Whether daunted by the bold act of the girl, or admiring her devotion to her father, the Indian drew himself back, exclaimed "Howgh!" and drew the cover again on his piece, went up to old Brand, who all this time looked him sternly in the face, and, shaking him by the hand, motioned at the same time to the others to be peaceable.

The other whites presently coming into camp, the Indians sat quietly down by the fire, and, when the supper was ready, joined in the repast, after which they gathered their buffalo robes about them, and quietly withdrew. Meanwhile Antoine, knowing the treacherous character of the savages, advised that the greatest precaution should be taken to secure the stock; and before dark, therefore, all the mules and horses were hobbled and secured within the corral, the oxen being allowed to feed at liberty—for the Indians scarcely care to trouble themselves with such cattle. A guard was also set round the camp, and relieved every two hours; the fire was extinguished, lest the savages should fire, by its light, at any of the party, and all slept with rifles ready at their sides. However, the night passed quietly, and nothing disturbed the tranquillity of the camp. The prairie wolves loped hungrily around, and their mournful cry was borne upon the wind as they chased deer and antelope on the neighbouring plain; but not a sign of lurking Indians was seen or heard.

In the morning, shortly after sunrise, they were in the act of yoking the oxen to the waggons, and driving in the loose animals which had been turned out to feed at daybreak, when some Indians again appeared upon the bluff, and descending it, confidently approached the camp. Antoine strongly advised their not being allowed to enter; but Brand, ignorant of Indian treachery, replied that, so long as they came as friends they could not be deemed enemies, and allowed no obstruction to be offered to their approach. It was now observed that they were all painted, armed with bows and arrows, and divested of their buffalo robes, appearing naked to the breech-clout, their legs only being protected by deerskin leggings, reaching to the middle of the thigh. Six or seven first arrived, and others quickly followed, dropping in one after the other, until a score or more were collected round the waggons. Their demeanour, at first friendly, soon changed as their numbers increased, and they now became urgent in their demands for powder and lead, and bullying in their manner. A chief accosted Brand, and, through Antoine, informed him "that, unless the demands of his braves were acceded to, he could not be responsible for the consequences; that they were out on the 'war-trail,' and their eyes were red with blood, so that they could not distinguish between white and Yutah scalps; that the party, with all their women and waggons, were in the power of the Indian 'braves,' and therefore the white chief's best plan was to make the best terms he could; that all they required was that they should give up their guns and ammunition 'on the prairie,' and all their mules and horses—retaining the 'medicine' buffaloes (the oxen) to draw their waggons."

By this time the oxen were yoked, and the teamsters, whip in hand, only waited the word to start. Old Brand foamed whilst the Indian stated his demands, but, hearing him to the end, exclaimed, "Darn the red devil! I wouldn't give him a grain of powder to save my life. Put out, boys!"—and, turning to his horse, which stood ready saddled, was about to mount, when the Indians sprang at once upon the waggons, and commenced their attack, yelling like fiends.

One jumped upon old Brand, pulled him back as he was rising in the stirrup, and drew his bow upon him at the same moment. In an instant the old backwoodsman pulled a pistol from his belt, and, putting the muzzle to the Indian's heart, shot him dead. Another Indian, flourishing his war-club, laid the old man at his feet; whilst others dragged the women from the waggons, and others rushed upon the men, who made brave fight in their defence.

Mary, when she saw her father struck to the ground, sprang with a shrill cry to his assistance; for at that moment a savage, frightful as red paint could make him, was standing over his prostrate body, brandishing a glittering knife in the air, preparatory to thrusting it into the old man's breast. For the rest, all was confusion—in vain the small party of whites struggled against overpowering numbers. Their rifles cracked but once, and they were quickly disarmed; whilst the shrieks of the women and children, and the loud yells of the Indians, added to the scene of horror and confusion. As Mary flew to her father's side, an Indian threw his lasso at her, the noose falling over her shoulders, and, jerking it tight, he uttered a delighted yell as the poor girl was thrown back violently to the ground. As she fell, another deliberately shot an arrow at her body, whilst the one who had thrown the lasso rushed forward, his scalp-knife flashing in his hand, to seize the bloody trophy of his savage deed. The girl rose to her knees, and looked wildly towards the spot where her father lay bathed in blood; but the Indian pulled the rope violently, dragged her some yards upon the ground, and then rushed with a yell of vengeance upon his victim. He paused, however, as at that moment a shout as fierce as his own sounded at his very ear; and, looking up, he saw La Bonté galloping madly down the bluff, his long hair and the fringes of his hunting-shirt and leggins flying in the wind, his right arm supporting his trusty rifle, whilst close behind him came Killbuck and the stranger. Dashing with loud hurrahs to the scene of action, La Bonté, as he charged down the bluff, caught sight of the girl struggling in the hands of the ferocious Indian. Loud was the war-shout of the mountaineer, as he struck his heavy spurs to the rowels in his horse's side, and bounded like lightning to the rescue. In a single stride he was upon the Indian, and, thrusting the muzzle of his rifle into his very breast, he pulled the trigger, driving the savage backward by the blow itself, at the same moment that the bullet passed through his heart, and tumbled him over stone-dead. Throwing down his rifle, La Bonté wheeled his obedient horse, and, drawing a pistol from his belt, again charged the enemy, into the midst of whom Killbuck and the stranger were dealing death-giving blows. Yelling for victory, the mountaineers rushed at the Indians; and they, panic-struck at the sudden attack, and thinking this was but the advanced guard of a large band, fairly turned and fled, leaving five of their number dead upon the field.

Mary, shutting her eyes to the expected death-stroke, heard the loud shout La Bonté gave in charging down the bluff, and, again looking up, saw the wild-looking mountaineer rush to her rescue, and save her from the savage by his timely blow. Her arms were still pinned by the lasso, which prevented her from rising to her feet; and La Bonté was the first to run to aid her, as soon as the fight was fairly over. He jumped from his horse, cut the skin rope which bound her, raised her from the ground, and, upon her turning up her face to thank him, beheld his never-to-be-forgotten Mary Brand; whilst she, hardly believing her senses, recognised in her deliverer her former lover, and still well-beloved La Bonté.[13]

"What, Mary! can it be you?" he asked, looking intently upon the trembling woman.

[13] Ruxton admits in a letter to his publisher (see Appendix A, below) that the story of the attack was written for dramatic effect; that the trappers really joined the Brand party previous to the Indian scare.

"La Bonté, you don't forget me!" she answered, and threw herself sobbing into the arms of the sturdy mountaineer.

There we will leave her for the present, and help Killbuck and his companions to examine the killed and wounded. Of the former, five Indians and two whites lay dead, grandchildren of old Brand, fine lads of fourteen or fifteen, who had fought with the greatest bravery, and lay pierced with arrows and lance wounds.[14] Old Brand had received a sore buffet, but a hatful of cold water from the creek sprinkled over his face soon restored him. His sons had not escaped scot-free, and Antoine was shot through the neck, and, falling, had actually been half scalped by an Indian, whom the timely arrival of La Bonté had caused to leave his work unfinished.

Silently, and with sad hearts, the survivors of the family saw the bodies of the two boys buried on the river bank, and the spot marked with a pile of loose stones, procured from the rocky bed of the creek. The carcasses of the treacherous Indians were left to be devoured by wolves, and their bones to bleach in the sun and wind—a warning to their tribe, that such foul treachery as they had meditated had met with a merited retribution.

The next day the party continued their course to the Platte. Antoine and the stranger returned to the Arkansa, starting in the night to avoid the Indians; but Killbuck and La Bonté lent the aid of their rifles to the solitary caravan, and, under their experienced guidance, no more Indian perils were encountered. Mary no longer sat perched up in her father's Conestoga, but rode a quiet mustang by La Bonté's side; and no doubt they found a theme with which to while away the monotonous journey over the dreary plains. South Fork was passed, and Laramie was reached. The Sweet Water mountains, which hang over the "pass" to California, were long since in sight; but when the waters of the North Fork of Platte lay before their horses' feet, and the broad trail was pointed out which led to the great

14 We have found no evidence that any whites were killed in the brush with the Indians. Ruxton is doubtless using a novelist's prerogative to produce a dramatic story.

valley of Columbia and their promised land, the heads of the oxen were turned *down* the stream, where the shallow waters flow on to join the great Missouri—and not *up*, towards the mountains where they leave their spring-heads, from which springs flow several waters—some coursing their way to the eastward, fertilising, in their route to the Atlantic, the lands of civilised man; others westward, forcing a passage through rocky cañons, and flowing through a barren wilderness, inhabited by fierce and barbarous tribes.

These were the routes to choose from: and, whatever was the cause, the oxen turned their yoked heads away from the rugged mountains; the teamsters joyfully cracked their ponderous whips, as the waggons rolled lightly down the Platte; and men, women, and children, waved their hats and bonnets in the air, and cried out lustily, "Hurrah for home!"

La Bonté looked at the dark sombre mountains ere he turned his back upon them for the last time. He thought of the many years he had spent beneath their rugged shadow, of the many hardships he had suffered, of all his pains and perils undergone in those wild regions. The most exciting episodes in his adventurous career, his tried companions in scenes of fierce fight and bloodshed, passed in review before him. A feeling of regret was creeping over him, when Mary laid her hand gently on his shoulder. One single tear rolled unbidden down his cheek, and he answered her inquiring eyes: "I'm not sorry to leave it, Mary," he said; "but it's hard to turn one's back upon old friends."

They had a hard battle with Killbuck, in endeavouring to persuade him to accompany them to the settlements. The old mountaineer shook his head. "The time," he said, "was gone by for that. He had often thought of it, but, when the day arrived, he hadn't heart to leave the mountains. Trapping now was of no account, he knew; but beaver was bound to rise, and then the good times would come again. What could he do in the settlements, where there wasn't room to move, and where it was hard to breathe—there were so many people?"

He accompanied them a considerable distance down the river, ever and anon looking cautiously back, to ascertain that he had not gone out of sight of the mountains. Before reaching the forks, however, he finally bade them adieu; and, turning the head of his old grizzled mule westward, he heartily wrung the hand of his comrade La Bonté; and, crying Yep! to his well-tried animal, disappeared behind a roll of the prairie, and was seen no more—a thousand good wishes for the welfare of the sturdy trapper speeding him on his solitary way.

Four months from the day when La Bonté so opportunely appeared to rescue Brand's family from the Indians on Black Horse Creek, that worthy and the faithful Mary were duly and lawfully united in the township church of Brandville, Memphis county, State of Tennessee. We cannot say, in the concluding words of nine hundred and ninety-nine thousand novels, that "numerous pledges of mutual love surrounded and cheered them in their declining years," &c. &c.; because it was only on the 24th of July, in the year of our Lord 1847, that La Bonté and Mary Brand were finally made one, after fifteen long years of separation.[15]

The fate of one of the humble characters who have figured in these pages, we must yet tarry a while longer to describe.

During the past winter, a party of mountaineers, flying from overpowering numbers of hostile Sioux, found themselves, one stormy evening, in a wild and dismal cañon near the elevated mountain valley called the "New Park."

The rocky bed of a dry mountain torrent, whose waters were now locked up at their spring-heads by icy fetters, was the only road up which they could make their difficult way: for the rugged sides of the gorge rose precipitously from the creek,

[15] This is clearly a fictionized ending to his story. On July 14, 1934, I addressed a letter to the "County Clerk and Recorder, Memphis County, Tennessee," inquiring if there was any record of a marriage of a man named La Bonté (possibly not his real name) to Mary Chase on July 24, 1847. From "Ed. B. Crenshaw, County Court Clerk," came this response: "Do not find any record relative to these parties." In fact there is no Memphis County, Tennessee.

scarcely affording a foot-hold to even the active bighorn, which occasionally looked down upon the travellers from the lofty summit. Logs of pine, uprooted by the hurricanes which sweep incessantly through the mountain defiles, and tossed headlong from the surrounding ridges, continually obstructed their way; and huge rocks and boulders, tumbling from the heights and blocking up the bed of the stream, added to the difficulty, and threatened them every instant with destruction.

Towards sundown they reached a point where the cañon opened out into a little shelving glade or prairie, a few hundred yards in extent, the entrance to which was almost hidden by a thicket of dwarf pine and cedar. Here they determined to encamp for the night, in a spot secure from Indians, and, as they imagined, untrodden by the foot of man.

What, however, was their astonishment, on breaking through the cedar-covered entrance, to perceive a solitary horse standing motionless in the centre of the prairie. Drawing near, they found it to be an old grizzled mustang, or Indian pony, with cropped ears and ragged tail (well picked by hungry mules), standing doubled up with cold, and at the very last gasp from extreme old age and weakness. Its bones were nearly through the stiffened skin, the legs of the animal were gathered under it; whilst its forlorn-looking head and stretched-out neck hung listlessly downwards, almost overbalancing its tottering body. The glazed and sunken eye—the protruding and froth-covered tongue—the heaving flank and quivering tail—declared its race was run; and the driving sleet and snow, and penetrating winter blast, scarce made impression upon its callous, insensible, and worn-out frame.

One of the band of mountaineers was Marcellin, and a single look at the miserable beast was sufficient for him to recognise the once renowned Nez-percé steed of old Bill Williams. That the owner himself was not far distant he felt certain; and, searching carefully around, the hunters presently came upon an old deserted camp, before which lay, protruding from the snow, the blackened remains of pine logs. Before these, which had been the fire, and leaning with his back against a pine trunk, and his legs crossed under him, half covered with snow, reclined the figure of the old mountaineer, his snow-capped head bent over his breast. His well-known hunting-coat of fringed elk-skin hung stiff and weather-stained about him; and his rifle, packs, and traps, were strewed around.

Awe-struck, the trappers approached the body, and found it frozen hard as stone, in which state it had probably lain there for many days or weeks. A jagged rent in the breast of his leather coat, and dark stains about it, showed he had received a wound before his death; but it was impossible to say whether to this hurt, or to sickness, or to the natural decay of age, was to be attributed the wretched and solitary end of poor Bill Williams.[16]

A friendly bullet cut short the few remaining hours of the trapper's faithful steed; and burying, as well as they were able, the body of the old mountaineer, the hunters next day left him in his lonely grave, in a spot so wild and remote, that it was doubtful whether even hungry wolves would discover and dis-inter his attenuated corpse.

[16] This report has no basis in fact. Old Bill Williams served as Frémont's guide in the disastrous expedition into the San Juan Mountains of Colorado in the winter of 1848–49. The next spring, when Williams and Dr. B. J. Kern went from New Mexico back to the mountains to recover the instruments and equipment left in the snow, both were killed by the Indians.

APPENDIX A

The Late George Frederick Ruxton[1]

HE READERS OF *Blackwood's Magazine*, who for six succeeding months have followed La Bonté and his mountain companions through the hardships, humours, and perils of "Life in the Far West," will surely not learn with indifference, that the gallant young author of those spirited sketches has prematurely departed to his long home, from that Transatlantic land whose prairies and forests he so well loved to tread, and the existence and eccentricities of whose wildest sons he so ably and pleasantly portrayed. Nearly a month has now elapsed since the London newspapers contained the mournful tidings of the death, at St. Louis on the Mississippi, and at the early age of twenty-eight,[2] of Lieutenant George Frederick Ruxton, formerly of her Majesty's 89th regiment, known to the reading world as the author of a volume of Mexican adventure, and of the above-named contributions to this Magazine. The former work has too completely gained the suffrages of the public to need commendation at our hands: it divides, with Madame Calderon de la Barca's well-known volumes, the merit of being the best narration extant of travel and general observation in modern Mexico.

Many individuals, even in the most enterprising periods of

---

[1] This sketch and appraisal of Ruxton by *Blackwood's Magazine* was published in its November, 1848, issue, immediately following the last installment of "Life in the Far West." In the first book edition this was used, with slight modifications, as an introduction. A fuller biography is found in our companion volume, *Ruxton of the Rockies*.

[2] Ruxton was actually twenty-seven at the time of his death. He was born July 24, 1821, and died August 29, 1848. See *Ruxton of the Rockies*, 3 and 310.

our history, have been made the subjects of elaborate biography, with far less title to the honour than our late departed friend. Time was not granted him to embody in a permanent shape more than a tithe of his personal experiences, and strange adventures, in three quarters of the globe; indeed, when we consider the amount of physical labour which he endured, and the extent of the fields over which his wanderings were spread, we are almost led to wonder how he could have found leisure even to have written so much. At the early age of seventeen, Mr. Ruxton quitted Sandwich,[3] to learn the practical part of a soldier's profession on the field of civil war then raging in the peninsula of Spain. He received a commission in a royal regiment of lancers, under the command of Don Diego Leon, and was actively engaged in several of the most important combats of the campaign. For his marked gallantry on these occasions, he received from Queen Isabella II the cross of the first class of the order of St. Fernando, an honour which has seldom been awarded to one so young. On his return from Spain he found himself gazetted to a commission in the 89th regiment; and it was while serving with that distinguished corps in Canada that he first became acquainted with the stirring scenes of Indian life, which he has since so graphically portrayed. His eager and enthusiastic spirit soon became wearied with the monotony of the barrack-room; and, yielding to that impulse which in him was irresistibly developed, he resigned his commission, and directed his steps towards the stupendous wilds, only tenanted by the red Indian, or the solitary American trapper.

Those who are familiar with his writings cannot fail to have remarked the singular delight with which the author dwells upon the recollections of this portion of his career, and the longing which he carried with him to the hour of death, for a return to those scenes of primitive freedom. "Although liable to an accusation of barbarism," he writes, "I must confess that the very happiest moments of my life have been spent in the

[3] Sandhurst.

wilderness of the Far West; and I never recall, but with pleasure, the remembrance of my solitary camp in the Bayou Salade, with no friend near me more faithful than my rifle, and no companions more sociable than my good horse and mules, or the attendant cayute which nightly serenaded us. With a plentiful supply of dry pine-logs on the fire, and its cheerful blaze streaming far up into the sky, illuminating the valley far and near, and exhibiting the animals, with well-filled bellies, standing contentedly at rest over their picket-fires, I would sit cross-legged enjoying the genial warmth, and, pipe in mouth, watch the blue smoke as it curled upwards, building castles in its vapoury wreaths, and, in the fantastic shapes it assumed, peopling the solitude with figures of those far away. Scarcely, however, did I ever wish to change such hours of freedom for all the luxuries of civilised life; and, unnatural and extraordinary as it may appear, yet such is the fascination of the life of the mountain hunter, that I believe not one instance could be adduced of even the most polished and civilised of men, who had once tasted the sweets of its attendant liberty, and freedom from every worldly care, not regretting the moment when he exchanged it for the monotonous life of the settlements, nor sighing and sighing again once more to partake of its pleasures and allurements."

On his return to Europe from the Far West, Mr. Ruxton, animated with a spirit as enterprising and fearless as that of Raleigh, planned a scheme for the exploration of Central Africa, which was thus characterised by the president of the Royal Geographical Society, in his anniversary address for 1845: "To my great surprise, I recently conversed with an ardent and accomplished youth, Lieutenant Ruxton, late of the 89th regiment, who had formed the daring project of traversing Africa in the parallel of the southern tropic, and has actually started for this purpose. Preparing himself by previous excursions on foot, in North Africa and Algeria, he sailed from Liverpool early in December last, in the *Royalist*, for Ichaboe. From that spot he was to repair to Walvish Bay, where we have already mercantile establishments. The intrepid traveller had received from their agents of the establishments such favourable account of the nations towards the interior, as also of the nature of the climate, that he has the most sanguine hopes of being able to penetrate to the central region, if not of traversing it to the Portuguese colonies of Mozambique. If this be accomplished, then indeed will Lieutenant Ruxton have acquired for himself a permanent name among British travellers, by making us acquainted with the nature of the axis of the great continent of which we possess the southern extremity."

In pursuance of this hazardous scheme, Ruxton, along with a single companion, landed on the coast of Africa, a little to the south of Ichaboe, and commenced his journey of exploration. But it seemed as if both nature and man had combined to baffle the execution of his design. The course of their travel lay along a desert of moving sand, where no water was to be found, and little herbage, save a coarse tufted grass, and twigs of the resinous myrrh. The immediate place of their destination was Angra Peguena, on the coast, described as a frequented station, but which in reality was deserted. One ship only was in the offing when the travellers arrived, and, to their inexpressible mortification, they discovered that she was outward bound. No trace was visible of the river or streams laid down in the maps as falling into the sea at this point, and no resource was left to the travellers save that of retracing their steps—a labour for which their strength was hardly adequate. But for the opportune assistance of a body of natives, who encountered them at the very moment when they were sinking from the influence of fatigue and thirst, Ruxton and his companion would have been added to the catalogue long of those whose lives have been sacrificed in the attempt to explore the interior of this fatal country.

The jealousy of the traders, and of the missionaries settled on the African coast, who constantly withheld or perverted that information which was absolutely necessary for the successful prosecution of the journey, induced Ruxton to abandon the attempt for the present. He made, however, several interesting excursions towards the interior, and more especially in the country of the Bosjesmans.

Finding that his own resources were inadequate for the accomplishment of his favourite project, Mr. Ruxton, on his return to England, made application for Government assistance. But though this demand was not altogether refused, it having been referred to, and favourably reported on by, the Council of the Royal Geographical Society, so many delays were interposed that Ruxton, in disgust, resolved to withdraw from the scheme, and to abandon that field of African research which he had already contemplated from its borders. He next bent his steps to Mexico; and, fortunately, has presented to the world his reminiscences of that country, in one of the most fascinating volumes which, of late years, has issued from the press. It would, however, appear that the scheme of African research, the darling project of his life, had again recurred to him at a later period; for, in the course of the present spring, before setting out on that journey which was destined to be his last we find the following expressions in a letter addressed to us:

"My movements are uncertain, for I am trying to get up a yacht voyage to Borneo and the Indian Archipelago; have volunteered to Government to explore Central Africa; and the Aborigines Protection Society wish me to go out to Canada to organise the Indian tribes; whilst, for my own part and inclination, I wish to go to all parts of the world at once."

As regards his second work, we shall not, under the circumstances, be deemed egotistical, if we here, at the close of its final portion, express our very high opinion of its merits. Written by a man untrained to literature, and whose life, from a very early age, had been passed in the field and on the road, in military adventure and travel, its style is yet often as remarkable for graphic terseness and vigour, as its substance every where is for great novelty and originality. The narrative of "Life in the Far West" was first offered for insertion in *Blackwood's Magazine* in the spring of the present year, when the greater portion of the manuscript was sent, and the remainder shortly followed.

The wildness of the adventures which he relates have, perhaps not unnaturally, excited suspicions in certain quarters as to their actual truth and fidelity. It may interest our readers to know, that the scenes described by the author are faithful pictures of the results of his personal experience. The following are extracts from letters addressed to us in the course of last summer:

"I have brought out a few more softening traits in the characters of the mountaineers—but not at the sacrifice of truth—for some of them have their good points; which, as they are rarely allowed to rise to the surface, must be laid hold of at once, before they sink again. Killbuck—that 'old hos' *par exemple,* was really pretty much of a gentleman, as was La Bonté. Bill Williams, another 'hard case,' and Rube Herring, were 'some' too.

"The scene where La Bonté joins the Chase family is so far true that he did make a sudden appearance; but, in reality, a day before the Indian attack. The Chases (and I wish I had not given the proper name)[4] did start for the Platte alone, and were stampedoed upon the waters of the Platte.

"The Mexican fandango *is true to the letter.* It does seem difficult to understand how they contrived to keep their knives out of the hump-ribs of the mountaineers; but how can you account for the fact that, the other day, 4,000 Mexicans, with 13 pieces of artillery, behind strong intrenchments and two lines of parapets, were routed by 900 raw Missourians; 300 killed, as many more wounded, all their artillery captured, as well as several hundred prisoners; and that not one American was killed in the affair? *This is positive fact.*

[4] In accordance with this suggestion, the name was changed to Brand. The mountaineers, it seems, are more sensitive to type than to tomahawks; and poor Ruxton, who always contemplated another expedition among them, would sometimes jestingly speculate upon his reception, should they learn that he had shown them up in print.—Note by the editor of *Blackwood's Magazine.*

"I myself, with three trappers, cleared a fandango at Taos, armed only with bowie-knives—some score Mexicans, at least, being in the room.

"With regard to the incidents of Indian attacks, starvation, cannibalism, &c., I have invented not one out of my own head. They are all matters of history in the mountains; but I have, no doubt, jumbled the *dramatis personæ* one with another, and may have committed anachronisms in the order of their occurrence."

Again he wrote to us as follows:

"I think it would be as well to correct a misapprehension as to the truth or fiction of the paper. It is *no fiction*. There is no incident in it which has not actually occurred, nor one character who is not well known in the Rocky Mountains, with the exception of two whose names are changed—the originals of these being, however, equally well known with the others."

His last letter, written just before his departure from England, a few weeks previously to his death, will hardly be read by any who ever knew the writer, without a tear of sympathy with the sad fate of this fine young man, dying miserably in a strange land, before he had well commenced the adventurous journey whose excitement and dangers he so joyously anticipated:

"As you say, human natur can't go on feeding on civilised fixings in this 'big village'; and this child has felt like going West for many a month, being half froze for buffler meat and mountain doins. My route takes me *via* New York, the Lakes, and St. Louis, to Fort Leavenworth, or Independence on the Indian frontier. Thence packing my 'possibles' on a mule, and mounting a buffalo horse (Panchito, if he is alive), I strike the Santa Fé trail to the Arkansa, away up that river to the mountains, winter in the Bayou Salade, where Killbuck and La Bonté joined the Yutes, cross the mountains next spring to Great Salt Lake—and that's far enough to look forward to—always supposing my hair is not lifted by Comanche or Pawnee on the scalping route of the Coon Creeks and Pawnee Fork.

"If anything turns up in the expedition which would 'shine' in Maga, I will send you a dispatch.—Meanwhile," &c. &c.

Poor fellow! he spoke lightly, in the buoyancy of youth and a confident spirit, of the fate he little thought to meet, but which too surely overtook him—not indeed by Indian blade, but by the no less deadly stroke of disease. Another motive, besides that love of rambling and adventure, which, once conceived and indulged, is so difficult to eradicate, impelled him across the Atlantic. He had for some time been out of health at intervals, and he thought the air of his beloved prairies would be efficacious to work a cure. In a letter to a friend, in the month of May last, he thus referred to the probable origin of the evil:

"I have been confined to my room for many days, from the effects of an accident I met with in the Rocky Mountains, having been spilt from the bare back of a mule, and falling on the sharp picket of an Indian lodge on the small of my back. I fear I injured my spine, for I have never felt altogether the thing since, and shortly after I saw you, the symptoms became rather ugly. However, I am now getting round again."

His medical advisers shared his opinion that he had sustained internal injury from this ugly fall; and it is not improbable that it was the remote, but real cause of his dissolution. Up to this time of writing (21st October), however, no details of his death have reached his afflicted friends, nor any account of it, other than that given by the public journals. From whatsoever it ensued, it will be a source of deep and lasting regret to all who ever enjoyed opportunities of appreciating the high and sterling qualities of George Frederick Ruxton.

Few men, so prepossessing on first acquaintance, gained so much by being better known. With great natural abilities, and the most dauntless bravery, he united a modesty and gentleness peculiarly pleasing. Had he lived, and resisted his friends' repeated solicitations to abandon a roving life, and settle down in England, there can be little doubt that he would have made his name eminent on the list of those daring and persevering men, whose travels in distant and dangerous lands have accumulated for England, and for the world, so rich a store of scientific and general information. And, although the few words we have thought it right and becoming here to devote to his memory, will doubtless be more particularly welcome to his personal friends, we are persuaded that none will peruse without interest this brief tribute to the merits of a gallant soldier, and accomplished English gentleman.

APPENDIX B

Who Were La Bonté and Killbuck?

SINCE THE FIRST publication of *Life in the Far West*, in 1848, readers have been conjecturing about the identity of Ruxton's heroes, La Bonté and Killbuck. Except for these two, Ruxton used the true names of the trappers and Mountain Men mentioned in his story. He wrote of his work:

"It is *no fiction*. There is no incident in it which has not actually occurred, nor one character who is not well known in the Rocky Mountains, with the exception of two whose names are changed—the originals of these being, however, equally known with the others."[1]

But although the incidents are facts, he admitted: "I have, no doubt, jumbled the *dramatis personæ* one with another, and may have committed anachronisms in the order of their occurrence."[2]

This jumbling of the actors and the sequence of events has made it difficult, if not impossible, to determine absolutely the identity of his two lead characters. It may be that each is a composite of more than one personality; though in view of Ruxton's statement it is presumed that each is largely, if not wholly, a particular historic person.

We had at first hoped to be able to identify La Bonté and Killbuck from episodes in the narrative, such as their being found in a starving condition at Independence Rock by the Sir William Drummond Stewart party in 1843. But Matt Field's and William Sublette's diaries of the trip and the writing of

---

[1] *Blackwood's Magazine* (November, 1848), 594 (reprinted above in Appendix A).
[2] *Ibid.*, 593.

William Clark Kennerly fail to mention any such incident. Nor can the horse stealing raid to California be placed absolutely in a definite year, or the personnel of the raiding party be named with certainty.

The incident of La Bonté finding his old sweetheart (referred to as Mary Brand) in the party that set out from the Mormon colony at Pueblo ahead of the regular company presents a better clue to his identity. The patriarchal family, which Ruxton called "Chase" and which his publisher changed to "Brand," is almost certainly that of Robert Crow, as indicated in the footnote on pages 208–209.

The Mormon colony that first settled near the site of Pueblo, Colorado, in the summer of 1846, was spoken of as the Mississippi Company, most of the families having come from Monroe County, Mississippi.[3] But this group, while moving west, had by prearrangement been joined at Independence, Missouri, by the Robert Crow family of Perry County, Illinois (about fifty miles southeast of St. Louis).[4] In view of this association and of Robert Crow's birth in Tennessee, it is understandable that Ruxton might speak of the "Brand" family as coming from Tennessee or Mississippi.

After spending the winter of 1846–47 at Pueblo on the upper Arkansas, Robert Crow was anxious, as Ruxton relates, to be on his way toward California. He had not fully aligned himself with the Mormons and did not hesitate to proceed with his party alone, ahead of the other families and the Mormon Battalion soldiers. Upon reaching Fort Laramie the Crow party waited there for two weeks, until Brigham Young's pioneer band came along, and then accompanied it westward. (The personnel and equipment of the Crow party are given above, in footnote 10, page 209.)

[3] See Hafen and Young, "The Mormon Settlement at Pueblo during the Mexican War," 121–36.

[4] *Autobiography of Pioneer John Brown, 1820–1896* (Salt Lake City, 1941), 63, 65–67, 75. The author of this autobiography was a member of the Mississippi company. His mother lived in Perry County, Illinois, and he was a cousin of Mrs. Robert Crow.

The Mountain Man and hunter who joined Crow's party was Lewis B. Myers. Could he be La Bonté? Literature of the fur trade has heretofore provided scant information about Myers. He was listed as an employee of Sarpy and Fraeb in their Fort Jackson venture on the South Platte in 1837–38.[5]

Interesting accounts of Lewis B. Myers are given, however, by various Mormon diarists. Heber C. Kimball recorded on June 7, 1847:

"The hunters have killed a long tailed deer and an antelope which were divided and distributed as usual. Bro. Crow's hunter also killed a deer, and Brother Rockwood went to ask if they were willing to divide according to the law of the Camp. Bro. Crow informed him that the man they employed was not a member of the Church and he would not feel willing to help kill meat only for their family, inasmuch as Brother Crow & he have made a bargain, the former furnishing a horse & ammunition, the latter agreeing to furnish all the meat the family will need. They have no flour nor breadstuff, and are not prepared to go on equal shares according to the laws of the Camp."[6]

William Clayton added: "Myers, the hunter, roasts the young antlers of the deer and eats them." On June 19 he records: "Myers killed two buffalo, but took only the tallow and tongues and left the rest to rot on the ground."[7]

Shortly after arrival in the Salt Lake Valley Myers went southward to explore. He returned on August 3 and reported plenty of timber on the east side of Utah Lake. On a second exploring tour he led a party northward to Miles Goodyear's trading post at the site of Ogden, Utah, and to the early trapper haven the fur men called Cache Valley and which still carries that name.[8]

---

[5] LeRoy R. Hafen, "Fort Jackson and the Early Fur Trade on the South Platte," in the *Colorado Magazine*, Vol. V, No. 1 (February, 1928), 10, 13.

[6] "Pioneer Journal of Heber C. Kimball," in the *Utah Genealogical and Historical Magazine*, Vol. XXXI, No. 2 (April, 1940), 83.

[7] *William Clayton's Journal*, 223, 245.

[8] Egan, *Pioneering the West, 1846 to 1878*, 115, 122.

In the spring of 1848 Robert Crow and family, his son-in-law Therlkill [Threlkel] and family, some of the other "Mississippi Saints," and Lewis B. Myers went to the site of Ogden and built log cabins. The following spring Crow, Therlkill, and Myers deserted their cabins and traveled north to Fort Hall. So say the Utah records, and then are silent.[9]

Believing that these men were on their way to the gold fields, we transferred our search to California libraries. State Librarian Mabel R. Gillis found a sketch of Lewis B. Myers which shows that he settled in Eldorado County, raised a fine family there, and died in 1893. A granddaughter, Mrs. Lee H. Bixby, whom I met in Pasadena in October, 1950, provided a photograph of Myers. All the children of Lewis B. Myers now are dead, and Mrs. Bixby, the oldest grandchild, having lost her parents when very young, knows but little of her grandfather. Nothing has been learned from the two or three other living descendants of Myers.

The sketch of Lewis B. Myers in *Historical Souvenir of El Dorado County, California, with Illustrations and Biographical Sketches of its Prominent Men and Pioneers* (Oakland, 1883), 252–53, gives a little information about Myers' early career along with his California experiences. The complete sketch follows:

Lewis B. Myers, one of the first men to reach California in 1849, was born in McConnellsville, Bedford County, Penn., Oct. 26, 1812. When 18 years of age he went to learn the cabinet maker's trade at St. Louis, Mo. From here he went in the employ of Benton Savery [Bent and St. Vrain], as a trapper to the Rocky Mountains, afterwards as an interpreter among the Sioux Indians. When the Mormons came along he joined in with them and went to Salt Lake City. In 1849 he left there with a company bound for California. They arrived at Sacramento about middle of July, and in a short time Myers was keeping a place at Brighton, constructed

[9] Milton R. Hunter, *Beneath Ben Lomond's Peak, A History of Weber County, 1824–1900* (Salt Lake City, 1944), 65, 69. See also "Journal History," in the Mormon Church Historical Library, Salt Lake City, Utah.

of willow poles and canvass, in which he sold meals and drinks. After two or three months he formed a partnership with Nathan Fairbanks and Louis Lane, and opened a store at Greenwood, in El Dorado county, no doubt the first one kept in the place. John Greenwood had kept a public house, then kept by Root, and there is little doubt but that it was there in 1848. Louis Lane soon died, and the business was continued by Fairbanks and Myers, who soon added a butchering business to the trade and took in Wm. P. Crone [Crow?] as a partner. Myers sold out and bought the Penobscot House, which he kept until 1854, when it passed into the hands of Page and Lovejoy. He then purchased the property known as "Chimney Rock" ranch, on which he still resides.

Mr. Myers was married en route across the plains, at Ragtown, on Carson river, to Miss Maria Lane, the ceremony took place on the 7th of June, 1849. The family consists of Lewis L., born March 25, 1850, and the first white child born at Greenwood, Margaret Louella, born January 31, 1852 (deceased), Ann Maria, born March 25, 1854, killed by accident when 3 years old, Mary Elizabeth, born January 27, 1856, now Mrs. Godfrey Smeder, of Oakland, William H., born Aug. 14, 1858, and George Grant, born Aug. 16, 1863. Mrs. Myers died Feb. 16, '82. She was the second white woman in Greenwood Valley. It has been Mr. Myers' good luck to raise a family of children that are interesting, intelligent and of good habits. His sons are steady young men of temperate habits.[10]

It is possible that Myers' name, Lewis (Louis) B., or L. B., may have suggested to Ruxton the name of "La Bonté" which he used for his hero. Myers' previous acquaintance with the Crow family and their inclusion in the Mississippi colony could explain Ruxton's assertion that La Bonté came from Mississippi.

Harriet Crow (probably the Mary Brand of the story) was run over by a wagon on June 8, 1847, but she recovered from

10 George W. Threlkel [Therlkill], Robert Crow's son-in-law, who came to California with Myers, settled in Long Valley, Placer County, California, where he reared his family. He died there on January 3, 1900. See his biographical sketch in W. B. Lardner and M. J. Brock, *History of Placer and Nevada Counties, California* (Los Angeles, 1924), 1013.

the accident.[11] However, we have found no further information about her.

Regarding the identity of Killbuck, the field is open. Such men as Joe Walker, Bill Williams, William Bent, Dick Wootton, Black Harris, John Hatcher, Rube Herring, and Jim Waters were famous Mountain Men who might in general answer the description of Killbuck. But they all appear in the story under their own names.

The known facts of the character and whereabouts of certain other well known fur trappers eliminate as possibilities such men as Thomas Fitzpatrick, Kit Carson, James Bridger, Philip Thompson, and Joe Meek.

To qualify as Killbuck the person must be a well seasoned and confirmed trapper and trader. He must be one whom Ruxton could have met on the upper Arkansas between January and May, 1847.

Ruxton gives but few particulars about Killbuck's past. He was born in Kentucky. He came into the Indian country early (no date is specified). In one place he is said to have been in the mountains twenty years; in another, thirty years prior to 1846–47. He had lived among various tribes and could speak a number of Indian languages. His first squaw was a Blackfoot. Hardness and cruelty were mixed with kindness and decency in his character. His journeys had carried him over most of the Western country, with trips into New Mexico. He had been on a horse-stealing raid to California. He was a good yarner, and in telling of his own experiences, he used the figurative and colorful language of the Mountain Men.

Were it not for Thomas L. ("Pegleg") Smith's wooden leg, he would certainly be a candidate for identification as Killbuck. Pegleg was born in Kentucky in 1801. As one of the older trappers, he traveled all over the West with occasional visits to New Mexico. He was a famous raider of California horses, and generally answers to the character of Killbuck. But he

11 *William Clayton's Journal*, 224.

could not have made the run on foot from the head of Bijou Creek to South Park to recover the horses stolen by the Arapahoes. Of course, Ruxton is writing fiction, and he could, if need be, give his hero two good legs. In fact, had he really been writing of Thomas L. Smith, it would not have been advisable for him to mention the wooden leg, since this would have revealed Killbuck's identity, which Ruxton did not want to do. Pegleg's known exploits in the West are so numerous and colorful that a full-length biography of him is overdue.

If we eliminate the Mountain Men already named, one of the most likely remaining candidates is John S. Smith. He was born at Frankfort, Kentucky,[12] in 1810.[13] After serving an apprenticeship to a tailor in St. Louis he came to the plains and Rocky Mountains in 1826.[14] He went first to the Blackfeet, then to the Sioux, and later to the Cheyenne, with whom he lived most of his later life. Among the Cheyenne he was called Po-ome ("Blackfoot"), because of his early association with that tribe.[15]

John S. Smith was a leading trader in the upper Arkansas country. Lewis H. Garrard, a young American adventurer, became acquainted with Smith several months before Ruxton did, and went south of Bent's Fort with the famous mountaineer on a trading expedition to the Cheyenne in November, 1846. Garrard remained with Smith for two or three months and came to know him well. He described him as "an unaccountable composition of goodness and evil, cleverness and meanness, caution and recklessness! I used to look at him with astonishment and wonder if he was not the devil incog. He and I often sang hymns, and a more sanctimonious, meek, at-peace-with-mankind look could nowhere be found than in his countenance; at other times, he *sacré-ed* in French, *caroho-ed* in Span-

[12] LeRoy R. Hafen, "A Report from the First Indian Agent of the Upper Platte and Arkansas," in *New Spain and the Anglo-American West* (Los Angeles, 1932), II, 128.

[13] Garrard, *Wah-To-Yah and the Taos Trail*, 95.

[14] Henry Inman, *The Old Santa Fé Trail* (New York, 1898), 279, 283.

[15] Garrard, *Wah-To-Yah and the Taos Trail*, 101, 170.

ish-Mexican, interpolated with *thunder strike you* in Cheyenne, or, at others, he genuinely and emphatically damned in American."

In telling of Smith's coming into the Far West, Garrard says that the old trader first went to the Blackfeet, then to the Sioux, and "subsequently wended his way, while pursuing the trail of a horse-stealing band of Arapahoes, to the headwaters of the Arkansas; and, in the quiet nooks and warm savanas of the Bayou Salade [South Park], took up his abode and a squaw, with the Cheyennes, with whom he has ever since remained."[16] This trailing of the Arapaho horse thieves and his sojourn with the Indians in Bayou Salade fit the adventure of Ruxton's Killbuck. Ruxton called the South Park Indians Utes, while Garrard says they were Cheyenne. Garrard writes much of Smith, and quotes his trapper talk.

Garrard traveled with Ruxton down the Arkansas in the spring of 1847 and met him again in August, 1848, at Buffalo, New York. At this second meeting the two young men talked of their western experiences and of Ruxton's "Life in the Far West," then running serially in *Blackwood's Magazine*. Garrard, just turned nineteen on June 29, 1848, was undoubtedly influenced by Ruxton's style of writing and presently produced his own excellent book, *Wah-to-Yah and the Taos Trail* (1850). His most extensive descriptions and quotations were of Mountain Men John S. Smith and John Hatcher. But Garrard did not reveal Ruxton's secret of the identity of Killbuck and La Bonté.

Another person who has given us a good picture of John S. Smith—and one that fits the Killbuck character—is Colonel Henry Inman. In his *The Old Santa Fé Trail* (1898), he writes:

"Uncle John Smith, as he was known to every trapper, trader, and hunter from the Yellowstone to the Gila, was one of the most famous and eccentric men of the early days. In 1826, as a boy, he ran away from St. Louis with a party of Santa Fe traders. . . .

16 *Ibid.*, 115, 117.

"During Sheridan's memorable winter campaign against the allied tribes in 1868–69, the old man, for he was then about sixty, was my guide and interpreter. He shared my tent and mess, a welcome addition to the few who sat at my table, and beguiled many a weary hour at night, after our tedious marches through the apparently interminable sand dunes and barren stretches of our monotonous route, with his tales of that period, more than half a century ago, when our mid-coninent region was as little known as the topography of the planet Mars."[17]

Colonel Inman tells at considerable length stories of several of Smith's experiences.

Whether Ruxton met Smith at or near Fort Pueblo (site of Pueblo, Colorado) during February to April, 1847, we are not sure; but the two men did travel together down the Arkansas to Fort Mann in the May following, Garrard reports.

The career of John S. Smith after 1847 does not figure in our problem of his possible identification as Killbuck, but it may be of interest to have his subsequent life outlined briefly. He continued to live and trade with the Cheyenne. Having the reputation of knowing the Cheyenne language better than any other white man, he was chosen by Agent Thomas Fitzpatrick as interpreter for the first Indian Agency established among the Cheyenne (1847) on the upper Arkansas. He served in a similar capacity most of the rest of his life. In 1851, following the Fort Laramie Treaty council, he accompanied the Indian delegation to Washington, D. C.

In 1858 he had Indian trade goods at the mouth of Cherry Creek branch of the South Platte; and there joined with the gold prospectors in founding Denver (Colorado). He accompanied Black Kettle and other chiefs to the peace talks of 1864 at Camp Weld. In November of that year he was with the Indians at Sand Creek when U. S. troops made a surprise attack on the unsuspecting village and killed over a hundred Indians. Smith's halfbreed son, Jack, was among those killed.

When the Cheyenne were removed to the Indian reserva-

17 Inman, *The Old Santa Fé Trail*, 279–81.

tion of Oklahoma, "Uncle John" Smith and his Cheyenne wife went with them. He continued as trader and interpreter until his death on June 29, 1871.

Was John S. Smith Ruxton's Killbuck?

INDEX

Sah-qua-manish (La Bonté's squaw): 95; carried off by enemies, 107
Salazar, Dolores: 190
Salt Lake: 81, 137, 232
Salt Lake desert: 84, 141
Sandhurst: 227n.
San Fernando Mission: 147, 148, 156
San Joaquin River: 146n.
Scalp dance: of Utes, 36–39
Scalping: by Indians, 21–22, 26, 102, 126; by whites, 21, 31, 65, 83, 88, 120, 124, 140
Shawnee Indians: 77
Shian Indians: *see* Cheyenne Indians
Sierra Nevada Mountains: 141n.
Sioux Indians: 33, 67, 69, 73, 76, 98, 99, 101, 102, 104, 140, 223
Slave trade (of Indians): 87n.
Slim-Face: 11
Smith, Jedediah: 138n.
Smith, John S.: 241–44
Smith, Joseph (Mormon leader): 195, 196, 199, 200, 201
Smith, Thomas L. (Pegleg): 138n. 240–41
Snake Indians: 76
Somes, Dick: 12
South Pass: 76, 130, 137
Spanish missions: of California, 148n.
Spanish Trail: 171, 172n.; *see also* Old Spanish Trail
Speyer, Albert: 7n.
Squaws: 35, 37; work of, 102–104; *see also* women
Stewart, William D.: 9n., 10n., 133n., 137n., 139n.
St. Louis: description of, 50–53
St. Vrain, Ceran; 5n., 186n.
St. Vrain, Marcelline; 6n., 73n.
Sublette: 77
Sublette, William L.: 8, 8n., 135, 137n.
Sweet Water River: 130
Sybille and Adams: 137n.

Taos: 176, 182, 185; fandango in, 186; fight in, 188
Tharp, William: 5n., 6
Therlkel, George W.: 209n., 239n.
Thompson, Philip: 240
Tobacco: 41, 44, 180
Trade: with Indians, 74, 77, 99, 179–81